Theories of the Stranger

'Vince Marotta's exploration of the idea of the stranger in the social sciences is a tour de force. Its critical insights combine to make an invaluable contribution to our understanding of the multiple ways the term has been and continues to be used, while pointing us in analytically productive directions.'

Peter Kivisto, Augustana College, U.S.A and
St. Petersburg State University, Russia

'Marotta presents a meticulous analysis of concepts of the stranger from Simmel's classical statement through ideas of the "marginal man" and cosmopolitanism to the emerging debate on the "cyborg" and "posthumanism". This is essential reading for those interested in the history of a key idea in social theory.'

Stephen Castles, University of Sydney, Australia

In our global, multicultural world, how we understand and relate to those who are different from us has become central to the politics of immigration in Western societies. Who we are and how we perceive ourselves are closely associated with those who are different and strange. This book explores the pivotal role played by 'the stranger' in social theory, examining the different conceptualisations of the stranger found in the social sciences and shedding light on the ways in which these discourses can contribute to an analysis of cross-cultural interaction and cultural hybridity. Engaging with the work of Simmel, Park and Bauman and arguing for the need for greater theoretical clarity, *Theories of the Stranger* connects conceptual questions with debates surrounding identity politics, multiculturalism, online ethnicities and cross-cultural dialogue. As such, this rigorous, conceptual re-examination of the stranger will appeal to scholars across the social sciences with interests in social theory and the theoretical foundations of discourses relating to migration, cosmopolitanism, globalisation and multiculturalism.

Vince Marotta is Senior Lecturer in Sociology at Deakin University, Australia and Managing Editor of the *Journal of Intercultural Studies* (Taylor & Francis). He is co-editor of *Intercultural Relations in a Global World* (2011, Common Ground Pub) and *Muslims in the West and the Challenges of Belonging* (2012, MUP Academic).

Routledge Studies in Social and Political Thought

For a full list of titles in this series, please visit www.routledge.com/series/RSSPT

112 **Jürgen Habermas and the European Economic Crisis**
Cosmopolitanism Reconsidered
Edited by Gaspare M. Genna, Thomas O. Haakenson, and Ian W. Wilson

113 **Genealogies of Emotions, Intimacies, and Desire**
Theories of Changes in Emotional Regimes from Medieval Society to Late Modernity
Ann Brooks

114 **Modernity and Crisis in the Thought of Michel Foucault**
The Totality of Reason
Matan Oram

115 **Crisis and Critique**
On the Fragile Foundations of Social Life
Rodrigo Cordero

116 **China in Early Enlightenment Political Thought**
Simon Kow

117 **Elementary Forms of Social Relations**
Status, Power and Reference Groups
Theodore D. Kemper

118 **Groundwork for the Practice of the Good Life**
Politics and Ethics at the Intersection of North Atlantic and African Philosophy
Omedi Ochieng

119 **Theories of the Stranger**
Debates on Cosmopolitanism, Identity and Cross-Cultural Encounters
Vince Marotta

Theories of the Stranger
Debates on Cosmopolitanism, Identity and Cross-Cultural Encounters

Vince Marotta

LONDON AND NEW YORK

First published 2017
by Routledge
2 Park Square, Milton Park, Abingdon, Oxon OX14 4RN

and by Routledge
711 Third Avenue, New York, NY 10017

Routledge is an imprint of the Taylor & Francis Group, an informa business

© 2017 Vince Marotta

The right of Vince Marotta to be identified as author of this work has been asserted by him in accordance with sections 77 and 78 of the Copyright, Designs and Patents Act 1988.

All rights reserved. No part of this book may be reprinted or reproduced or utilised in any form or by any electronic, mechanical, or other means, now known or hereafter invented, including photocopying and recording, or in any information storage or retrieval system, without permission in writing from the publishers.

Trademark notice: Product or corporate names may be trademarks or registered trademarks, and are used only for identification and explanation without intent to infringe.

British Library Cataloguing in Publication Data
A catalogue record for this book is available from the British Library

Library of Congress Cataloging-in-Publication Data
A catalog record for this book has been requested

ISBN: 978-1-4724-1719-0 (hbk)
ISBN: 978-1-315-55123-4 (ebk)

Typeset in Times New Roman
by Apex CoVantage, LLC

Cover image: Mount Vesuvius, Naples, courtesy of Daniel Mazzarella

Contents

	Acknowledgements	vi
1	Introduction	1
2	Theories of the stranger	9
3	The death of the 'classical stranger'?	23
4	Georg Simmel, the stranger and the sociology of knowledge	32
5	Civilisation, culture and the 'marginal man'	46
6	The hybrid of modernity	60
7	The cosmopolitan stranger: mark II	79
8	The multicultural civil sphere and the universality of binary codes	91
9	The cyborg stranger and posthumanism	106
10	Conclusion: Intercultural knowledge and the 'professional stranger'	120
	Index	130

Acknowledgements

This book has been in the making for a while, and there are many people who have helped me refine and strengthen my argument. I would like to thank Peter Beilharz and Fuyuki Kurasawa for their critical comments when this project was in its infancy. My gratitude also goes to my students and seminar participants who were exposed to some of these ideas and were willing to challenge some of my claims. I appreciate the institutional support that the *Alfred Deakin Institute for Citizenship and Globalisation* has provided and the friendship of its director, Fethi Mansouri. My thanks also go to my employer Deakin University for providing study leave to finish the majority of this book. I also owe a huge thanks to Paula Muruca for her meticulous copy-edit and for her friendship. I am particularly indebted to my editor from Ashgate, Neil Jordan, for his patience and the faith he showed in the manuscript.

Although this book is a theoretical exploration of the idea of the stranger, it is steeped in my personal experiences of migration that was instigated by my parents so many years ago. I would like to dedicate this book to my late parents Stella and Giuseppe, who were strangers to Australia but gave their children the opportunities that were not available in Naples in the early 1960s. Thank you, Mum and Dad.

1 Introduction

The forces of decolonialisation, the global movement of refugees entering Europe, North America, and Oceania, but also various parts of Asia and the Middle East, and the rise of the global international student market have meant that cities and various regional centres across the globe have become sites of 'super diversity' (Vertovec, 2007). The 'cultural stranger' is now a familiar sight, at least for some sections of the host community. Although the observation that we live in a 'world of strangers' is not a new, *who* these strangers are has altered. The idea that we live in a 'world of strangers' was popularised by US sociologists trying to comprehend the social and cultural changes caused by rapid urbanisation after World War II (Lofland, 1973; Meyer, 1951). The strangers that were increasingly present in US cities were both immigrants and those moving from the rural South to the industrial cities of the North. Living in a 'world of strangers' has changed in a global, transnational and multicultural world. In social theory and sociology and cultural studies, this empirical change has been reflected in a greater focus on issues to do with the construction of identity, Otherness and the role of social and cultural boundaries. These theoretical and conceptual concerns are not necessarily a navel-gazing exercise; they are partly a reaction to, and a reflection of, the complex and contradictory empirical realities of global and transnational processes. For example, such paradoxical processes are found in the political cultures of many Western countries where popular nationalist movements and centre-right parties, expressing anti-immigration and Islamophobic views, coexist with human rights activists, nongovernmental organisations (NGOs), and community organisations espousing a more inclusionary political culture. Thus, whereas this book contributes to a conceptual discussion of the stranger in social and cultural thought, it is engaging and responding to the realities of living with strangers and supports the view that theory and practice are not mutually exclusive.

Studies that address the stranger rarely dedicate much space to unpacking its various meanings and, at times, have added to the conceptual confusions surrounding the category. Is it a figure or a process? Does it allude to a hermeneutical condition or a societal condition? Is it an existential or ontological condition? Does it constitute difference, or does it blur differences? What does the signifier 'stranger' signify? Does it have a referent, or has it become a floating signifier? These questions cannot be adequately addressed without providing a systematic account of the various permutations of the stranger and their interconnection. My assessment of the stranger draws on a methodological approach that focuses on the role of ideas in conceptualising the social world. Specifically, I will be critically drawing on a field of studies known as the History of Ideas. This does not mean that my approach shuns a materialist understanding; rather in some cases conceptions of the stranger are embedded in preexisting and interconnected economic and political relations, for example, racial and gender relations.

The stranger and the History of Ideas

In 1966 the sociologist Robert A. Nisbet published an influential study identifying the key sociological ideas (Nisbet, 1966), at least those sociological ideas that had originated in Europe and North America. Following the work of Arthur O. Lovejoy, Nisbet called them 'unit-ideas in sociology'. Such ideas, argues Nisbet, must have generality in that they are discernible across influential minds of a particular age. They need to have continuity in that they are observable across the early as well as the late phases of the period under study. Such ideas also must be distinctive in that they must participate in what makes a discipline different from other disciplines. Finally, unit ideas in sociology have to be searchlights that light up a part of the sociological landscape (Nisbet, 1966, pp. 5–6). Nisbet designates five unit-ideas in sociology: *community, authority, status, the sacred* and *alienation*. For Nisbet, the idea of the stranger was not seen as germane to Western sociology. This is surprising considering that Western sociology and its understanding of European modernity is intrinsically connected to processes of colonialism, enslavement, dispossession and appropriation of the colonial Other (Bhambra, 2014, p. 3). Nonetheless, the idea of alienation resonates, for Nisbet, with estrangement because alienation 'is a historical perspective within which man is seen as estranged, anomic, and rootless when cut off from ties of community and moral purpose' (1966, p. 6). This strangeness signifies an existential experience of homelessness. Another study outlines core dichotomies that have become fundamental to sociological understanding (Jenks, 1998, p. 4). These core dichotomies, according to Jenks, are relevant to understanding contemporary issues, such as the politics and identities of different genders and sexual orientations, and in articulating the experiences of different racial and ethnic groups and beliefs (1998, p. 3). Some of the contents of the book include structure/agency, culture/nature, local/global, subject/object, sex/gender and race/ethnicity. Binary thinking, for Jenks, seems to be how we understand the world, and if identities and beliefs of others are important to making sense of the contemporary world, then it seems odd that the binary of us/them or insider/outsider was not included. The works of Nisbet and Jenks do not address the role of the stranger in sociological thought nor how it has contributed to a particular worldview. Whereas the stranger remains marginal to their analysis, the category of the stranger has become central to many recent studies (see Amin, 2012; Simpson, 2013). What is missing in these recent accounts, however, is a systematic and rigorous assessment of the different theoretical approaches and the multiple constructions of the stranger found in social and cultural thought.

Nisbet's approach and the examination of the unit-ideas or core dichotomies of sociology can be contextualised within a body of thought known as the 'History of Ideas'. Arthur O. Lovejoy, known as the father of this approach, attempted to make intellectual history a self-conscious endeavour. There have been recent attempts to reformulate and reconceptualise the practice of intellectual history, and I will critically situate theories of the stranger within this body of work.

To categorise the History of Ideas as a discipline is problematic, but according to Lovejoy, it is possible to identify a common research agenda. The discipline has its own objectives, program and research procedures, and its own institutional locus (*The Journal of the History of Ideas*). In Lovejoy's *The Great Chain of Being* (1933), he outlines some of these ideas and conceptual tools underlying the History of Ideas. By embracing these procedures and concepts, Lovejoy maintains that one can better locate the prominent ideas of a single philosopher or a whole epoch of thinking. The writer or the particular period under study may not explicitly express these ideas and concerns; nonetheless, Lovejoy contends that certain ideas are unconsciously present.

> [T]here are explicit *assumptions*, or more or less *unconscious mental habits*, operating in the thought of an individual or a generation. It is the beliefs which are so much a matter of course that they are rather tacitly presupposed than formally expressed and argued for, the ways of thinking which seem so natural and inevitable that they are not scrutinized with the eye of logical self consciousness, that often are most decisive of the character of a philosopher's doctrine, and still oftener of the dominant intellectual tendencies of an age.
> (Lovejoy, 1933, p. 7)

Lovejoy categorises these epochal tendencies as 'unit-ideas' and contends that they seem to be working just below the surface of consciousness. In some cases Lovejoy's description of these 'unit-ideas' assumes some totalising perspective in which the 'total life-history of individual ideas' are mapped out to identify the alliances and interplay with other ideas' (1938, p. 9). Such an approach, according to Lovejoy, develops a 'fresh perspective' and provides greater intelligibility over a social reality that 'sometimes appears dull, unrelated, and more or less incomprehensible' (1938, pp. 9–10). For Lovejoy, the History of Ideas 'has its own reason for being', and this reason is self-knowledge – in the sense not only of seeking truth but also of analysing error. The historian of ideas succumbs to our need to interpret and reflect; in other words, the discipline exemplifies the 'quest for intelligibility' inherent in the human condition (Lovejoy, 1933, pp. 22–3). Lovejoy implies that underlying the work of scholars are unexpressed and unintended ideas that extend beyond their time and space. More recently, Hausheer argues that this field of knowledge attempts to 'trace the birth and development of some ruling concepts of civilisation and culture through long periods of mental change' and to 'lay bare the origins and nature . . . of often implicit, deeply embedded, formative ideas, concepts and categories . . . by means by which we order and interpret a major part of our experience' (2013, pp. xxxvi–xxxvii). Informing the

History of Ideas is a belief in the existence of grand narratives that explain the origins of key ideas and thus provide intelligibility of our messy social world.

Lovejoy's approach has been criticised because it ignores context. The 'contextualist method' insists that our ideas constitute a response to more immediate circumstances and that we should, in consequence, study not texts in themselves but rather the context of other happenings which explains them. This critique is evident in Skinner's assessment of the History of Ideas (Skinner, 1969). Unlike Lovejoy, Skinner identifies the meaning of the text with the intentions of its author and argues that it is difficult to 'credit a writer a meaning he could not have intended to convey, since that meaning was not available to him' (1969, p. 9). More specifically, Skinner argues that the major problem with Lovejoy's approach 'is that the doctrine to be investigated so readily becomes hypostatized into an entity' (Skinner, 1969, p. 10). As a consequence,

> [T]he historian duly sets out in quest of the idea he has characterized, he is very readily led to speak as if the fully developed form of the doctrine was always in some sense immanent in history, even if various thinkers failed to 'hit upon' it, even if it 'dropped from sight' at various times, even if an entire era failed to 'rise to a consciousness' of it.
>
> (Skinner, 1969, p. 10)

In conclusion, what Lovejoy characterises as the 'quest for intelligibility', Skinner pejoratively labels as a 'mythology of coherence' (1969, p. 16). Historians of Ideas may be imparting or imposing an intelligibility and consciousness that is not present.

In addition, Lovejoy's approach adopts a reflective theory of language that has been pervasive since the early twentieth century. This view of language assumes that it is 'an essentially transparent medium for the expression of ideas and emotions or the description of the external world' (Jay, 1982, p. 86). Lovejoy's 'unit-idea' is premised on the view that the scholars and writers expressing these ideas are detached from the public, intersubjective world. The focus is on the text that, through language, expresses certain key ideas. Yet, with the linguistic turn came a problematisation of this conventional paradigm of language. Furthermore, Lovejoy does not reduce meaning to intention, and for Lovejoy, understanding, in particular identifying and interpreting the 'unit-ideas', is a one-way process. It is the historian of ideas who is able to identify and locate these ideas that are inaccessible to the writer. It is difficult however to detach oneself from one's historicity, and thus it is impossible to locate the underlying meaning of a text or epoch from a perspective outside history because interpretation is dialogical. In contrast to Lovejoy, understanding is an intersubjective process rather than a distanced analysis, and as Jay writes, 'human beings are thrown into a world already linguistically permeated and language is prior to humanity and speaks through it' (1982, p. 94).

Finally, one of the central problems of Lovejoy's approach to intellectual history is its emphasis on continuity rather than difference. This critique is clearly expressed, according to Poster (1982), in Michel Foucault's *Archaeology of Knowledge*. Unlike the intellectual historian who provides a clear and coherent narrative of the move from the Renaissance to the Reformation, from the Enlightenment to Romanticism, then to Realism and so on, Foucault's approach 'remains at one site, digging in all directions, unearthing the specificities of a particular discourse' (Poster, 1982, p. 145).

In certain respects the present study is 'unearthing the specificities' of the stranger and does not assume a perfect coherence within or between different theories of the stranger; my approach adopts the attitude of a presumption rather than an expectation of coherence (Bevir, 1997, pp. 168, 183). In contrast to the traditional approach to intellectual history, I take a more dialectical stance and argue that this presumption of coherence needs to be integrated with a presumption of difference. For example, Bevir asserts that adopting the conceptual priority of coherence means 'that a norm of coherence governs the process of interpretation' but one that is still able to ascertain inconsistencies (1997, p. 183). In light of 'poststructuralist' critiques, this position is still problematic. Underlying Bevir's norm of coherence is an essentialist view of identity. He argues that if one assumes a norm of coherence then one should also assume that individuals have stable identities (1997, p. 184). Bevir ignores recent critiques of intellectual history and assumes that a unified and sovereign subject operates beyond the restrictions of language and culture. In contrast, my examination of the theories of the stranger implies that these discourses cannot be detached from political and cultural contexts; consequently, scholars who contribute to these discourses represent particular worldviews that affect their conceptual and cultural horizons. As an interpreter I cannot avoid the intellectual climate within which I am immersed; thus the focus of this study may tell as much about my own interests and theoretical predispositions than the worldviews of those writers who contribute to the different permutations of the stranger.

Although the conceptual framework adopted here owes its intellectual debt to Lovejoy, it is influenced by recent reinterpretations of intellectual history where continuity and difference are dialectically interwoven. Although I want to establish the idea of the stranger as a key explanatory concept within the social sciences, I do not accept the intellectually conservative position of the History of Ideas. Focusing on ideas does not mean I want to limit 'the meaning of words to "original" or even "essential" meanings' or claim that, ' "Tracings" inevitably lead to origins that then determine the trajectories in usage and meaning to the present' (Agnew, 2014, p. 312). In other words, there is no original meaning to the stranger that can be located in a specific period or thinker. Any reference to the 'classical stranger' assumes an 'origin' to the stranger which then determines how later generations of thinkers conform to or depart from this authentic version. In contrast, *Theories of Strangers* will demonstrate that the very existence of a 'classical stranger' is questionable.

While I make a strong claim that within social and cultural thought, different theories on the stranger exist, I do not assume that these theories are unified and unproblematic nor that we can locate an original 'classical stranger'. I accept

Agnew's view that 'many of the ideas whose genealogies we are most anxious to trace never simply sprang into being fully formed' (2014, p. 313). Subsequently, I critically examine how the idea of the stranger is constructed within these theories using the work of Simmel, Park and Bauman as reference points to illustrate both its coherence and diversity. To treat these writers as a point of reference for any discussion of the stranger is not to fall into the trap of originary thinking. Rather I draw on these thinkers to shed light on the inherent contradictions within the discourse on the stranger.

To demonstrate the diverse, contradictory and multilayered dimension to the stranger, Chapter 1 will provide a systematic description and analysis of the stranger in contemporary social thought. The intention is not to provide a genealogy of the stranger but to extrapolate key themes and characteristics emerging from the theories of the stranger. I identify psychoanalytic, phenomenological/sociological, existential and postcolonial approaches. These approaches are not mutually exclusive, and the chapter aims to demonstrate these overlaps and to make explicit what has been implicit and, at times, unacknowledged in discussions of the stranger. Whereas the objective of the chapter is conceptual clarity, this only emerges through the recognition that the stranger is a contradictory and slippery category. The allusive nature of the stranger as an idea, is exemplified by my critique of the so-called existence and demise of the 'classical stranger' in a diverse, mobile, transnational and global world. As Chapter 2 outlines and critiques, what has replaced it is the universalisation of the stranger (universalisation thesis).

A portion of *Theories of Strangers* will establish the relevance and importance of the stranger to the social theory of Simmel, Park and Bauman. This is not to suggest that a definitive understanding of these scholars is possible by concentrating solely on their conception and use of the stranger; rather, this analysis illuminates a different perspective on their work that has been so far underexplored. While each chapter examines the multiplicity of the stranger in each thinker's oeuvre, it suggests that an in-between stranger underlies their work. This idea becomes increasingly important in the social sciences for theories of knowledge and intercultural knowledge. Chapter 3 first highlights the dialectical nature of Simmel's thought, second, the way in which he conceptualises the existence of a social actor who stands between two boundaries, and finally, his commitment to discovering a third possibility to the epistemological problems of his time. Throughout this analysis it is the stranger, both in its existential and sociological dimension, which features prominently in Simmel's account of new forms of knowledge. My analysis of Simmel also disrupts and problematises the very existence of the 'classical stranger' in his work thereby questioning the role it has played in the social sciences.

Chapter 4 emphasises Park's theoretical credentials, a fact often underestimated by scholars writing on Park. Park's social theory is informed by a particular conception of culture and civilisation, and his conceptualisation of strangerhood affects both his understanding of these terms and how they are interconnected. I explore, for example, how Park's famous notion of the 'marginal man' deepens his understanding of the relationship between civilisation and culture. I demonstrate that, for Park, it is the marginal man that epitomises the social, cultural and economic modality of civilisation and that the emergence of the marginal man exposes some of the existing tensions within the sociology of knowledge and the ways to overcome what Park regards as the narrow and constricting views of both the culture of 'whites' and 'Negros'.

Chapter 5 deals with the work of the sociologist Zygmunt Bauman. Bauman's work has become the focal point for various debates on modernity, the Holocaust, globalisation and postmodern ethics, especially in Europe. Nonetheless, I suggest that Bauman's sociology is partly a commentary on the sociology of strangerhood. Bauman's conception of modernity as the 'will-to-order' leads him to an analysis of Otherness/strangerhood because modernity's obsession with order requires the suppression and marginalisation of those who represent ambivalence. The stranger, as Bauman argues, is neither an enemy nor a friend. It is these 'ambivalent people' who upset the binary nature of knowledge, but as I argue, these ambivalent people are not necessarily associated with the stranger as Other.

Chapters 6, 7 and 8, apply some of these arguments and approaches to the stranger to specific topics such as cosmopolitanism, the nature of a multicultural civil sphere and the cyborg stranger. In each case we see that the debate about the role of the 'classical stranger' is foregrounded in conceptualisations of the cosmopolitan, the multicultural civil sphere and the cyborg and explore how the in-between stranger both enhances and diminishes these ideas. The last chapter revisits the connection between the sociology of knowledge and the in-between stranger, only this time to ponder the role of the latter in developing intercultural knowledge. Drawing on a body of work known as critical intercultural hermeneutics, I contemplate a more active and transformative role for the stranger as Other in cross-cultural encounters and the construction of intercultural knowledge.

The gendered nature of the stranger

Throughout my exploration of the stranger, there has been little work conducted on how the qualities of the stranger can be reconceptualised from a feminist perspective. Most of the work examined here assumes a gender-neutral and in some cases a gender-blind account of the stranger. Simmel, Park and Bauman make no attempt to distinguish the experience of women as strangers, whereas theories of the stranger have altogether ignored gender. It is not that women have not been studied as strangers or outsiders, rather what these studies adopt is an idea of the stranger that is already gender blind (Durbin, 2016; Prashizky and Remennick, 2012). In other words, they adopt a view of the 'classical stranger' that is already gendered. As a consequence, I will adopt the masculine pronoun when discussing the stranger, not because I want to exclude the experiences of women but to highlight the gender-blind approach adopted by various thinkers. There will be times however when the gendered dimension of the discourse on the stranger needs to be foregrounded to contest particular accounts of the stranger.

References

Agnew, J., 2014. By Words Alone Shall We Know: Is the History of Ideas Enough to Understand the World to Which Our Concepts Refer? *Dialogues in Human Geography*, 4(3), pp. 311–319.

Amin, A., 2012. *Land of Strangers*. Cambridge: Polity.

Bevir, M., 1997. Mind and Method in the History of Ideas. *History and Theory*, 36(2), pp. 167–189.

Bhambra, G.K., 2014. *Connected Sociologies*. London: Bloomsbury Academic.

Durbin, S., 2016. *Women Who Succeed: Strangers in Paradise?* Hampshire: Palgrave Macmillan.

Hausheer, R., 2013. Introduction. In: H. Hardy, ed. *Isaiah Berlin Against the Current: Essays in the History of Ideas*. 2nd edition. Princeton, NJ: Princeton University Press, pp. xxxi–lxxxiii.

Jay, M., 1982. Should Intellectual History Take a Linguistic Turn? Reflections on the Habermas and Gadamer Debate. In: D.L. Capra and S.L. Kaplan, eds. *Modern European Intellectual History: Reappraisals and New Perspectives*. Ithaca: Cornell University Press, pp. 86–110.

Jenks, C. ed., 1998. *Core Sociological Dichotomies*. London: Sage.

Lofland, L.H., 1973. *A World of Strangers: Order and Action in Urban Public Space*. New York: Basic Books.

Lovejoy, A.O., 1933. *The Great Chain of Being: Study of the History of an Idea*. Reprint 1961. Cambridge: Harvard University Press.

Lovejoy, A.O., 1938. *Essays in the History of Ideas*. Reprint 1948. Baltimore: Johns Hopkins Press.

Meyer, J., 1951. The Stranger and the City. *American Journal of Sociology*, 56(5), pp. 476–483.

Nisbet, R., 1966. *The Sociological Tradition*. London: Heinemann.

Poster, M., 1982. The Future According to Foucault: The Archaeology of Knowledge and Intellectual History. In: D.L. Capra and S.L. Kaplan, eds. *Modern European Intellectual History: Reappraisals and New Perspectives*. Ithaca: Cornell University Press, pp. 137–152.

Prashizky, A. and Remennick, L., 2012. "Strangers in the New Homeland?" Gendered Citizenship among Non-Jewish Immigrant Women in Israel. *Women's Studies International Forum*, 35(3), pp. 173–183.

Simpson, D., 2013. *Romanticism and the Question of the Stranger*. Chicago: The University of Chicago Press.

Skinner, Q., 1969. Meaning and Understanding in the History of Ideas. *History and Theory*, 8(1), pp. 3–53.

Vertovec, S., 2007. Super-Diversity and its Implications. *Ethnic and Racial Studies*, 30(6), pp. 1024–1054.

2 Theories of the stranger

The stranger is a complex and multifaceted concept and cannot be confined solely to the experience of cultural otherness. There are many quite different understandings and theories of the stranger, and it has become a popular concept in the work of many writers. Moreover, it is an interdisciplinary concept that has appeared in the fields of psychoanalysis, phenomenology, sociology, existentialism and postcolonialism. A systematic and comprehensive study of these different perspectives is long overdue because scholars have conflated these different dimensions without acknowledging the distinctions or the overlap between them. We need to consider how and in what ways these different disciplines have engaged with the stranger and what they contribute to our understanding of it. The following discussion critically examines what or who constitutes the stranger and then focuses on different approaches and how they complement and differ from each other. Contrary to previous insights, this chapter shows that the category of the stranger is internally differentiated, multidimensional and multilayered. The multilayered dimension of the stranger is articulated in terms of the intra-subjective, the inter-subjective and as a societal condition. In turn, these different levels of analysis have led to a reconceptualisation of the proximity/distance scheme underlying the so-called classical idea of strangeness. Later chapters demonstrate how these ideas are manifested in the work of key scholars on the stranger as well as how they can be applied to examine the cosmopolitan subject, the multicultural civil sphere and the cyborg stranger.

Who is the stranger?

The answer to this question seems obvious. The stranger is someone who is not like me. This implies that the stranger is a social construct because who the stranger is not only depends on who the 'me' is but also on the temporal and spatial context. In other words, the constitution of the stranger changes across time and space and changes according to the self who is doing the construction. Therefore, if the stranger is such a fluid concept, can it ever be definitively defined? Maybe not. And maybe we should avoid attempts to define it because it is the very fluidity of the category that makes it such a powerful and influential idea. Yet, this fluidity does not mean that a systematic study of its internal contradictions and connections to other ideas is not possible. By tracking its different permutations, we can shed light on its limitations and strengths while allowing us to rethink how our contemporary world is being understood.

There have been several attempts to unpack the idea of the stranger. Kearney and Semonovitch's (2011) phenomenological study provides a comprehensive discussion on the differences and overlaps between the stranger, the foreigner and the Other. They suggest that whereas there are similarities among these concepts, they are not identical (2011, p. 3). For example, when we speak of strangers as foreigners, they are usually the ones we see. They reveal their faces as someone who has an identity and a name; they bring with them 'papers and fingerprints, an accent and place of origin' and they can be constructed as an enemy, an alien or a guest (Kearney and Semonovitch, 2011, p. 5). In this register the foreigner is an embodied stranger. The Other, however, is invisible and cannot be categorised in political, psychological or social terms. It is 'so unexpected and transcendent that it eludes our knowledge' and becomes totally alien such as the 'Other as other rather than the other-for-me' (Kearney and Semonovitch, 2011, pp. 5–6). In contrast to the stranger as foreigner, the stranger as Other has no name or face and could be categorised as the 'absolute Other' that we encounter in the work of Derrida and Levinas, according to Kearney and Semonovitch (2011, p. 6). Once the stranger can be tracked, categorised and named, it becomes a foreigner; on the other hand, if it alludes to the uncanny, to the terrifying and to elements of surprise, the stranger indicates Otherness. In contrast to the foreigner and the other, Kearney and Semonovitch argue that the stranger is placed in between these categories:

> The Stranger occupies the threshold between the Other and the Foreigner. It is a hinge that conceals and reveals, pointing outward and inward at the same time. Foreigner is the stranger we see; the Other is the Stranger we do not see. Two sides of the same visage – visible and invisible, inner and outer, immanent and transcendent.
>
> (2011, p. 6)

The stranger represents the space in between inside and outside. It signifies an embodied and corporeal actor but also an intangible, slippery and unconscious process. This multiplicity, according to Kearney and Semonovitch, is evident in the phenomenologies of the stranger found in the work of Husserl, Levinas and Derrida. Such distinctions are insightful and timely because they allows us to unpack how certain ideas are increasingly conflated while also highlighting a central idea among theories of the stranger that position the stranger as in between. Kearney and Semonovitch conclude that these accounts 'remind us that Strangeness is not something added to selfhood from without but inhabits the very tenor of its lived experience' (2011, p. 17).

Seidman (2013) moves away from defining the Other in these terms, suggesting instead that the Other has been used too loosely and should be differentiated according to a specific understanding of difference. On one hand, the Other has been seen as a non-normative status; for example, women are seen as the Other to men, or the Arab or Muslim seen through 'Western' eyes is the Other to the European Christian. Seidman claims that in this register using the category of the

Other is inappropriate because any reference to a non-normative status is better connected to a sociology or politics of difference. The difference that signifies a non-normative status may lead to social and cultural structural disadvantage across a variety of spheres but not *all* of them. Using the example of an American working-class man who may suffer disadvantages because of his class (status) position, Seidman argues that these 'blue-collar men are also white and heterosexual [and] would retain [their] gender, racial and sexual privilege' (2013, p. 5). In contrast to the sociology of difference, any reference to the Other should 'signal a condition of systematic symbolic exclusion' across all social, cultural, economic and political fields. Constructed in these terms, the Other is 'represented not merely as deficient or eccentric, but as defiled or fundamentally debased and grotesque'. The Other becomes 'a grave social threat' and thus becomes 'symbolically associated with a condition of excess and ungovernability' (2013, p. 6). The Other is less than human, and this is why, for Seidman, a sociology of the Other differs from a sociology of difference. The category of the stranger, on the other hand, should only be used within the sociology of difference rather than the sociology of the Other because it signifies a lower normative status. For Seidman, strangers refer to status difference (included but subordinated), whereas the Other is excluded and systematically subordinated (Seidman, 2013, p. 5). Here, similar to Kearney and Semonovitch, the stranger is not conceptualised as the Other, but in contrast to Kearney and Semonovitch, the constitution of the Other for Seidman relies on its visibility as a social threat. This difference collapses when Seidman links the Other to the unconscious. He develops a 'psychology of Othering' (2013, pp. 18–19) in which negative reactions to the Other are understood as 'largely unconscious memories of forbidden desires and bodily pleasures' (2013, p. 6), which allow 'selves to reclaim a sense of existential security and coherence by externalizing and controlling unsettling psychological or bodily processes' (2013, p. 14). Seidman provides no rationale for the conceptual shift from a sociological to psychological reading of Othering.

These studies indicate the confusion over the category of the stranger. For example, the stranger is both associated with difference (the foreigner) but simultaneously different from the foreigner. The stranger is not the Other – as in Kearney and Semonovitch's reading – whereas it refers to an invisible Othering process – according to Seidman. The following sections attempt to provide a systematic account of the different theoretical approaches to the stranger, bringing some coherence to what has been a haphazard approach in social and cultural theory.

The psychoanalytic stranger: the intra-subjective mode

Seidman's notion of the Other needs to be contextualised within the psychoanalytical explanation of the stranger reminiscent of Kristeva's (1991) work. In this approach the stranger is conceptualised at the intra-psychic level and connected to Freud's notion of the 'uncanny' and unconscious processes. The psychoanalytic representation, at least initially, does not view self and Other as external counterparts; rather the psychoanalytical approach, especially as expressed by Freud, claims that the Other is part of the self and that we are our own Others. The Other is always the Other within, and the purpose of this repressed Other is to protect the stable and fixed self. As Alphen notes,

> The uncanny other is a creation, the result of repression. This repression is motivated by the 'need' to defend the coherence of the self and to conserve its fragile unity and integrity.
>
> (1991, p. 13)

This uncanny Other is intrinsically part of the constitution of the subject because it is 'a return of that which has been repressed and was once part of the self' (Alphen, 1991, p. 13). The self and Other are not distinct parts of the individual, and so Otherness, within this perspective, is not so different to the self.

The psychoanalytic view of the stranger as the 'uncanny Other' does not signify an embodied stranger, at least not in the first instance. Kristeva (1991) represents the quintessential scholar of this perspective. She examines the historical construction of strangeness within European literature and social thought and draws on the psychoanalytic stranger to make some sociological observations about our responses to the stranger as foreigner. Drawing on Freudian psychoanalysis, she claims that we have a love/hate relationship with an internal Other, which she categorises as our 'uncanny strangeness' (1991, p. 192). The use of psychoanalysis, therefore, is then 'experienced as a journey into the strangeness of the Other and oneself, toward an ethics of respect for the irreconcilable' (1991, p. 182). It is through the acknowledgment of our inner strangeness, claims Kristeva, that we learn to relate to the external Other – neighbours, visitors, immigrants – as an ethical subject. If we do not resolve this psychic tension within the self, the uncanny strangeness is displaced onto an alien Other. We start to project our own sense of Otherness onto the cultural and social stranger, and 'the strange appears as a defence put up by a distraught self' (Kristeva, 1991, p. 183). Kristeva reformulates the ethnological perspective because she locates the process of self-understanding as an internal journey. In other words, self-understanding is not achieved through the study and contact with otherness, rather greater self-knowledge is only possible by acknowledging our self-estrangement. 'Henceforth', writes Kristeva, 'we know that we are foreigners to ourselves, and it is with the help of that sole support that we can attempt to live with others' (1991, p. 170). Without facing our ambivalent relationship with our 'uncanny strangeness', there will always be an abyss between those who are rooted and the uprooted foreigner (Kristeva, 1991, p. 17). It is only by recognising our internal Otherness that we come to realise our commonality with the stranger as foreigner. It is through this recognition that the boundaries between self and Other dissolve and the notion of the foreigner loses its specificity.

> By recognising *our* uncanny strangeness we shall neither suffer from it nor enjoy it from the outside. The foreigner is within me, hence we are all foreigners. If I am a foreigner, there are no foreigners.
>
> (Kristeva, 1991, p. 192)

The danger with the psychoanalytic formulation of a universal estrangement is that it may lead to interpreting societal problems such as xenophobia, exclusionary nationalism and racism as a projection of unconscious struggles. Both Seidman and Kristeva reduce negative reactions to an external cultural stranger to unconscious memories of forbidden sexual or emotional desires. This implies that explanations for racism and racialisation lie within the psychology of the individual, minimising the historical and political sources of these negative reactions. Moreover, it is unclear how Seidman plans to identify the suppressed, collective, unconscious sexual memories among large groups. Rather than focusing on external social, economic and political forces to unravel the mystery of the human condition and the problems that arise from cross-cultural contact, Kristeva and Seidman imply that the answers are located in the depth of our unconscious. This interpretation echoes the position expressed in *The Authoritarian Personality* (Adorno et al., 1969): a classic study on racism and authoritarianism. Adorno et al. understand authoritarianism in terms of psychic processes and, as a consequence, tend to diminish the influence of sociological and historical factors in understanding racism. Similarly, Kristeva and Seidman interpret our reaction to the stranger as foreigner in terms of our relationship with an internal Other. The implication is that the political, economic and social inequalities that the stranger as foreigner experiences can be construed as stemming from our unconscious desires and anxieties rather than embedded in either the institutionalised structures of the host society or the historical and colonial relationships among different social, racial, and cultural groups. Kristeva and Seidman's position may therefore support solutions to societal inequalities that focus on individuals and their desire to resolve their psychic struggles. In developing a psychology of Othering, there may be a tendency to interpret problems with cross-cultural contact as reflecting psychological anxieties that may leave the material inequalities experienced by marginalised groups unquestioned. There may be a role for the unconscious in explaining our relationship to the stranger as foreigner, but unconscious factors by themselves are not fully determinant of a subject's personality or his or her reaction to the foreigner. Other factors – sociological, cultural and historical – have been shown to coexist and interact with psychological ones (Anderson, 1981). Kristeva's use of the stranger shifts from the intra-subjective to the intersubjective because our psychic struggle with our inner uncanny stranger has repercussions for our relationship to the cultural stranger. It is only with the phenomenological/sociological approach that the focus shifts decidedly towards the intersubjective reading of the stranger.

Phenomenological perspective: The intersubjective mode

The central figure in formulating a phenomenological theory of the stranger is Alfred Schutz. More recently the phenomenologies of the stranger have been traced from Husserl, Heidegger, Levinas and Merleu-Ponty to the hermeneutics of Ricouer and the deconstruction of Derrida (Kearney and Semonovitch, 2011). Phenomenology should not be seen solely as a field of philosophy but should also be understood as a field of inquiry (Detmer, 2013) that deals with the nature of experience and its underlying structures. It seeks to understand how consciousness of objects and subjects is disclosed to the human mind and our subjective experience of them. This shifts the level of analysis away from unconscious sources, evident in the psychoanalytical perspective on the stranger, and focuses on intentionality as an act of consciousness that directs the subject outwards rather than inwards. Thus consciousness is always relational and is directed to something outside itself, or as the phenomenologists claim, consciousness is always 'consciousness of' something. Human action and experience become its domain, and it attempts to provide a 'rational and systematic understanding of that domain' (Luckmann, 1978, p. 10) through the formulation of various explanatory categories such as 'the natural attitude', 'life-world', 'horizon' and 'intersubjectivity'. I will outline the salient features of these ideas and their relation to Schutz's phenomenology of the stranger.

The life-world or the 'world of daily life' refers to the intersubjective world that exists prior to our being born into it. This life-world is experienced and interpreted by our contemporaries and predecessors as an organised world. All knowledge of this world is based on previous experiences, including our own and those that are passed down from previous generations (Schutz, 1945, pp. 533–4). The 'natural attitude' is that stock of knowledge that exists in this intersubjective world and is common to all of us (Schutz, 1945, p. 534). In this attitude 'the existence of the life-world and the typicality of its contents are accepted as unquestionably given until further notice' (Schutz, 1970, p. 116). This common knowledge of our everyday world arises from the shared perspectives that we achieve through our everyday interaction. For Schutz, the world and its meaning is not a 'private world of the single individual' (Schutz, 1945, p. 534), rather it is constructed intersubjectively. Yet, this is not Husserl's transcendental intersubjectivity, focused as it is, on the singularity of the ego. Rather shared meaning occurs when we position ourselves in the place of the Other and identify our experiences with this Other subject. Shared meaning is more likely if we know something about the Other's past and the context in which the Other is communicating his messages. The shared meanings arise in the social world because the interlocutors use common signs, language and actions that are embedded in a shared system of significations. The meanings attached to the Other's words or actions will rely on all past and anticipated meaning brought to the interaction. Meaning will rely on knowing the Other and placing oneself in the shoes of the Other as well as prior knowledge of the words and signs used in the exchange.

> The interpreter puts himself in the place of the other person and imagines that he himself is selecting and using the signs. He interprets the other's person subjective meaning as if it were his own. In the process he draws upon his whole personal knowledge of the speaker, especially the latter's ways and habits of expressing himself.
>
> (Schutz, 1967, p. 38)

What happens when this organised and taken-for-granted life-world becomes problematic and is disrupted? Schutz (1945, p. 554), drawing on Kierkegaard, refers to these moments as 'leaps' that are subjectively experienced as shocks. The reality that is experienced by us as the natural one, 'we are not ready to abandon our attitude toward it without having experienced a specific shock which compels us to break through the limits of these 'finite' provinces of meaning and to shift the accent of reality to another one' (Schutz, 1945, p. 552). Rather than viewing these 'shocks' as isolated incidences, Schutz argues that they are part of the life-world; 'they themselves pertain to its reality' (1945, p. 552). He applies the phenomenological outlook to various everyday experiences to illustrate the underlying structures of the life-world and the pervasive nature of these shocks: for example, Schutz investigates why, as a consequence of 'shocks', 'well-informed citizens' accept some types of knowledge and exclude others (1976a, p. 122) and explores the experience of 'shocks' to 'Homecomers' who find on their return that their life-world and the knowledge of that world has drastically changed to the extent that their 'natural attitude' no longer coincides with those they left behind (Schutz, 1976b, pp. 112–113); and finally, Schutz examines how strangers experience a 'shock' within their life-world when they arrive in the host society. What is noteworthy is that the essay on the stranger is written from the perspective of the stranger rather than the host; it is the stranger not the host that experiences a 'shock' in his life-world. In addition, it is important to note that Schutz's stranger is gender blind. The stranger is usually male and enters a host society embedded in patriarchal relations.

For Schutz, the stranger is an 'adult individual of our time and civilisation who tries to be permanently accepted or at least tolerated by the group which he approaches' (1976c, p. 91). Strangeness, for this individual, entails physical closeness but social and cultural distance. It is this specific dimension of strangeness that allows Schutz to argue that the experience of the stranger can be extended to other social situations because 'their validity [is not] restricted to this special case [the immigrant]' (1976c, p. 91). The stranger here is not necessarily the foreigner, rather it can also allude to a general condition experienced by anyone. Non-immigrants can experience the strangeness of the stranger without being represented as a cultural Other in the eyes of the host. One can be physically close to certain individuals or groups while feeling socially and cultural distant from them. For example, Schutz includes those who want to enter an exclusive social club, those approaching the family of their prospective brides, those from a working-class background entering university, or someone from the city settling in a rural area. Whereas non-immigrants can be strangers, for Schutz, the personal 'crisis' that they endure is milder than the immigrant stranger. Therefore Schutz's phenomenological approach to the proximity/distance experienced by the stranger as foreigner can be generalised beyond the specific experience of this stranger. The potential for us all to be strangers was a theme also evident in the psychoanalytic perspective and, as will be shown later, reappears in other approaches. What is also significant in Schutz's essay on the stranger is what he excludes from his definition: for example, he jettisons visitors who have temporary contact with the established group, children, 'primitives' and 'contacts between individuals and groups of different levels of civilization' (Schutz, 1976c, p. 91). It is never explained why these individuals should be excluded from his definition of the stranger, especially after he has pointed to the generalised nature of the stranger experience. It is as if these 'primitive' strangers cannot be understood through a Western philosophical lens. As we shall see later, the postcolonial approach to the stranger makes this contact between different 'civilisations' essential in understanding how power inequalities are intrinsically embedded in the category of the stranger. Likewise, feminists have been critical of Schutz's understanding of we-relations or intersubjective experiences because it ignores how individuals relate to each other as dominant (male/host) and subordinate (female/stranger) (Lengermann, 1995).

Although Schutz mentions that the stranger is concerned with assimilating or being accepted by the host, his analysis focuses less on the assimilation and adjustment process and more on the 'situation of approaching'. In other words, what happens to strangers as foreigners – psychologically, culturally and socially – when they approach a world they do not comprehend and thus lack the stock of knowledge to go on in the everyday world of the host? Strangers do not share the taken-for-granted, basic assumptions or worldview of host members, and thus they 'become essentially the man [sic] who has to place in question nearly everything that seems to be unquestionable to members of the approached group' (Schutz, 1976c, p. 96). The stranger's life-world and natural attitude stand in opposition to that of the host group. For Schutz, the problem of the stranger needs to be approached in terms of the 'constitutive phenomenology of the natural attitude' (Nasu, 2006, p. 388). The host members can be said to be in the 'natural attitude' in the sense that 'the existence of the life-world and the typicality of its content are accepted as unquestionably given until further notice' (Schutz, 1978, p. 257). Unlike strangers, host members – until moments of 'shock' – do not reflect upon nor are they conscious of what they take for granted; strangers transcend both their natural attitude and that of the host because their experience is situated in another life-world. Through his investigation of the experiences of the stranger, Schutz's phenomenology makes believing in the taken for granted an 'object of inspection and interrogation' (Natanson, 1998, p. 7). It is through observing and examining the everyday experiences of the stranger that we can demonstrate how the familiar life-world of the host becomes strange to the immigrant. As a result of this discrepancy, an intercultural hermeneutical problem arises where 'the stranger cannot assume that his interpretation of the new cultural pattern coincides with that current with the members of the in-group' (Schutz, 1976c, p. 100). This places the stranger in a position in which the cultural and language code of the host is – in the short term – inaccessible. The phenomenological perspective thus raises epistemological questions that – as will be demonstrated in later chapters – have become increasingly important in the discourse on the stranger.

As mentioned earlier, Schutz's examination confines itself to the stranger's personal crisis rather than the experiences of the host. He disregards how the appearance of the stranger into the host's locality may challenge the host's natural attitude and life-world and in return change the host's reaction to the stranger. If we adopt the perspective of the host, a slightly different interpretation emerges. Focusing on the host's reaction has repercussions for how the stranger is perceived and treated and, in turn, aggravates the stranger's personal crisis. For example, strangers also threaten the host's life-world because they question the host's taken-for-granted view of their own society and their cultural and social beliefs. Threatening the host's worldview could lead to anxieties and negative reactions towards strangers and thus feed into the stranger's personal crisis and shock. The phenomenological approach confines itself to the stranger's perspective ignoring how this view is partly constructed via the host's response to the stranger. Ironically whereas the phenomenological reading of the stranger depends on the intersubjective mode, this mode is not extended to understanding how the stranger's response is partly constituted through the host's reaction. From a phenomenological perspective we need to rethink the stranger-host relation to demonstrate the co-constitutive nature of this relation in which the personal crisis of the stranger and host are intrinsically intertwined.

The existential stranger and the universalisation thesis

Previous accounts of the stranger have focused on the intra- and intersubjective mode, but another important existential understanding has emerged, invoking a more general societal condition. Sociological discussions on the stranger tend to marginalise or overlook its existential dimension. Harman's (1988) seminal text on the 'modern stranger' purports to overlook the 'existential literature in which strangeness is seen as inherent in life itself' in favour of a 'sociological analysis of the stranger'. Yet, this arbitrary separation between sociology and existentialism ignores the fruitful conversation between these two bodies of knowledge that has existed through an area of studies known as 'existential sociology' (Kotarba and Johnson, 2002). As I will show later, this distinction – between the existential and sociological – is blurred in the discourse on the stranger. Harman herself slips from the sociological to the existential in her assessment on the differences between the 'modern' and the 'classical' conception of the stranger. She states that the modern stranger 'is an outsider on the inside' (1988, p. 44) who 'searches for meaning, for authenticity' (1988, p. 135) and tries 'to validate the estrangement of modern existence as an authentic being-in-the-world' (1988, p. 136). She adopts the language of existentialism to formulate a sociological definition of the 'modern stranger'. If existentialism addresses itself to the predicament of the human subject in a world where the stability of institutions and the permanence of things and customs is threatened, then Harman's 'modern stranger' speaks to these concerns. Further evidence of the porous boundary between the existential and sociological versions of the stranger can be found in Schutz's version of the stranger's objectivity. For Schutz, strangers' objectivity should not be interpreted in terms of the 'critical attitude' that arises when they adopt the standards of home, thus perceiving the host world through the eyes of an outsider. Contrary to this position, the stranger's objectivity is the outcome of an existential crisis.

> The deeper reason for his objectivity, however, lies in his own *bitter experience* of the limits of the 'thinking as usual', which has taught him that a man may lose his status, his rules of guidance, and even his history and that *the normal way of life is always far less guaranteed than it seems.* Therefore, the stranger discerns, frequently with a *grievous clear-sightedness, the rising of*

> *a crisis which may menace the whole foundation of the 'relatively natural conception of the world'*, while all those symptoms pass unnoticed by the members of the in-group, who rely on the continuance of their customary way of life.
>
> (Schutz, 1976c, p. 104, my emphasis)

Schutz's account seems to be describing an existential condition in which strangers question the nature of reality and their place in the world. What was once taken for granted and allowed the stranger to see the world as coherent and stable is now contingent and fragmentary. The stranger's veil of ignorance has been lifted, and what the stranger thought was real – the taken-for-granted world – is in fact illusionary. What passes unnoticed by host members is made conscious to the stranger 'with grievous clear-sightedness'. The stranger's insight is a double-edged sword: it is a clear but tragic vision of a new reality that has lost its old foundations. The stranger's natural attitude can no longer be a guide for the self and the world. Whereas Schutz confines this existential crisis of self-estrangement and uncertainty to the stranger, this sense of disconnection and disorientation resulting from economic, social and cultural change has been interpreted as a common experience within modernity. It is here where the intra- and societal modes of understanding the stranger finally meet.

There has been a growing body of work that has interpreted this disconnection, disorientation and loss of certainty that the stranger experiences as a ubiquitous state of affairs within modern Western societies. This was especially the case for those existentialist writers who were critical of a Western capitalist modernity characterised by bureaucratic rationality, consumerism, massification, conformity and materialism. In this broader existential register, the stranger can no longer be confined to the experience of the immigrant or the foreigner, rather it refers to a state of being which large numbers of people experience in the 'West' because the traditional social, cultural and religious foundations that were the pillars of the West have apparently disappeared. This existential crisis of Western, capitalist societies has led to the self-estrangement of modern individuals that denotes the loss relationship that the self has with an internalised authentic other; as a consequence, we have become more anxious and alienated. These generalisations have led to a discussion of the 'existential marginal self', the self that has lost the security of absolutes and no longer stands on terra firma but is disoriented and directionless (Muller, 1987). For Wilson (1978), this existential outsider/stranger is also evident in the modernist literature of Kafka, Dostoevsky, Camus and Sartre. For the existential outsider, the only important distinction is between being and nothingness (Wilson, 1978, p. 37).

The appearance of the existential outsider has been associated with the loss of a metaphysical home. This is evident in the work of Heidegger, in which he explores the relationships among modernity, homelessness, estrangement and our sense of being in the world. Heidegger's *Letter on Humanism* (1977a) and *Building Dwelling Thinking* (1977b) clearly articulate the ontological reading of the stranger and its connection to a state of homelessness. Homelessness, for Heidegger, is not understood in terms of its material concern, for example, the material condition of lacking a roof over one's head or the displacement of thousands of war refugees. On the contrary, homelessness is understood ontologically: it is that 'which prevents us from making ourselves at home, from dwelling poetically in what he calls the "house of being"' (Lewandowski, 1995, p. 142). Heidegger explicitly connects an ontologised view of the stranger with an existential homelessness when he argues that 'homelessness is coming to be the destiny of the world' and 'estrangement of man has its roots in the homelessness of the modern man' (Heidegger, 1977a, p. 219). Underlying this pessimistic attitude is a notion of home associated with the spiritual unity found between humans and things. This ontological, conservative paradigm assumes that we have lost our metaphysical 'home' or roots because we live in a modern society that is overly rationalistic, bureaucratic and soul destroying. Heidegger's critique of modernity is mediated through a language of authenticity because he presupposes that what was once an authentic self, the modernising experience has destroyed or suppressed.

This critique of a rationalistic and bureaucratic modernity and the experience of being an existential stranger can also be found in the work of sociologists within the phenomenological tradition. According to these accounts, the notion of metaphysical home has become increasingly meaningless in a global and plural modern world, and consequently individuals have become increasingly disoriented, alienated and estranged. Berger et al. (1973) have observed that the notion of homelessness epitomises modern consciousness and suggests that there has been a 'pluralization of Life-Worlds'. As a result, it has been difficult for modern individuals to maintain a 'home-world' which can 'serve as the meaningful centre' for their life in society (Berger et al., 1973, p. 66). According to Berger et al., the development of the homeless mind is closely connected with the destabilisation of modern identity. Due to the rise of technological production and bureaucratic rationality, modern identity has become more open, differentiated, reflective and individuated (Berger et al., 1973: 76–9). Berger et al. conclude:

> The final consequence of all this can be put very simply . . . *that man has suffered from a deepening condition of 'homelessness'*. The correlate of the migratory character of his experience of society and of self has been what might be called a metaphysical loss of 'home'.
>
> (1973, p. 82)

This passage implicitly illustrates that the existential stranger relates to a condition of loss, especially the loss of a secure and stable self. Berger et al. are concerned with the emergence of global estrangement because it is suggestive of a loss of ontological security; in other words, the modern condition has threatened one's sense of being in the world. The movement of people, or 'the migratory character' of modern subjects, and the destruction of the authentic self (Heidegger) reflect modernity's moral, social and existential crisis. This 'homelessness' myth, however, presupposes that we, at one time in the distant past, have been rooted within a single, all-inclusive order (Shotter, 1993). Heidegger and Berger et al. assume that a moral and an existential order once existed and that the modern condition has somehow undermined this order and the rooted individual that supposedly supported it. Thus the existential stranger refers both to an intra-subjective experience but also to a societal condition characterised by existential homelessness that is brought about by modern rationalising and bureaucratic processes. Whereas the theme of global estrangement appears in the existential reading of the stranger, it is also apparent in the phenomenological and psychoanalytical accounts.

The postcolonial stranger

The final perspective on the stranger originates within postcolonial thought, particularly the seminal text by Sara Ahmed (2000) on encountering strangers. Ahmed's work emphasises how the historical and the political are essential in understanding the idea of the stranger. Unlike Seidman and Kearney and Semonovitch, she does not distinguish the stranger from the Other because, for Ahmed, the stranger as Other is constituted through power relations that are embedded in the past as much as the present. Ahmed's postcolonial approach does not assume that we have overcome colonialism, rather she places it as central to the constitution of modernity (2000, p. 10). At one level, her idea of 'strange encounters' has some affinities with Schutz's phenomenology of the stranger. Schutz argues against Husserl's 'transcendental subject' because it ontologises identity, whereas he conceives identity as constructed through our encounters with others. Ahmed also speaks of the importance of encounters to the constitution of subjectivity because identity 'itself is constituted in the "more than one" of the encounters: the dissemination of an "I" or "we" requires an encounter with others' (2000, p. 7). Reminiscent of Schutz's phenomenology, she concludes, 'the encounter itself is ontologically prior to the question of ontology (the question of the being who encounters)' (2000, p. 7). Yet, what distinguishes Ahmed's observation from Schutz's is that these encounters are mediated by historical processes that presuppose other faces, bodies, spaces and times that have already impinged on encounters and thus 'fix others in regime of difference' (Ahmed, 2000, p. 8). These strange encounters, therefore, are not equal encounters between similar selves as Schutz's account tends to assume, rather they take place within power differentials. These strange encounters should be situated within broader historical relationships of power and antagonism. For example, colonial encounters involve a spatial and temporal dislocation that transforms both the colonisers and colonised subjects, but these transformations are not equal, both in their qualitative and quantitative traits. How others are constituted and transformed depends on relationships of power. Ahmed's postcolonial approach also contests the very category of the stranger evident in the phenomenological and existential account. In such accounts the stranger has been fetishised as a figure that has a life of its own. This conceals the 'histories of determination which already exists in constructing the stranger as dangerous and menacing' (Ahmed, 2000, p. 4) and thus displaces them from social and material relations. For example, constituting the stranger as the figure of the immigrant or foreigner 'grants the stranger the status of a figure which has a referent in the world' (2000, p. 5) and denies the different ways in which one can be displaced from home. Stranger fetishism works to conceal differences and merges different forms of displacement under one category (2000, p. 5). It is at this moment that Ahmed is critical of the universalisation thesis because the figure of the stranger 'assumes a life of its own only insofar as it is cut off from the histories of its determination' (2000, p. 6). This fetishisation and ahistorical understanding of the stranger is also evident in Schutz's argument to exclude the 'primitive' or contact between different civilisations in any discussion of the stranger. The postcolonial approach – in contrast to Seidman – constitutes the stranger as the cultural Other and, unlike the phenomenological and existential accounts, is embedded in past and present power relations.

Conclusion

Framing different versions of the stranger as signifying the intra-subjective, inter-subjective and a general societal condition has allowed us to clarify how the stranger is manifested in ways which were absent before. To be drawn into whether the stranger is the foreigner or the Other or whether it conflates with a specific type of difference or Othering process leads us into an intellectual black hole. My typology – like all typologies – is not fully reflective of reality, but it attempts to bring some order to a substantial body of literature on the stranger and, at the same time, is not overly concerned with trying to locate a definitive understanding of the stranger. This framework allowed us to demonstrate the fluid and flexible nature of the stranger. For example, at the intra-subjective level the stranger is an internal Other (Kristeva and Seidman), but this internal Other transforms into an external foreigner as soon as we move into the intersubjective mode (Kristeva, Schutz and Ahmed). In addition, it is at this intersubjective mode that we also see the existential definition of the stranger (Schutz and Harman) appear and manifest into a societal condition (Berger and Heidegger). These modes of interpreting the stranger should not ignore the historical and material conditions of the stranger that the postcolonial approach foregrounds.

References

Adorno, T., Frenkel-Brunswik, E. Levinson, D. and Sanford, N., 1969. *The Authoritarian Personality*. New York: Norton.
Ahmed, S., 2000. *Strange Encounters: Embodied Others in Post-Coloniality*. London: Routledge.
Alphen, E., 1991. The Other Within. *In*: R. Corbey and J. Leerssen, eds. *Alterity, Identity, Image: Selves and Others in Society and Scholarship*. Amsterdam: Rodopi, pp. 1–16.
Anderson, J.W., 1981. The Methodology of Psychological Biography. *Journal of Interdisciplinary History*, xi(3), pp. 455–475.
Berger, P.L., Berger, B. and Kellner, H., 1973. *The Homeless Mind: Modernization and Consciousness*. New York: Random House.
Detmer, D., 2013. *Phenomenology Explained: From Experience to Insight*. New York: Open Court.

Harman, L.D., 1988. *The Modern Stranger: On Language and Membership*. Berlin: Moutonde Gruyter.
Heidegger, M., 1977a. Letter on Humanism. *In*: D.F. Krell, ed. *Martin Heidegger Basic Writings*. New York: Harper & Row, pp. 189–242.
Heidegger, M., 1977b. Building Dwelling and Thinking. *In*: D.F. Krell, ed. *Martin Heidegger Basic Writings*. New York: Harper & Row, pp. 319–340.
Kearney, R. and Semonovitch, K., 2011. At the Threshold: Foreigners, Strangers, Others. *In*: R. Kearney and K. Semonovitch, eds. *The Phenomenologies of the Stranger: Between Hostility and Hospitality*. New York: Fordham University Press, pp. 3–29.
Kotarba, J.A. and Johnson, J.M. eds., 2002. *Postmodern Existential Sociology*. Walnut Creek, CA: Alta Mira.
Kristeva, J., 1991. *Strangers to Ourselves*. New York: Wheatsheaf.
Lengermann, P., 1995. A Feminist Investigation of the Sociology of Alfred Schutz. *Sociological Theory*, 13(1), pp. 25–36.
Lewandowski, J.D., 1995. Modernity and Its Vicissitudes. *Cultural Critique*, 29, pp. 139–162.
Luckmann, T., 1978. *Phenomenology and Sociology: Selected Readings*. Penguin: Harmondsworth, England.
Muller, R.J., 1987. *The Marginal Self: An Existential Inquiry into Narcissism*. Atlantic Highlands: Humanities Press International.
Nasu, H., 2006. How Is the Other Approached and Conceptualized in Terms of Schutz's Constitutive Phenomenology of the Natural Attitude? *Human Studies*, 28, pp. 385–396.
Natanson, M., 1998. Alfred Schutz: Philosopher and Social Scientist. *Human Studies*, 21(1), pp. 1–12.
Schutz, A., 1945. On Multiple Realities. *Philosophy and Phenomenological Research*, 5(4), pp. 533–576.
Schutz, A., 1967. The Phenomenology of the Social World. *In*: C. Calhoun, J. Gerteis, J. Moody, S. Pfaff and I. Virk, eds. *Contemporary Sociological Theory*. Reprint 2012. Chichester: John Wiley and Sons, pp. 35–45.
Schutz, A., 1970. Some Structures of the Life-World. *In*: I. Schutz, ed. *Collected Papers: Studies in Phenomenological Philosophy*, Vol. III. The Hague: Martinus Nijhoff, pp. 115–132.
Schutz, A., 1976a. The Well-Informed Citizen: An Essay on the Social Distribution of Knowledge. *In*: A. Brodersen, ed. *Alfred Schutz Collected Papers II: Studies in Social Theory*. The Hague: Martinus Nijhoff, pp. 120–134.
Schutz, A., 1976b. The Homecomer. *In*: A. Brodersen, ed. *Alfred Schutz Collected Papers II: Studies in Social Theory*. The Hague: Martinus Nijhoff, pp. 106–119.
Schutz, A., 1976c. The Stranger: An Essay in Social Psychology. *In*: A. Brodersen, ed. *Alfred Schutz Collected Papers II: Studies in Social Theory*. The Hague: Martinus Nijhoff, pp. 91–105.
Schutz, A., 1978. Some Structures of the Life-World. *In*: T. Luckmann, ed. *Phenomenology and Sociology: Selected Readings*. Penguin: Harmondsworth, pp. 257–274.
Seidman, S., 2013. Defilement and Disgust: Theorising the Other. *American Journal of Cultural Sociology*, 1(1), pp. 3–25.
Shotter, J., 1993. Rhetoric and the Roots of the Homeless Mind. *Theory, Culture & Society*, 10, pp. 41–62.
Wilson, C., 1978. *The Outsider*. London: Picador.

3 The death of the 'classical stranger'?

Berger et al. (1973) have shown that the condition of the existential stranger has been universalised and that since the early 1970s this has been a recurrent theme in social theory. Yet, what distinguishes current approaches from previous accounts is that the former are less pessimistic about the experience of universal strangerhood. Instead of categorising the stranger as an individual figure, such as the foreigner, the state of strangeness has become a general experience. Dessewffy accepts the universalisation thesis when he notes that the curiosity we feel towards the exotic Other has turned into an 'astonishment over our own personalities spilt into irreconcilable roles' (1996, p. 600). Within this contemporary universalisation thesis is a growing critique of the 'classical stranger' as an explanatory category. Underlying this thesis is a consensus that we can identify a 'classical' version of the stranger in the work of Simmel, characterised by one who comes today and stays tomorrow. This version, according to its critics, is now redundant because it assumes that the stranger is entering a nation-state that is closed and sovereign and that the host identity is fixed and stable.

Harman (1988) was one of the first scholars to raise some of these concerns when she argued that there are certain assumptions underlying the category of the 'classical stranger': it assumes that the origins and identity of the stranger are distinct from the host group; that the approached homogenous host group has a 'definable, integrated, shared and self-contained identity'; and that the 'rigid rules of membership are only available to those "inside"' (1988, p. 3). Her analysis of the modern stranger draws on David Riesman's (1955) typology of 'tradition-directed', 'inner-directed' and 'other-directed' modes of social organisation, and their relationship to social character, to highlight the shortcomings of the 'classical stranger'. She asserts that the classical stranger assumes a particular type of social organisation that no longer exists. For example, she observes that the classical interpretation of strangers, which has been advocated by scholars such as Simmel and Schutz, perceives its subject as autonomous, self-contained actors who formulate their identities separately from those who construct them as different. In this account the stranger approaches a host group that is assumed to have a definable, integrated, shared and self-contained identity. According to Harman, the Simmelian stranger enters a society immersed in 'tradition-directed' activities and practices. This is distinct from the modern, highly globalised world that contemporary strangers enter. Such a society is characterised by increased personal mobility, consumerism, mass production, rapid capital accumulation and technological change. This mode of social organisation fosters individuals who are better able to cope in a society without strict and self-evident tradition-directed rules and norms. Contemporary strangers enter societies that do not encourage tradition-directed individuals but individuals who are inner directed (Riesman, 1955, pp. 29–30). In this type of society, social and cultural boundaries, and hence membership and identity, are becoming porous and flexible. The inner-directed individual is a unique and self-directed actor. In an inner-directed social modality, we are more likely to be perceived as strangers because our mobility leads us to places where we are constructed as non-members (Harman, 1988, pp. 56–7).

Harman argues however that with the emergence of the 'other-directed' society, the constitution of the stranger and its relationship to solidarity alters. In the other-directed mode of social organisation, other people become the basis and direction of conformity. This differs from a tradition-directed society where tradition is the source of conformity and an inner-directed society where the self is the organising principle. Harman claims that in contrast to previous modes of social organisation, the other-directed society is based on social proximity rather than spatial proximity. Social actors become members of clubs, associations and organisations that transcend spatial distance and begin to associate with people beyond their primary group. Social proximity is maintained through a language of membership, and belonging depends on how fluent one is in the common language of particular organisations, clubs and groups. Understanding others occurs only through that which is communicable through symbols. Harman notes 'speech communities emerge on the basis of privatized language' (1988, p. 62). The other-directed actor becomes cosmopolitan in a cosmopolitan world, and the distinction between the familiar and the stranger is blurred. Social boundaries, so important to the classical experience of strangeness, and thus the basis of solidarity, have all but disappeared. It is social rather than physical proximity, for Harman, which unites members through a language of membership. Physical proximity, once the basis of community and belonging, has been superseded by social proximity based on a common language. Speaking the appropriate language, or what Harman categorises as 'communicative normalization', allows actors to be accepted by the group or association to which one seeks membership. A 'discursive strangeness' has replaced the classical view of strangeness because individuals orient more to each other as members who speak the same language. Those who defy the language of membership or who are unable to appropriate the specific language game are represented as deviant (Harman, 1988, p. 61). Communication and hence language, for Harman, are the key to deciphering the new modes of strangeness and familiarity.

> Strangeness is no longer a temporary condition to be overcome, but a way of life. The group, once formulated as homogenous and self-contained, does not clearly exclude the stranger. Rather, it is the one who is *unfamiliar with the language of strangeness* . . . who becomes an anomaly when overtures of membership orientation are made in a 'world of strangers'.
>
> (Harman, 1988, p. 44)

Harman's formulation of the modern stranger is no longer connected to the foreigner or the Other. The modern stranger is one who is engaged in an ongoing quest for membership from within: modern subjects are outsiders on the inside; their strangeness is not visible through external signs such as language, skin colour, customs and dress. Harman's version of the stranger no longer equates it with alterity or to those who are 'radically Other'; it also re-conceptualises the proximity/distance dimension of the classical stranger because modern strangers unlike the 'classical stranger' are physically distant but culturally and socially near.

Since the publication of Harman's text, an increasing number of scholars have been eager to put the last nail in the coffin of the 'classical stranger'. Beck (1996), Papastergiadis (2000), Stichweh (1997) and more recently Rumford (2013) have all written their own obituaries. Beck suggests that the classical notion of the stranger relies on the existence of 'simple modernity' in which there is a clear distinction between who the 'locals' are and who the strangers are (1996, p. 386). Under 'reflexive modernisation', in which people live in a turbulent global risk society and face contradictory global and personal risks, 'the social construction of the stranger can no longer be limited to the cultural self-understanding of a closed circle, thus the definition of the self becomes particularly problematic' (Beck, 1996, p. 388). Under the conditions of individualisation, the self becomes fragmented and internally differentiated. In a global and mobile world, the 'classical stranger' is no longer a distinct category. Beck notes, 'reflexive modernity generalises the category of the stranger to one whose central characteristics is *universal strangeness*' (Beck, 1996, p. 388, emphasis in the original). From a Beckian perspective, Schutz perceived the life-world of both the host and the stranger as unproblematic, whereas for Beck, these life-worlds are themselves fragile because they assume the existence of self-contained societies/life-worlds untouched by global processes.

Others such as Stichweh (1997) maintain that the classical representation and understanding of the stranger is no longer relevant to contemporary society. Adopting a systems approach, Stichweh suggests that in an urban, functionally differentiated setting, strangers either become invisible or omnipresent. In this milieu, the category of the stranger loses its function of indicating a distinct social figure, such as the foreigner. Modern individuals, according to Stichweh, relate to each other neither as friend or enemy, rather in a highly urbanised environment we treat one another with indifference. From this premise Stichweh reinstates the universalisation thesis. If late modernity is understood as a highly differentiated social modality, then difference becomes something that constitutes the very basis of this society rather than being confined to the margins. The overcoming of strangeness is no longer a strategic problem for modern society; as a result, Stichweh, like Harman before him, comes to the conclusion that we are witnessing the disappearance of the 'classical stranger' as a cultural outsider, and as a consequence, the conventional view of strangeness no longer holds because 'marginality has become a condition of membership' (Harman, 1988, p. 44). Strangeness, for people in the West, is now a common experience, and ironically difference has been erased. If we are all strangers, then no one is a stranger.

A further problem with Simmel's 'classical stranger', according to Papastergiadis, is that it is embedded in a series of dichotomies: us/them, modern/traditional and insider/outsider. Whereas the stranger oscillates between these positions, 'it presupposes that these prior positions are fixed and counter-posed according to a binary logic' (Papastergiadis, 2000, p. 13). These assumptions, according to Papastergiadis, have led to an essentialist view of identity. Difference under an essentialist viewpoint is defined in oppositional terms where boundaries are maintained between the migrant and host. This representational model and the boundaries that support it are untenable in contemporary society (Papastergiadis, 2000, p. 14). Papastergiadis maintains that the relationship between the stranger and the local underlying Simmel's version of estrangement may now have changed. In a mobile and global society, our encounters with strangers have drastically multiplied to the extent that strangers are no longer at the margins of the everyday life of locals. Rather, the host's relationship to alterity has become entrenched in the everyday practices of social interaction. Papastergiadis concludes that strangers are more ubiquitous to our social surroundings, and thus physical proximity has not necessarily led to increasing social and cultural distanciation towards the other. This challenges the very constitution of the 'classical stranger': the physical proximity that we experience with those who come today and stay tomorrow does not necessarily lead to social and cultural distance. In a transnational and 'superdiverse' global world where strangers are increasingly part of our locality, Papastergiadis believes that we are becoming more open to and embracing of those who come today and stay tomorrow. Papastergiadis's approach differs from previous critiques of the 'classical stranger' because, although he agrees that the nature of strangeness has changed, his critique is not premised on the disappearance of the 'classical stranger'. The 'classical stranger' is more ubiquitous, which has led to a positive change in the host's attitude to the stranger as foreigner.

Rumford's work on the globalisation of strangeness provides the most rigorous attempt to rethink the category of the stranger in light of contemporary processes. In our global and mobile world, the stranger is no longer one who will come today and stay tomorrow, rather the stranger is one who is here today and gone tomorrow. According to Rumford, 'we no longer live in societies in which it is easy to distinguish who has "come today and will stay tomorrow" and ethnicity and other markers of difference no longer necessarily signify someone who is not "of" society' (Rumford, 2013, p. 6). The experience of being a stranger has now been extended to host members because they are no longer sure who constitutes 'they' or the 'other'. Rumford – reminiscent of the existential dimension – refers to a general 'sense of disorientation resulting from . . . an experience of globalization in which previously reliable reference points have been eroded and we encounter strangers where previously we encountered neighbours' (2013, p. 7). Strangeness becomes a societal condition in which not only is the stranger difficult to identify, but our own identity is also in question. Following a long line of thinkers and reminiscent of the psychoanalytical perspective to the stranger, Rumford concludes that we become strangers to others but also to ourselves. The experience of globalisation has led to self-estrangement because we have loss firm and fixed foundations, and we are increasingly disconnected to those who we once thought were part of our community. Globalisation 'pushes' down on people and has resulted in restricted access to global networks and reduced choices.

The universalisation of strangeness: A critique

The critique of the classical stranger is part of a long tradition in the social and behavioural sciences. It argues that, due to the enormous qualitative and quantitative changes that have occurred over the last two hundred years, we have seen the fall and rise of particular personality types. The leading exponents of this approach were members of the Frankfurt School such as Wilhelm Reich and Erich Fromm. Reich, writing in the 1920s and early 1930s, attempted to demonstrate that 'every social order creates those character forms which it needs for its preservation'. He concludes that the character structure represents 'the crystallization of the sociological processes of a given epoch' (in Held, 1980, p. 116). Fromm, in his discussion of the theoretical basis of freedom in modern society, states, 'Different societies or classes within society have specific social character, and on its basis different ideas develop and become powerful' (1942, pp. 239–40).

Through the work of Harman we have already encountered the classic sociological work in this field, David Riesman's *The Lonely Crowd*. Riesman relates the changing social and economic structure of US society to the social character of particular groups in the US. Likewise, there is a tendency within the universalisation thesis to assume that the 'social character' of contemporary society no longer reflects the condition that existed during Simmel's and Schutz's time. This temporal approach implies a linear perspective in which there is a break from one society to another, for example, from a society in which the stranger is the exception to a society in which the stranger is the norm. What is overlooked in the universalisation thesis is that to speak of a shift to a society of strangers is to adopt a temporal view in which the characteristics of different societies and the strangers that emerge from them do not overlap.

The issue with the 'stranger/difference as the norm' thesis is that it adopts an ahistorical account of difference in which past relations with strangers and their material and social conditions are conveniently put aside. Difference may have entered the 'centre' of Western societies, but this does not mean that difference has lost its Othering proprieties. A distinction also needs to be made between the 'difference' that those in the West experience and the 'difference' that non-Western and non-white individuals face in Western societies. Being a stranger in the latter case, as the postcolonial approach as indicated, is embedded in power relations that extend beyond time and space. Furthermore, to claim that markers of difference no longer help us to identify who belongs to the host society goes against the backlash to multiculturalism and diversity and the securitisation of migration occurring across the Western world. Visible markers are continually being used to marginalise and discriminate against religious and cultural groups.

The rise of Islamophobia and negative attitudes towards 'boat people' and refugees speaks to the continued presence of an 'us and them' mentality and the fear of cultural and religious strangers in the political culture of the West. The condition of strangeness in which we are physically close, but increasingly socially and cultural distant to others, may no longer be confined to our experience of the 'classical stranger'. Nonetheless, to conclude from this position that the 'stranger' – that comes today and stays tomorrow and who signifies difference and Otherness – has disappeared goes against the current political and social realities of many Western countries.

The universalisation thesis is also connected to the experience of homelessness and the de-territorialisation of place and place identification. The thesis is too quick to dismiss the relationship between place and identity. Research within urban sociology continues to focus on the importance of place identification. Cuba and Hummon have shown that this literature 'has challenged both the popular and social-scientific images of the placelessness of the contemporary landscape and self' (1993, p. 112). In fact, the idea that we are all strangers and place has lost its significance in a mobile and global world disregards how place identities affiliate the self with significant locales. Whereas these localities are changing due to a mobile populace, this does not mean that place has become inconsequential. The implication is that a sense of existential homelessness may be evident at the regional or national level, but at the local level one may still forge a sense of attachment or home. On the other hand, we find that people who have little or no connection to their local community have a strong affinity to their region, country or to the 'international community'. Place identification can be located at the local, regional or national level and brings with it the development of a sense of belonging and order with one's social-spatial world (Casakin et al., 2015). Nonetheless, place identification may also function to control social relations or strengthen notions of belonging (Hugh-Jones and Madill, 2009). Place identity – whether it is subjectively or objectively understood – is still relevant in understanding someone's place in the world. These findings suggest that if one accepts the apparent ubiquitous nature of being a stranger and homelessness, then a more complex and enriching narrative about the relationship among home, place and identity is being overlooked.

Finally, the universalisation of strangeness is premised on the observation that as a consequence of the global movement of people, in particular the emergence of a global mobile workforce, there are increasing strangers in the West who come today and are gone tomorrow. This does not mean, however, that these transnational workers or international students who may come from Asian or African countries are not treated as 'classical strangers' by the host. During the period that they reside in the host society, they are in the 'classic' sense physically close but socially and cultural distant. This period of temporary migration, which could last from a few months to a couple of years, could still be understood from a phenomenological perspective. Temporary migrants may experience the personal crisis or 'shock' outlined by Schutz, and thus their experience, however temporary, could still be understood through the lens of the 'classical stranger'. Living in increasingly 'super-diverse' worlds has meant that what was once an anomaly during the early part of the twentieth century – contact with strangers – has now become the norm. The distinction between physical proximity and cultural distance has broken down for an increasing number of host members in the West, but this does not mean that the experience of temporary mobile migrant workers cannot be understood in terms of the 'classical stranger'. They are still physically close and culturally distant even when they are mobile. Globalising and transnational processes are making us more mobile, and hence there are more strangers, but this mobility does not make them less Othered. The universalisation thesis assumes a kind of existential crisis within the West, but this condition does not mean that Othering has ceased.

Moreover, to what extent does the idea of the universalisation of homelessness or strangeness reflect or capture the social conditions of the everyday lives of people? In other words, the existential reading of global estrangement overlooks the material dimension and the privileges that are inherent in choosing to be 'homeless'. The current feeling of disorientation and homelessness, claims Massey, may be restricted to a particular section of the 'first world' trying to make sense of the arrival of the Other to their shores. She concludes that 'it is not proximity that is itself unsettling, but also the nature of the social relations, and most particularly in their aspect of power relations, of which proximity is the geography' (Massey, 1992, p. 11). Accounts of the universalisation of homelessness conflate the idea of homelessness with metaphors such as heartlessness, indifference, rootlessness, anomie (for Berger) and mobility and empowerment (for Harman). In this conflation the notion of homelessness tends to lose its material, economic and political connotations. The unintended consequence of using an existential conception of global estrangement is that it tends to distance itself from any material concern with the condition of homelessness. This makes it difficult to associate homelessness with economic and political powerlessness and thus material deprivation. Homelessness is a multidimensional and socially constructed category and should not be conflated with an ontological state of rootlessness (Somerville, 1992).

The last two chapters have shown that the category of the stranger is multifaceted; it ranges from the psychoanalytic to phenomenological and from existential, sociological and postcolonial approaches. It includes slippages, tensions and contradictions among these approaches. These tensions and contradictions are particularly evident when scholars both reject and draw on the 'classical stranger'. For some scholars, the experience of the classical stranger can no longer be used as an explanatory model to reflect the structural, systemic and cultural changes of our global, mobile contemporary society. Other scholars, explicitly and implicitly, argue that the classical stranger still provides a conceptual framework with which to interpret the very same global, multicultural and post-modern processes. Shields suggests that the dissolution of the distinction between near and far reflects the condition of the classical sociological stranger; in addition, the classical stranger illustrates how presence and proximity are 'no longer an indication of inside status, of citizenship, or of cultural membership' (Shields, 1992, p. 195). What was once far away – the stranger – is now near. The 'distances that once separated all the categories of "Otherness" from the local sphere of "our" everyday life appear to have collapsed or at least are undergoing important changes' (Shields, 1992, p. 194). For Shields, the classical sociological stranger provides an interpretive scheme with which to grasp the postmodern condition. Ironically, what for some scholars is a conceptually flawed category is for Shields the key to unlocking the postmodern condition. The assumption that we have moved from the classical to a modern understanding of the stranger is arbitrary because the 'classical' and the 'modern' stranger represent two sides of the same coin. The boundary between the classical and the modern stranger is porous. To assert, therefore, that the changing structure of society leads to the death of the classical stranger is to ignore the fluid boundaries between the traditional and the modern and the multiple dimensions of modernity (Eisenstadt, 2000; Wittrock, 2000) along with the different types of strangers that move in and out of these borderlands. The following chapter locates multiple versions of the 'classical stranger' in the work of Simmel and, in doing so, questions the essentialist reading found in the discourse on the death of the 'classical stranger'.

References

Beck, U., 1996. How Neighbours Become Jews: The Political Construction of the Stranger in an Age of Reflexive Modernity. *Constellations*, 2, pp. 378–396.

Berger, P.L., Berger, B. and Kellner, H., 1973. *The Homeless Mind: Modernization and Consciousness*. New York: Random House.

Casakin, H. Hernandez, B. and Riuz, C., 2015. Place Attachment and Place Identity in Israeli Cities: The Influence of City Size, *Cities*, 42, pp. 224–230.

Cuba, L. and Hummon, D.M., 1993. Identification with Dwelling, Community and Region. *The Sociological Quarterly*, 34(1), pp. 111–131.

Dessewffy, T., 1996. Strangerhood without Boundaries: An Essay in the Sociology of Knowledge. *Poetics Today*, 17(4), pp. 599–615.

Eisenstadt, S.N., 2000. Multiple Modernities. *Daedalus*, 129(1), pp. 1–30.

Fromm, E., 1942. *The Fear of Freedom*. Reprint 1960. London: Routledge and Kegan Paul.

Harman, L.D., 1988. *The Modern Stranger: On Language and Membership*. Berlin: Moutonde Gruyter.

Held, D., 1980. *Introduction to Critical Theory: Horkheimer to Habermas*. Berkeley: University of California Press.

Hugh-Jones, S. and Madill, A., 2009. "The Air's Got to Be Far Cleaner Here": A Discursive Analysis of Place-Identity Threat. *British Journal of Social Psychology*, 48, pp. 601–624.

Massey, D., 1992. A Place Called Home? *New Formations*, 17, pp. 3–15.

Papastergiadis, N., 2000. *The Turbulence of Migration: Globalization, Deterritorialization and Hybridity*. Cambridge: Polity Press.

Riesman, D., 1955. *The Lonely Crowd: A Study of the Changing American Character*. New York: Doubleday Anchor Books.

Rumford, C., 2013. *The Globalization of Strangeness*. London: Palgrave.

Shields, R., 1992. A Truant Proximity: Presence and Absence in the Space of Modernity. *Environment and Planning D: Society and Space*, 10(2), pp. 181–198.

Somerville, P., 1992. Homelessness and the Meaning of Home: Rooflessness or Rootlessness? *International Journal of Urban and Regional Research*, 16(4), pp. 529–539.

Stichweh, R., 1997. The Stranger – On the Sociology of Indifference. *Thesis Eleven*, 51, pp. 1–16.

Wittrock, B., 2000. Modernity: One, None, or Many? European Origins and Modernity as a Global Condition. *Daedalus*, 129(1), pp. 31–60.

4 Georg Simmel, the stranger and the sociology of knowledge

It has been well documented that the idea of the stranger can be traced back to a short essay written by the German philosopher and sociologist Georg Simmel. It has been more than a century since Simmel wrote the paper, and its significance has not diminished; scholars continue to draw on the essay, as evidenced by its citations. Part of this literature concerns itself with the extent to which Simmel's category relates to other concepts, whereas other studies – as Chapter 2 demonstrated – investigate whether Simmel's stranger can still describe the experience of cultural and religious Others in a global, mobile and 'super-diverse' world where cross-cultural contacts are more frequent and intense. In these latter works, the heuristic value of Simmel's category has now been questioned. This rich literature, however, confines itself to Simmel's essay on the stranger and rarely contextualises the stranger within his broader intellectual project: especially, his critique of binary thinking; his observations on the construction of historical knowledge; and his romantic conception of individuality evident in his comments on the genius and the cosmopolitan subject. Contextualisation along these lines provides a more expansive, deeper and multiple understanding of the Simmelian stranger. The final part of this chapter will demonstrate how Simmel's insights on these matters can provide a unique contribution to the sociology of knowledge and, more specifically, to rethinking the debate surrounding standpoint epistemologies. Contrary to the claims that the 'classical stranger' has become archaic, I argue that what constitutes the 'classical stranger' needs to be rethought and that what we find in Simmel is multiple readings of the 'classical stranger' that still resonate with contemporary debates in social theory.

Marginality theory

The literature on Simmel's stranger can be divided into two broad camps. On the one hand, we have those studies that attempt to engage with the category and refine it. Whereas on the other hand, we have studies – as the previous chapter has shown – that question the empirical value of Simmel's stranger. The issue of whether Simmel's stranger is compatible with other sociological categories has generated an intense debate. McLemore (1970) argues that it is Robert Park's 'marginal man' rather than the 'newcomer' who best exemplifies Simmel's stranger. Levine, a leading Anglo-American scholar on Simmel's stranger, emphasises that it is solely associated with a personality type (Levine, 1977, 1985). It is only by focusing on this personality type that Levine is able to conclude that there have been 'distortions', 'confusions' and 'misunderstandings' surrounding the literature on the stranger (1985, p. 73). Unlike McLemore, Levine maintains that the stranger cannot be linked to Park's 'marginal man' the experiences of ethnic groups in the US, the enemy within or the intruder. Levine concludes that the 'precise nature of Simmel's contribution in the excursus on "Der Fremde" can now be specified. It deals almost exclusively with the question of the characteristics of the status of the individual Sojourner' (1977, p. 27). More recently, Alexander (2004, p. 88) argues that Simmel's stranger cannot be associated with those who are excluded such as the poor and new immigrants because Simmel's category 'is very different from the economically disadvantaged or exploited class, the theoretical category for those impoverished by an impersonal economic order and its elite'. For Alexander, Simmel's stranger is not capable of understanding the underlying representational systems used by the core group to construct and interpret individuals in terms of polluted representations. The stranger is both an objective and subjective status, and it is when polarising categories are applied that an 'us and them' mentality is adopted. Simmel's account of the stranger, according to Alexander, is incapable of conceptualising strangeness in this way because 'it is the construction of difference, not commonality that makes potentially marginal groups into dangerous ones that are strange' (Alexander, 2004, p. 91).

Whereas Alexander's critique will be taken up in more detail in a Chapter 7, these observations are rather limited because they rarely move beyond Simmel's essay on the stranger. The following discussion connects Simmel's observation on the stranger to his overall theoretical project, to his construction of historical knowledge and to his reflections on cosmopolitanism, romantic individuality and the genius. It is only by placing Simmel's account of the stranger within his broader work that we can appreciate its nuances, complexity and depth. I take seriously Weinstein and Weinstein's suggestion that none of Simmel's works 'should be considered in abstraction from others if one wishes to give adequate understanding of the systematic coherence in his thought' (1990, p. 350).

Simmel and the 'third way'

It has been noted that a dialectical pattern of thinking underlies Simmel's philosophical and sociological writings (Weinstein and Weinstein, 1989, p. 49). Simmel's 'studies of society are not fundamentally interactionist or functionalist, formalist or impressionist' but essentially demonstrate this dialectic (Weinstein and Weinstein, 1989, p. 52). This dialectic expresses itself both in the way Simmel addresses various philosophical and sociological questions and in his conceptualisation of how particular individual types can transcend binary thinking. The development of a third type of consciousness can be located in Simmel's account of the stranger, the third element, and his discussion on the historian and 'the genius'. Wessely (1990) argues that Simmel searches for a third category that will move beyond the distorting philosophical language of binary oppositions:

> He constantly searches for 'third' categories which might comprehend opposites and make us comprehend how mutually exclusive forces and principles do not annihilate each other but create, in their interaction, new forms by finding, as it were, a third way out of a dilemma.
>
> (1990, p. 376)

This 'third way' is evident in Simmel's critique of nineteenth- and early twentieth-century philosophy because it has evolved a way of thinking that can no longer effectively comprehend modern society. Philosophy, maintains Simmel, tends to accept a dualistic framework. In philosophy 'one must say Yea or Nay, there is no third way', and its 'whole conceptual logic is felt to be so undesirably constricting, and at the same time its solutions are so rarely derived from any previously discovered third factor . . . or third possibility' (Simmel, 1976a, pp. 259–60). The ensuing analysis identifies this 'third possibility' in Simmel's account of the stranger and the construction of historical knowledge.

Simmelian strangers

Chapter 1 on theories of the stranger illustrated that the category of the stranger can be conceptualised in multiple ways and that this can been extended to Simmel's own account of the stranger. I want to suggest that the 'classical stranger' that has come to be associated with Simmel is not a homogenous and undifferentiated category; a close reading of Simmel's seminal essay within the context of his overall work highlights its multiple meanings. According to the conventional interpretation, Simmel's stranger is a commentary on a specific individual type that involves a particular social and spatial relation. This points to the importance of space in Simmel's thought. Simmel's overall position on space is not confined to a spatial determinism or a social constructivist perspective (Lechner, 1991). For Simmel, spatial forms of objects or social configurations should not be understood as causes but rather as effects that shed light on the character of social formations (Simmel, 1997, p. 138). In other words, *geometric distance* may produce *metaphoric distance* such as neighbourliness or strangeness, and these two forms of distance can be understood as operating simultaneously in Simmel's work (Ethington, 1997). It is not just social distance between self and other that determines strangeness, rather spatial configurations impact on social processes. Strangeness then exposes a dialectical spatial relation between proximity and distance. In the phenomenon of the stranger, 'distance means that he, who is [physically] close by, is [socially and culturally] far, and strangeness means that he, who also is [socially and culturally] far, is actually [physically] near'. In this spatial reading, Simmel conceptualises the stranger as a positive relation; it is a specific form of interaction (1999, p. 185). From this point onwards, however, this spatial reading of the stranger coexists with a conceptualisation of the stranger that emphasises metaphoric distance. The strangeness that the stranger experiences towards the host signifies physical proximity and social and cultural distance, and this I would argue represents one version of the 'classical' conception of the stranger. What is important here – because it has repercussions for how contemporary interpretations of the stranger are conceptualised – is that what constitutes 'far' and 'near' depends on whether spatial and metaphoric distances are applied.

The 'classical' understanding of the stranger incorporates the spatial (physical) 'near' but metaphoric (socially and culturally) 'far'. This, however, is disrupted when Simmel locates underlying commonalities between the host and the stranger. For example, a stranger may share with the host a common national identity, similar social and occupational identity or a common human nature. These universal features, claims Simmel, 'extend beyond ourselves and connect us only because they connect a great many people' (1999, p. 187). The more these 'similarities assume a universal nature', the more likely they will be based on detached, dispassionate and unemotional relations. In this situation the host and the stranger are simultaneously physically and socially close. These commonalities have the potential to upset the boundary between host and the stranger and paradoxically mean that the proponents of the universalisation thesis may have got it wrong. Rather than the universalisation of strangeness making the 'classical stranger' obsolete, universalism is built into the very construction of Simmel's 'classical stranger'.

Nonetheless, whereas at some fundamental level there are some similarities between the stranger and the host group, these ties do not run very deep. According to Simmel, 'with the stranger one has only certain more general qualities in common, whereas the relation with organically connected persons is based on similarity of just those specific traits which differentiate them from the merely universal' (1999, p. 186). Moreover, strangers are not organically connected to the host because of their mobility, 'which constitutes the formal relation of the stranger' (Simmel, 1999, p. 186). This mobility means that strangers are 'not bound up organically, through established ties of kingship, locality or occupation' (Simmel, 1999, p. 186). This conception of stranger in which one is connected (at the level of generality) and disconnected (at some personal 'organic' level) is consistent with Simmel's dialectical view of the relationship between the individual and society. For Simmel, there is a constant tension between 'the instinct driving to individuality and the instinct driving to dissolution into the community' (in Watier, 1993, p. 71). Watier notes that Simmel's conception of the individual encompasses the 'ability to blend into generality which allows the development and preservation of the most personal aspects' (1993, p. 74). This condition is also evident in the position of strangers who simultaneously have some affinities with the host community because they share a common human condition, but they preserve their distinctiveness and hence their difference because they are 'organically' different to the host.

Another dimension to the stranger that has been mostly overlooked in the literature on Simmel's stranger is aligned with the process of Othering and indirectly affiliated with postcolonial and cultural studies readings of the stranger. Simmel speaks of a type of 'strangeness' in which we deny the humanity of the Other. It is this 'sort of "strangeness" in which this very connection on the basis of a general quality embracing the parties is precluded' (Simmel, 1999, p. 187). The Otherness is heightened when groups reject the common connection we have with strangers. In these situations the interaction between self and Other transforms from a positive to a negative relation, and our relationship with the stranger becomes a non-relation. Simmel offers the example of the Greeks and the barbarians as a non-relation with strangers 'in which the general characteristics one takes as peculiarly and merely human are disallowed to the other' (Simmel, 1999, p. 186). Denying the Other their humanity effectively negates their existence. The non-relation that exists with the stranger suppresses what ties us together as human beings. It denies the possibility of an encounter with the stranger that could be both physically and socially close.

We can also locate an existential dimension to the 'classical stranger', which is sometimes understated in studies on Simmel. This dimension relates to a sense of dread or existential angst as one comes to the realisation that we are connected to forces beyond our control. There are larger processes working behind the everyday, mundane world of individuals in which what was thought as unique and individual 'is only fulfilling a general human destiny' (Simmel, 1999, p. 187). A loss of uniqueness and hence a rising sense of self-estrangement, for Simmel, 'easily enters even the most intimate relationships' (Simmel, 1999, p. 187); for example, what we thought as a love that had never existed before is a general condition experienced by many. Estrangement, continues Simmel, usually arises 'at the moment when this feeling of uniqueness vanishes from the relationship' (1999, p. 187) and when 'similarity, harmony and closeness are accompanied by the feeling that they are actually not the exclusive property of this particular relation, but stem from a more general one' (Simmel, 1999, p. 187). Reminiscent of the existential self, strangeness is connected to a sense of loss, renunciation or relinquishment indicating some recognition that one's experience is not unique or different but rather part of something greater than oneself. The feeling of existential strangeness then emerges when – in the face of overwhelming universal forces – we lose our sense of self as a unique individual with a set of unique experiences.

It is in Simmel's examination of different types of individuality (Simmel, 1964a) that we find the genesis of this existential reading of strangeness. Simmel notes that the philosophical outlook of the eighteenth century emphasises a quantitative individualism that treats the individual as a unit and as a separate entity, whereas the 'new individualism' of the nineteenth century emphasises the qualitative aspect of the individual. This new individualism, argues Simmel, is clearly expressed in Romanticism and is characterised by its claims to uniqueness and incomparability (1964a, p. 81). Simmel tends to adopt this 'new individualism' in his analyses of such topics as tact, discretion, confidence, reserve and secrecy. For Lipman, Simmel 'tends to accept the nineteenth-century interpretation of individuality as definitive'. He repeatedly 'emphasizes the uniqueness that springs from internal complexity and external incomparability rather than the individuality that is associated with atomic discreteness and subservience to universal law' (1965, p. 135). Hence, one dimension of Simmel's stranger echoes the existential self who experiences alienation and the loss of individuality or uniqueness. This existential self who has lost touch with his or her authentic self reappears in Simmel's critique of the quantitative and calculative nature of the money economy. In several places in *The Philosophy of Money*, Simmel refers to a 'distinctive and essential being' which is slowly being suppressed by technology, money and the domination of means over ends (Simmel, 1990, pp. 483–4).

Thus a close reading of Simmel's essay suggests that the stranger is manifested in multiple ways and that therefore what is represented as the 'classical stranger' needs rethinking. The 'classical stranger' can be associated with those who come today and stay tomorrow, and this has definite links to Schutz's phenomenological account of the stranger as immigrant. Nevertheless, what is also present in Simmel's account is a conception of the stranger linked to the Other who is not here but distant (the barbarian). Finally, the existential dimension of the stranger – later adopted by existential sociologists – reflects the loss of a unique individuality. Overall, Simmel's existential account of the stranger indicates a concern with how the romantic notion of individuality was threatened by a rational, bureaucratic and capitalist modernity. Simmel's writing on the stranger is the beginning of the third phase of his work, which was 'devoted to the philosophy of life and a critique of modernity' (Fuchs, 1991, p. 2).

Differentiated individuals, the cosmopolitan and 'the genius'

These multiple constructions of the 'classical stranger' not only suggest that contemporary critical views of this idea are too narrow, but they also ignore how Simmel's 'classical stranger' shares characteristics with other individual types found in his work. For example, Simmel illustrates how differentiated societies develop highly differential individuals who have a broad education and a diverse range of experiences (Simmel, 1976b, p. 104). Due to their cultivated life, differentiated individuals foster, according to Simmel, 'cosmopolitan sentiments' which contrast with the 'one-sided personalities' for whom common humanity exists only in their own limited, particular form. These one-sided personalities 'are incapable of empathizing with other people and therefore cannot become aware of what is common to all' (Simmel, 1976b, pp. 104–5). The cosmopolitan is the personality type that, for Simmel, emerges under modern conditions and has the ability to perceive the universal within the particular and the particular in the universal. Simmel's 'cosmopolitan individual' seems to describe his own dialectical thinking, which allows one to transcend boundaries by identifying universals while simultaneously constructing boundaries by highlighting particularities.

The characteristics of the 'classical stranger' are also found in Simmel's account of a third type of consciousness. Such a consciousness is evident in the authentic aesthetic sensibility where the subjective is experienced as universally valid and the universal is dialectically interwoven with the particular. In his later works Simmel rejects instrumental reason and systematic theorising and replaces it with aesthetic reflection (Fuchs, 1991, p. 9). This aesthetic, third type of consciousness finds its expression in the work of historians. The 'aesthetic secret of the historian[s]' lies in their 'ability to invest a purely individual – even unique entity with this sort of universality' (Simmel, 1977, p. 92). The in-between aesthetic consciousness denotes an ability to be close, yet distant, to objectify, but also be immersed in the subjectivism of the phenomenon under study. The aesthetic sensibility encourages a dialect between subject and object. Simmel refutes historical realism's claim that historical knowledge is possible insofar as it constitutes a mirror image of the event as it actually happened. Simmel contests this conception of history – which emphasises the process of distanciation on the part of the historian – as a copy or reproduction of its subject matter. In contrast, Simmel wants to 'emphasize both the proximity and distance between history and its subject matter' (1977, p. 87). This is reminiscent of the stranger who has something in common with the host but also remains distant due to 'organic differences'.

At one level, historians need to recreate the mental acts of historical subjects by reducing as much as possible the intellectual, social and cultural distance between themselves and historical actors. The historian, for Simmel, needs to transcend the boundaries between self and Other. This is only possible because, similar to the commonalities between the stranger and the host, 'the historical person and the historian have the same nature' and 'unless this condition is satisfied, the observable acts of historical persons would simply be unintelligible notions of physical objects' (Simmel, 1977, p. 87). Simmel emphasises the importance of proximity to historical knowledge, for instance, placing oneself in the position of the Other; according to the realist, however, this proximity does not mean that the historian's subjectivity becomes part of the interpretive process. In other words, historical realism wants to eliminate the historian's subjectivity from inquiry so that they can represent things as they actually occurred. This, according to Simmel, is not possible because if the historian's 'personal identity is eliminated, then there is nothing left for [them] to use in order to comprehend whatever lies beyond it' (Simmel, 1977, p. 88). He concludes that the 'more idiosyncratic ideas which the historian only requires through personal experience and which are inseparable from his own personality provide indispensable raw material for the understanding of another person' (Simmel, 1977, p. 88). Although realist historians want to distance or isolate their personalities from the historical interpretation and adopt the perspective of the Other, this process, for Simmel, is flawed. Historical knowledge cannot be conceived solely as a copy of the events 'as they actually occurred'. Rather, historical interpretation represents a transformation of experienced reality; thus, historical knowledge does not entail the elimination of subjectivity because 'this would destroy the possibility of historical knowledge' and 'the elimination of this most complete form of subjectivity would be self-defeating' (Simmel, 1977, p. 90). Simmel concludes that 'objectivity [the process of distanciation] cannot be detached from its subjective foundation [the proximity of the historian's own individuality], nor can these elements of subjectivity be eliminated from the results of historical knowledge' (1977, p. 91). Therefore the obstacle thought to limit or restrain knowledge – subjectivism – is also a condition under which knowledge is possible (Simmel, 1977, p. 89). Subjectivity and objectivity are intrinsically connected, and to suggest that they are contradictory processes misrepresents how knowledge is constructed.

Historical knowledge or understanding is not solely concerned with the naturalistic reproduction of the historical person because it extends beyond this pattern of congruence (Simmel, 1977, p. 94). Rather, historical understanding is about sharing in 'the mental life of persons who have nothing in common with us' (Simmel, 1977, p. 94). Similar to the historian, it is the 'genius', for Simmel, who has the special ability to connect with others beyond time and space:

> The genius seems to create knowledge out of himself, knowledge that the ordinary person can discover only through the basis of experience. On the basis of the slightest hints and allusions, he constructs an internally consistent and convincing picture of the intellectual processes, ideational associations and passions of historical persons, even though the actual examples of this cast of mind disappeared long ago.
>
> (Simmel, 1977, p. 95)

In a vague and somewhat fanciful manner Simmel attempts to identify the origins of the genius's interpretive powers. The ability of the genius to transcend, but also be close to the historical person, is related to unconscious forces:

> I interpret this phenomenon as a process whereby one becomes conscious of an inheritance that is unconscious or latent. In some form or other, earlier generations have transmitted their organic modifications to later generations; in some obscure fashion, the organic modifications are related to mental processes.
>
> (Simmel, 1977, p. 95)

This 'inheritance', according to Simmel, is favourably disposed in the mind of the genius because it is 'stored in his organism as genetically transmitted recollections'. These individuals can find traces of other characters and 'results and traces of earlier mental processes' in these 'genetically transmitted recollections'. As a result, the ability of historians to become conscious of an inheritance allows them to experience the same mental processes of those who are different whether they are one's contemporary or not (Simmel, 1977, p. 96). The boundary between self and other is not only maintained but also transcended. Geniuses/historians are different, but because of their special abilities they can also reflect on the universality of the human condition.

There is a continuity of experience between the historian as genius and the Other. The alterity of the Other is not closed to the historian because the Other, as a consequence of the 'genetically transmitted recollections', is in effect part of the self. Past, present and future are inextricably linked, but the organic connection between people of different times is only accessible or comprehensible through the mind of the historian/genius. They represent an aestheticism that expresses the proximity between subject and object while concomitantly maintaining distance and detachment. They signify the condition of the stranger, who through both commonality and organic differences, reinforces and blurs the distinction between self and other. In these observations, Simmel celebrates 'the cult of the creative genius who alone manages to escape from the iron cage of alienated culture . . . and expresses the deep pessimism underlying the "tragic consciousness" of German intellectuals at that time' (Fuchs, 1991, p. 3).

The third element, the stranger and the sociology of knowledge

There is an important connection among Simmel's 'classical stranger', the sociology of knowledge and debates on standpoint epistemologies that have been ignored in the contemporary dismissal of the 'classical stranger'. Pels's work on the relationship between the intellectual and the stranger argues that the sociology of knowledge has been haunted by the 'cognitive profits of marginality' (2000, p. 191). In other words, the marginal situation of strangers has allowed them a different, 'radical' and transgressive type of knowledge that generates a critique of 'conventional' knowledge.

This transformative and transgressive nature of the stranger is evident in Simmel's account, and he occasionally falls into the trap of romanticising and uncritically accepting the 'cognitive profits of marginality'. For example, strangers have a 'bird's-eye view' that both allows them to incorporate the particular views of the parties while not being immersed in the particularities of the opposing parties. The objectivity of strangers is characterised by their ability to be both remote and near or indifferent and involved (Simmel, 1999, p. 186). They are able to perceive the particular within the universal or the universal in the particular. Although the 'bird's-eye view' of the stranger can be considered as 'objective', this objectivity is not associated with the scientific method or the peep-show theory of knowledge in which scientists stand above the world they study. Scholars have claimed or implied that Simmel's category of the stranger adopts this neutral, transcendent knowledge (Jansen, 1980, p. 30; Pels, 2000, p. 182). Although this is partly true, this interpretation overlooks Simmel's nuanced view of objectivity, its relationship to the stranger and the construction of historical knowledge. First, Simmel ponders the connection among objectivity, subjectivism and the stranger:

> The "distinctive" objective attitude of the stranger does not signify . . . mere passivity and detachment: but is a distinct structure composed of remoteness and nearness, indifference and involvement. . . . Objectivity is by no means non-participation, a condition that is outside the distinction between subjective and objective orientations. It is rather a positive and definite kind of participation, in the same way that the objectivity of a theoretical observation clearly does not mean that the mind is a passive tabula rasa on which things inscribe their qualities.
>
> (Simmel, 1999, p. 186)

Simmel's view of objectivity undermines the positivist conception of knowledge based on the scientific method of neutrality, wherein subjectivism hinders rather than assists in the construction of true knowledge. Instead, Simmel argues that knowledge construction is a process that fuses objectivism with subjectivism and that the positivist notion of objectivity is illusory because objectivism relies on the incorporation of the subjective. Simmel's account of the 'third element' has affinities with the stranger's position and his ability to be 'objective'. First, the third element changes the content and quality of the relationship between individuals and groups: '[th]e appearance of the third party indicates transition, conciliation, and abandonment of absolute contrast (although, on occasion, it introduces contrast)' (Simmel, 1964b, p. 145).

The third element allows the construction of hybrid knowledges because it offers a different side to each of the element and 'yet fuses these different sides in the unity of its personality' (Simmel, 1964b, p. 135). Simmel constructs the third element as either a mediator and/or a non-partisan, and its function is to bring the two elements together by identifying their shared interests. The third element thus transcends the individual interests of the single elements. The 'objectivity' of the third element, for instance, the ability to be both indifferent and involved, becomes the vehicle with which the particularity of the two sides can be overcome and their underlying commonalities identified (Simmel, 1964b, pp. 148–9). The third element overcomes the problem of misunderstanding that exists between the two culturally different groups. The third party can place itself in close proximity to the two opposing groups while simultaneously distancing itself from each position. Similar to strangers, the third element is able to be 'objective' because it can be simultaneously detached and involved; it can stand outside and beyond the respective views. As demonstrated in the preceding discussion, Simmel's discussion of the third element, and its ability to move from the particular to the universal and back again, is reinforced in his account of the differentiated, cosmopolitan individual, the historian and the genius.

Conclusion: standpoint epistemologies

Simmel's major contribution to theories of the stranger is that it offers the opportunity to rethink the debate on standpoint epistemologies. A central argument of standpoint epistemologies is that the Enlightenment view of knowledge – as disinterested and context free – is misleading. This critique is usually directed at scientific knowledge and other forms of knowledge that adopt the positivist scientific method. This method is premised on a particular type of objectivity that is supposedly neutral and adopts a 'view from nowhere'. Feminist standpoint epistemology has been particularly critical of universal and context-free knowledge. It questions the idea that knowledge comes from a 'view from nowhere' and instead claims that 'each person can achieve only a partial view of reality from the perspective of his or own position in the social hierarchy' (Harding, 1991, p. 59). Standpoint epistemology is also critical of Karl Mannheim's (1936, 1993) idea of free-floating intellectuals, who float above the situated and have a disinterested, impartial, value-free and detached perspective. In contrast, Harding concludes that 'the view from the perspective of the powerful is far more partial and distorted than that available from the perspective of the dominated' because the powerful have a vested interest in 'obscuring the unjust conditions that produce their unearned privileges and authority than do the dominated groups in hiding the conditions that produce their situation' (in Michael, 1996, p. 95). Haraway is also critical of a version of objectivity which works to serve the 'hierarchical and positivist orderings of what counts as knowledge' (1988, p. 580) and questions the supposed vantage point of the subjugated, especially when it is appropriated by academics who occupy less marginal positions. There is a danger of romanticising and uncritically accepting this marginal position, and thus we must not assume that the marginal is an innocent position. What we need, according to Haraway, is a 'passionate detachment' or an 'embodied objectivity', both of which transcend the relativist position of standpoint epistemologies as well as the totalising project of positivist scientific knowledge (Haraway, 1988, pp. 585, 588). Haraway's 'passionate detachment' resonates with Simmel's notion of 'subjective objectivity' underlying the construction of historical knowledge in which the notion of 'objectivity' acknowledges the role of the historians' situated position and thus their involvement in the construction of historical knowledge.

On one level Simmel's discussion of the third element and its relationship to the stranger suggest an approach to knowledge construction that adopts a 'view from nowhere' or a 'bird's-eye view' that is not available to those who are situated. The stranger's hybrid knowledge sits uncomfortably with Simmel's suggestion that the construction of historical knowledge cannot be separated from the historian's subjectivity. It is their social and cultural situation that partly contributes to the construction of historical knowledge and the historical person. Nonetheless, although Simmel and Haraway may agree that the construction of knowledge cannot be context or situation free, Simmel would disagree with standpoint epistemology's assumption that 'true' representation can only be achieved through self-representation. This goes at the very heart of identity politics and the standpoint epistemology that informs it. Standpoint epistemology assumes that the representation of the Other – the historical or marginal person – by another – in this case the historian or the stranger – distorts the image, beliefs, values, acts, needs and wishes of the Other, and thus the Other can only be seen through the distorted eyes of the historian and interpreter. Thus self-representation is the only way of grasping the true nature of the Other. For example, only Chinese women can represent Chinese women, only Muslims can represent Muslims and only Jews can represent Jews. This position becomes problematic because Simmel's account of the stranger and the historian emphasises both the commonality and differences between self and Other. The representation of Otherness is possible because we are both socially close at some fundamental level and also distant to the Other due to our 'organic differences'. From Simmel's perspective, radical forms of standpoint epistemologies overstate our differences at the cost of illuminating our commonalities.

Simmel's account of the historian suggests that the distinction between auto-representation – or self-representation – and hetero-representation – or representation by others – is overdrawn because it assumes that we have only one identity dominating all others (Heller, 1998). In a world of multiple and hybrid identities, 'one of [our] identities will gain preference in one situation, and the other in another, every auto representation will be also a hetero-representation' (Heller, 1998, p. 351). Simmel's work on the stranger and the construction of historical knowledge can shed light on how we can break down the binaries between self and Other and the systems of knowledge that support it. Simmel supports one of the key arguments of standpoint epistemology: that knowledge is contextual and situated; for example, the historian's subjectivity is indispensable to historical knowledge. Nonetheless, his work also implies that the radical forms of standpoint epistemology – which privileges the knowledge of the marginal position and argues that the identity of the Other can only be achieved through self-representation – provides an incomplete understanding of knowledge construction. Whereas self-representation tends to reinforce the binary between self and Other, Simmel's work on the stranger suggests that commonality and difference contributes to our understanding of what makes us human. As standpoint epistemology has argued, knowledge cannot be constructed from a 'view from nowhere', but as Simmel points out neither is it solely situated. To see the world differently, there is a third possibility that Simmel advances in which knowledge construction incorporates the subjective and the specificity of the situated while also acknowledging the commonalities between those who are situated (the historical subject) and those who are detached from the situated experience (the historian).

To understand how knowledge is constructed through the interaction between self and Other, Simmel's reflections on the stranger suggests that one can never be completely detached or totally immersed. One has to be cautious of accepting this position at face value. Although Simmel's observation on the construction of historical knowledge raises some concerns with standpoint epistemologies, his acceptance that the stranger adopts a 'bird's-eye view' is still problematic. Is such a third position – a dwelling between the subjective and objective perspectives, between the particular and universal – possible? The in-between stranger is alleged to transcend standpoint epistemologies, but the in-between perspective collapses into another standpoint. As demonstrated further in Chapter 9, Simmel succumbs to the ideology of the third in which the incommensurability between self and Other can be overcome and gives way to a middle or common ground where we can reason or converse with Others. Such a common ground is not impossible to find, but the in-between stranger does not have privileged access to it, rather it may be found through a critical conversation between self and Other.

Whereas many studies have acknowledged Simmel as the 'father' of the 'classical stranger' in the social sciences, this literature confines itself to his essay on the stranger and adopts a one-dimensional view of the Simmelian stranger. By demonstrating the multifaceted nature of the 'classical stranger' and its relation to Simmel's overall theoretical project, I have questioned previous interpretations of the 'classical stranger' but also how different versions of it continue to have relevance to current epistemological debates.

References

Alexander, J., 2004. Rethinking Strangeness: From Structures in Space to Discourses in Civil Society. *Thesis Eleven*, 79, pp. 87–104.
Ethington, P.J., 1997. The Intellectual Construction of "Social Distance": Toward a Recovery of Georg Simmel's Social Geometry. *Cybergeo: European Journal of Geography*, no. 30, [online] Available from: http://cybergeo.revues.org/227.
Fuchs, S., 1991. From Theory to Critique of Modernity: The Development of Simmel's Sociology. *Michigan Sociological Review*, 5, pp. 1–18.
Haraway, D., 1988. Situated Knowledges: The Science Question in Feminism and the Privilege of Partial Perspective. *Feminist Studies*, 14(3), pp. 575–599.
Harding, S., 1991. *Whose Science? Whose Knowledge?* Milton Keynes: Open University Press.
Heller, A., 1998. Self-Representation and the Representation of the Other. *In*: R. Bauböck and J. Rundell, eds. *Blurred Boundaries: Migration, Ethnicity, Citizenship*. Aldershot: Ashgate, pp. 341–354.
Jansen, S.C., 1980. The Stranger as Seer or Voyeur: A Dilemma of the Peep-Show Theory of Knowledge. *Qualitative Sociology*, 2(3), pp. 22–55.
Lechner, F.J., 1991. Simmel on Social Space. *Theory, Culture and Society*, 8(3), pp. 195–201.
Levine, D., 1977. Simmel at a Distance: On the History and Systematics of the Sociology of the Stranger. *Sociological Forces*, 10(1), pp. 15–29.
Levine, D., 1985. *The Flight from Ambiguity: Essays in Social and Cultural Theory*. Chicago: University of Chicago Press.
Lipman, M., 1965. Some Aspects of Simmel's Conception of the Individual. *In*: K.H. Wolff, ed. *Essays on Sociology, Philosophy and Aesthetics*. New York: Harper Torchbooks, pp. 119–138.
Mannheim, K., 1936. *Ideology and Utopia: An Introduction to the Sociology of Knowledge*. Reprint 1985. San Diego: Harcourt Brace Jovanovich.
Mannheim, K., 1993. The Sociology of Intellectuals. *Theory, Culture & Society*, 10(3), pp. 69–80.
McLemore, S.D., 1970. Simmel's "Stranger": A Critique of the Concept. *The Pacific Sociological Review*, 13(2), pp. 86–94.
Michael, J., 1996. Making a Stand: Standpoint Epistemologies, Political Positions, Proposition 187. *Telos*, 108, pp. 93–103.
Pels, D., 2000. *The Intellectual as Stranger: Studies in Spokespersonship*. London: Routledge.
Simmel, G., 1964a. Individual and Society in Eighteenth and Nineteenth Century Views of Life. *In*: K.H. Wolff, ed. *The Sociology of Georg Simmel*. New York: The Free Press, pp. 58–84.
Simmel, G., 1964b. The Quantitative Aspect of the Group. *In*: K.H. Wolff, ed. *The Sociology of Georg Simmel*. New York: Free Press, pp. 87–174.
Simmel, G., 1976a. The Crisis of Culture. *In*: P.L. Lawrence, ed. *Georg Simmel: Sociologists and European*. London: Nelson & Sons, pp. 253–266.
Simmel, G., 1976b. The Meaning of Culture. *In*: P.L. Lawrence, ed. *Georg Simmel: Sociologists and European*. London: Nelson & Sons, pp. 243–249.

Simmel, G., 1977. *The Problems of the Philosophy of History*. New York: The Free Press.
Simmel, G., 1990. *The Philosophy of Money*. London: Routledge.
Simmel, G., 1997. The Sociology of Space. *In*: D. Frisby and M. Featherstone, eds. *Simmel on Culture: Selected Writings*. London: Sage, pp. 137–169.
Simmel, G., 1999. The Stranger. *In*: G. Lemert, ed. *Social Theory: The Multicultural and Classical Readings*. Boulder, CO: Westview Press, pp. 184–189.
Watier, P., 1993. Simmel and the Image of Individuality. *Current Sociology*, 41(2), pp. 69–75.
Weinstein, D. and Weinstein, M., 1989. Simmel and the Dialectic of the Double Boundary: The Case of the Metropolis and Mental Life. *Sociological Inquiry*, 59(1), pp. 48–59.
Weinstein, D. and Weinstein, M., 1990. Dimensions of Conflict: Georg Simmel on Modern Life. *In*: M. Kaern, ed. *Georg Simmel and Contemporary Sociology*. Boston: Kluwer, pp. 341–355.
Wessely, A., 1990. Simmel's Metaphysics. *In*: M. Kaern, B.S. Phillips and R.S. Cohen, eds. *Georg Simmel and Contemporary Sociology*. Dordrecht: Kluwer Academic, pp. 375–384.

5 Civilisation, culture and the 'marginal man'

The previous chapter demonstrated that the Simmelian 'classical stranger' is not an undifferentiated category and that, therefore, its usefulness and heuristic value is far from lost. This chapter explores the work of the Chicago sociologist Robert Park and his contribution to theories of the stranger. Issues to do with identity, the stranger and its relationship to the host are made possible via the concept of hybridity (Papastergiadis, 2000). Park's work on civilisation and culture and his conceptualisation of the 'marginal man' not only allow him to conceive the world theoretically but highlight his important contribution to a social theory of hybridity via the category of the stranger. Park's spatial analysis, expressed both in terms of his conceptualisation of the urban environment and his understanding of intercultural and interracial interaction, is a key conceptual framework in his oeuvre. Emerging from Park's distinction between civilisation and culture is the hybrid self, or in Park's words, the 'marginal man'. Although Simmel influences Park's notion of the 'marginal man', it is Frederick Teggart's view of history and Edward B. Reuter's work on the 'mulatto' that allow Park to broaden and deepen his conception of hybridity. I outline the major characteristics of this new personality type and illustrate the extent to which it aligns with some of the characteristics of the 'classical stranger'. Hence, Park's work is pivotal because he is one of the first Anglo-American sociologists to link the stranger to the idea of hybridity, a concept that has become increasingly influential in cultural and ethnic studies.

The sociology of space

Harman has questioned Park's contribution to a discourse of the stranger and strangeness. Whereas the 'marginal man' concept has led to fruitful research on those who live in between cultures, according to Harman, Park has ignored the 'proximity and membership orientation' (1988, pp. 20–21). Harman goes on to claim that the concept is peripheral 'sociologically because it was not initially grounded in the very concepts – familiarity/strangeness – which it was introduced to aid'. In the final analysis, Harman finds Park's concept 'meaningless and regressive' (Harman, 1988, pp. 20–21). This assessment is exceedingly harsh considering that spatiality, for Park, becomes a key sociological tool that allows sociologists to comprehend intersubjectivity and the sociology of knowledge in terms of distance and proximity. 'In society we not only live together, but at the same time we live apart, and human relations can always be reckoned, with more or less accuracy, in terms of distance' (Park, 1925, p. 166).

The importance of distance is illustrated clearly when Park examines the relationship between different racial and cultural groups. Distance becomes crucial in analysing the emergence of racial consciousness. One's 'blackness' or 'Orientalness' is the result of the social and cultural distance that exists between the self and other (Park, 1924, p. 257). Racial consciousness, for Park, is a state of mind where racial groups become acutely aware of the distance that separates them. Conflict or tensions between different groups are less likely to occur when they preserve their 'proper distance'. This attitude is associated, for Park, with the saying that 'the Negro is all right in his place' (1924, p. 257). Park's examination of the distance and proximity between racial groups lacks any critical reflection on how white society conceptualises and determines what is the 'proper distance' and the 'right place' for the Negro. Neither does he investigate how the processes of racialisation and the unequal power relationship between whites and blacks affect the construction of racial identities. Nonetheless, Park does explore how familiarity and distance can partly explain the emergence of prejudice and racism.

Prejudice, for Park, originates when the social and cultural boundaries between racial groups are crossed and it 'seems to be more or less instinctive and spontaneous disposition to maintain social distances' (1924, p. 259). Park adopts a socio-psychological approach in explaining the rise of racism and accepts that the type of interaction that occurs between individuals influences self-identification and behaviour. He contends that it is the fear of the Other, and the competition that the Other brings for the available economic resources, that encourages racist attitudes. Prejudice, continues Park, is not an aggressive act, but a conservative force insofar as it tries to maintain the social order by preserving the social distance upon which that order rests. This was particularly the case with Chinese migration into the US's 'frontier society'. Before the appearance of the Oriental, asserts Park, a particular type of 'democracy' was evident; this 'democratic' regime allowed for the reduction of social distances among groups and fostered closer social relations. The Oriental changed this situation because he 'looked strange, he spoke a quaint language, and he developed habits of industry and thrift that were intolerable to those who had to compete with him' (Park, 1924, pp. 258–9). The host (Anglo-American white man) found it difficult to have close social relations with a stranger who was a direct competitor; this difficulty resulted, according to Park, in an increase in the social distance between whites and the Oriental. This analysis links well with the classical stranger and the strangeness associated with it. The Oriental is physically close but socially and culturally distant. It is the strangeness experienced by the host that leads to misunderstanding and thus prejudice towards the stranger. Echoing the phenomenological understanding of different life-worlds, Park stresses that people from different cultural and racial backgrounds have 'differences in the universe of discourse' (Park, 1943, p. 306; Park and Miller, 1921, p. 267). The 'universe of discourse' designates the 'fund of fundamental ideas and assumptions which are understood and taken for granted but not, under ordinary circumstances, debatable' (Park, 1943, p. 306). These differences, in what phenomenology has labelled the 'natural attitude', lead to misunderstanding and thus prejudice between the host and the stranger, and as a consequence of these discrepancies, Park claims that different racial and cultural groups will find it difficult assimilating into US society.

Proximity, distance and the sociology of knowledge

Park's use of spatial concepts to analyse cultural and racial interaction and communication has implications for the sociology of knowledge. Park's interest in the intersubjective nature of knowledge construction reveals an intellectual curiosity with intercultural communication. In particular, he is fascinated with how social distance becomes an explanatory tool to comprehend the incommensurability between strangers. Park's interest in the sociology of knowledge is evident when he examines Karl Mannheim's work and its relationship to racial ideologies (Park, 1943, p. 305). The 'universe of discourse' can take the form of ideologies, especially racial ideologies, that become an impediment to effective communication between cultures. The 'final obstacle to communication', writes Park, 'is self-consciousness' (Park, 1925, p. 176), which is the consciousness of individual differences. These individual differences are the 'basis of all our reserves, personal and racial' (Park, 1925, p. 175). When expressed as racial differences, racial self-consciousness intensifies and the social distance between 'the alien and the native peoples' increases (Park, 1926, p. 253). However, Park does not advocate that we should always overcome distance because a certain amount of isolation and private space provides the condition for a 'sound personal existence' and a 'wholesome society' (1925, p. 176). In 'primitive' societies, for example, isolation and distance from strangers are socially and morally important. They are important morally because maintaining distances through social, cultural and symbolic boundaries allow members of the group to recognise their similarities (Park, 1939, p. 87). Conversely, greater proximity, and hence greater communication among groups, may intensify group conflict, but it may also lead to a greater understanding of the Other. Physical closeness to the stranger, rather than leading to social and cultural distance, may result in greater social and cultural proximity. Strangeness, thereby, diminishes. Closer proximity to those who are different results in mutual understanding and empathy. In the language of Schutz, the lifeworld of strangers begins to merge, and incommensurability diminishes.

> But conflict, and particularly cultural conflict, in so far as it brings into the light of understanding impulses and attitudes of which we would otherwise remain unconscious, inevitably increases our knowledge not merely of ourselves but of our fellows, since the attitudes and sentiments which we are able to appreciate and understand, no matter how indirectly expressed, when we find them in the minds of others.
>
> (Park, 1938, p. 50)

Notwithstanding the 'conflict' between different racial and cultural groups, proximity to the cultural and racial stranger leads to greater knowledge of oneself and those who are different. Intimate relations with strangers can overcome cultural incommensurability. 'Personal relations and personal friendships are the great moral solvents. Under their influence all distinctions of class, of caste, and even race, are dissolved' (Park, 1926, p. 254).

Park's ideas on proximity and distance and their role in fostering cross-cultural understanding is a precursor to contact theory, which argues that greater contact with those who are cultural and racially different will promote more tolerant and positive attitudes to culturally and religiously diverse Others. Contact theory posits that interpersonal contact among people of different races will produce positive change in social relations. When people of different groups interact with each other, they should come to understand each other better, and 'familiarity [will] breed liking' (Pettigrew and Tropp, 2006, p. 766; Pettigrew et al., 2011). Yet, both Park and contact theory tend to ignore the historical and political context of contact and the power relations that underlie it.

Strangeness – being physically close but socially and culturally distant – can also be overcome when we acknowledge our common humanity. Park notes that

> when we say, as we often do, that human nature is fundamentally everywhere and always the same, we mean simply that when we are able to penetrate to the motives behind customs and conduct which at first seemed strange, outlandish and forbidding, they inevitably turn out to be motives such as might have moved us under similar circumstances.
>
> (Park, 1926, p. 253)

It is this universal human nature which makes it possible for different groups to communicate with each other. Communication, for Park, is a process where one individual can 'assume, in some sense and to some degree, the attitudes and point of view of another' (Park, 1919, p. 122). It 'is only to the extent that we are able to enter imaginatively into the lives and experiences of others that we regard them as human like ourselves' (Park, 1926, p. 253). Proximity to the Other does not necessarily lead to incommensurability because, through empathic understanding, we can transcend the racial barriers and the 'universe of discourse' that exist between groups and allow us to accentuate our commonalities rather than our differences. The Otherness of strangers can be overcome if we detach ourselves and adopt the perspective of the Other. The role of empathy, as it was for Simmel, is essential in conversing across difference.

Civilisation and the hybrid self

Park's intellectual interest in the sociology of space – in particular, how distance and proximity are conveyed through the social interaction between racial groups – and his distinction between culture and civilisation lead him to an analysis of cultural hybridity. Park is one of the earliest American sociologists to be concerned with the clash of cultures. In fact, Park intimates that modernisation and hybridisation are synonymous terms. Hybridisation occurs at the frontiers of civilisation where the population is mobile, changing and cosmopolitan (Park, 1929a, p. 377).

The expansion of Western Europe into the colonies resulted in racial intermingling and the creation of 'frontier cities' (Park, 1934). It is through these 'frontier cities' that civilisation is imposed on traditional cultures. 'Civilisation', as a process of rationalisation, mitigates the mores and customs of the Other. Western civilisation's contact with the Other, argues Park, results in the emergence of a 'zone of transition' where cultural fusion and hybridity develops (Park, 1934, p. 133). Cultural frontiers or zones of transition are 'the point of contact between the Oriental and the Occident and where new cultures and centers emerge' (Park, 1934, p. 137). Geographical isolation results in accentuating racial differences, whereas through the spread of civilisation, cultural contact increases, and cultural fusion becomes the norm. It is the hybrid individual that encapsulates the meeting between two cultures and the extent and character of European cultural contact (Park, 1934, p. 132).

In Park's attempt to formulate a 'scientific' sociology, he stresses that a key research agenda is to study those social and cultural communities on the margins of US society. The local immigrant neighbourhood captures the tension between the old pre-industrial social order and the emerging modern industrial society (Park, 1916, 1925). Park notes that the city is an ideal place to study the emergence of 'natural areas' or 'moral regions'. These places are the result of the natural spatial distribution of the population in the city, and they are the resting place of those individuals who are 'more transitory and less stable'. The 'natural areas', 'where life is freer, more adventurous and lonely than elsewhere', tend to attract certain individuals such as bohemians and hobohemians (Park, 1929b, p. 196). In addition, unlike rural communities, the city rewards the outcasts.

> In a small community it is the normal man, the man without eccentricity or genius, who seems most likely to succeed. The small community often tolerates eccentricity. The city, on the contrary, rewards it. Neither the criminal, the defective, nor the genius has the same opportunity to develop his innate disposition in a small town that he invariably finds in a great city.
> (Park, 1916, p. 48)

Although the modern metropolis rationalises social life and dissolves cultural and class distinctions, it concomitantly encourages other types of strangers to flourish. These strangers are not necessarily those who are culturally different from the host. They may be individuals such as eccentrics, criminals or 'the defective' who all find a home in the urban crowd. Ironically, urban strangers find their existential homes in an environment that from the perspective of a traditional worldview, is a place of homelessness. Moreover, the stranger, as represented through the cultural and racial hybrid, is also lured to the metropolis. The mixed blood, notes Park, 'gravitates to the cities, and particularly to the great cities, which have always been the final refuge of the detribalized, and emancipated' (Park, 1934, p. 136).

History and the 'marginal man'

As I have shown, Park's conceptualisation of civilisation is synonymous with cultural hybridisation, and the marginal subject emerges from this process. The constitution of the hybrid subject, according to Park, is the result of economic, political and cultural imperialism (1937, p. 376). The literature on Park and the 'marginal man' (Bulmer, 1997; Lal, 1990; Lyman, 1990; Maines et al., 1996; Raushenbush, 1979), however, pays little attention to his conception of history and its relationship to the hybrid self. Park argues that it is only possible to understand the emergence of cultural hybridity if we view history as a series of abruptions and unexpected occurrences.

This view of history draws on the work of the historian Frederick Teggart. According to Park, Teggart, unlike his contemporaries who conceived of civilisation and society as the result of evolutionary processes, adopted a 'catastrophic theory of civilisation' and history (Park, 1928, p. 345) based on productive competition, conflict, and cooperation. In contrast to nineteenth-century intellectuals, Park did not believe in the 'universality of natural causation' where one could detect the underlying laws of social change (Burrow, 1966, p. 107). Park, following Teggart, believes these laws of social change are not discernible because revolutions and the global movement of people always destabilise the march of history. These events inevitably lead to the breakdown of an existing social order. Teggart observes that the main factor provoking social change was the 'release' from the traditions and mores of one's society. People would be released from 'their unconscious commitment to these habits, ways, and customs and in this state of liberation' (Lyman, 1990, pp. 78–9) they would adopt new roles and identities. This condition arose when migration patterns led to borderland settlements where different cultures intermingled.

Drawing on this perspective of migration, Park insists that the movement of people occurs either through invasion or through 'peaceful penetration'. Either way it provides for the 'secularization of society and the individualization of the person' (Park, 1928, p. 351). The secularisation of society arises because 'migration as a social phenomenon' manifests itself 'in changes in [social and religious] custom and in the mores' and more importantly is revealed 'in the changed type of personality which it produces' (Park, 1928, p. 350). Individuality and freedom become pervasive in times of 'release', and more importantly, for Park, a new personality type emerges out of the interaction and mixing of people. In his paper *Human Migration and the Marginal Man*, Park conceptualises this new personality type as the cultural hybrid and links the 'marginal man' with the Simmelian stranger:

> The cultural hybrid is a man living and sharing intimately in the cultural life and traditions of two distinct peoples; never quite willing to break, even if he were permitted to do so, with his past and his traditions, and not quite accepted, because of racial prejudice, in the new society in which he now sought to find a place. He was a man on the margin of two cultures and

two societies, which never completely interpenetrated and fused. The emancipated Jew was, and is, historically the marginal man, the first cosmopolite and citizen of the world. He is par excellence, "the stranger", whom Simmel, himself a Jew, has described with such profound insight and understanding.
(Park, 1928, p. 354)

The characteristics of the marginal Jew is also evident in the 'city man, the man who ranges widely, [and] lives preferably in a hotel' (Park, 1928, p. 355). Other times Park includes the racial hybrid under the marginal man category. '[T]he marginal man is a mixed blood, like the Mulatto in the United States or the Eurasian in Asia, but that is apparently because the man of mixed blood is one who lives in two worlds, in both of which he is more or less a stranger' (Park, 1928, p. 356).

A major limitation of Park's category is its attempt to encompass various individuals who do not necessarily have compatible experiences due to their different social, cultural and racial backgrounds. The marginal man concept conflates racial and cultural hybridity, and as Harman notes, this leads to a 'confusing and contradictory profile' because the category is not associated to any continuum of familiarity or strangeness (1988, p. 20). As a consequence, Jews – who may not be visibly different – could be perceived by the host as a member and thus be physically and socially close. Racial hybrids however, may be physically close but, because of their physical appearance, are socially and culturally distant. In other words, to include Simmel's stranger, the emancipated Jew (cultural hybrid), the racial hybrid (the mulatto), the urban dweller and the transitory traveller under the category of the 'marginal man' is to overlook the different types of strangeness that each may experience. For example, the urban dwellers – such as bohemians in the US – may experience strangeness in the sense that they are physically close but are socially distant to other urban dwellers. In other words, they may feel socially alienated from mainstream white society and thus their experience may be closer to existential strangers. Yet, when compared to the racial hybrid, they are racially close to other urban dwellers because they are white. By treating the category of the 'marginal man' and the stranger as undifferentiated categories, Park falls into the trap of what Ahmed (2000) has called fetishising the stranger as a figure, which ignores how this figure is embedded in power relations and a racist ideology. Therefore, the experiences of the stranger as the racial hybrid are drastically different to the 'city man' as the stranger. The former refers to the stranger as Other, whereas the latter is an existential stranger.

Hybrid consciousness and ambivalence

Although Park includes multiple individuals under the category of the 'marginal man', a hybrid consciousness tends to be confined to the racial and cultural hybrid. The social and cultural condition of the cultural hybrid encourages an ambivalent psychological state. First, these in-between subjects are less nationalistic because they 'look across national boundaries' and are attracted to the 'frontier cities' which are part of the 'cosmopolitan civilisation' (Park, 1934, p. 137). In-between subjects, moreover, eschew particularistic sentiments such as those expressed through fanatical nationalism, and they favour a culture that conforms to their broader intellectual and cultural perspective. The hybrid, who adopts the role of the cosmopolitan and stranger, 'becomes, relatively to his cultural milieu, the individual with the wider horizon, the keener intelligence, the more detached and rational viewpoint' (Park, 1937, p. 376). An enlightened and cosmopolitan attitude becomes a core feature of hybrid subjectivity. In Park's words, '[H]e learns to look upon the world in which he was born and bred with something of the detachment of a stranger' (1928, p. 351).

The experience of hybridity, at least according to these observations, is generally positive; cultural and racial hybrids have a more open and flexible mind, and they are more 'objective' and 'rational' than those confined to a particular worldview or to their 'universe of discourse'. The hybrid self plays the 'role of the intermediary and interpreter between the two races and two cultures' (Park, 1934, p. 136). Due to their marginal position, racial hybrids for instance are able to transcend the particular 'universe of discourse' associated with whites and Negroes. The 'marginal man', because of his proximity and distance from both racial groups, can simultaneously enter the lives and experiences of these groups and expose their humanity and subjectivism. Drawing on the work of the African-American sociologist Du Bois, Park believes that the hybrid subject has access to the world of the self (white race) and the Other (the Negro), and this double perspective or 'double consciousness' (Du Bois, 1903, p. 5), for Park, allows him to develop a universal, objective understanding of the world. The character of the hybrid subject echoes those intellectual qualities associated with Simmel's historian; the 'marginal man', however, focuses more on the quality of objectivism.

Yet, these positive attributes of the marginal self are offset by less endearing characteristics. The 'marginal man' has a divided self because an internal conflict rages between the old self, linked to his primary group, and the new self, associated with the host group. As such, the 'marginal man' becomes homeless because he wanders from the warm security of his primary group, which he has now abandoned, to the cold freedom of the new group, in which he is not quite at home (Park, 1928, p. 355). The 'marginal man' occupies a social and cultural space that is neither part of the centre (dominant group) nor part of the periphery (the subordinate group); rather, the place where the 'marginal man' resides is an in-between place, a place in limbo. In Park's original manuscript jottings on the 'marginal man', he describes the place where the marginal self resides at the 'borderlands' (Lindner, 1996, p. 49). Park suggests that out of this suspended state, a sense of homelessness or rootlessness arises. Homelessness here tends to be associated with an existential experience because it designates a state of social alienation from both the primary and host group. Park also contends that the 'marginal man' experiences 'moral dichotomy, inner turmoil and intense self-consciousness' (1928, p. 355). The 'marginal man', as Park constructs him, experiences ambivalent feelings: he not only experiences positive attributes like a keener intelligence and a wider horizon, but he is also prone to psychological anxieties. The 'marginal man' is distinct from members of the host and primary group, and this distinction provides him with an intellectual perspective not available to those who belong; this very same difference, however, makes him an existential wanderer and an outcast. Although Park draws on Simmel's category of the stranger to depict the 'marginal man's' social and cultural position, the 'marginal man', unlike Simmel's stranger, has an unfulfilled urge to belong that becomes the cause of his psychological and existential crises. In places, the 'marginal man' becomes the marginal existential subject addressed in Chapter 2.

The Negro and the racial hybrid

When Park addresses the experiences of individuals from other marginalised groups, a process of Othering the stranger occurs. For example, the ethnic outcast of the ghettoes represent, for Park, the irrational and 'suppressed impulses', whereas the 'marginal man' exemplifies intellect and rationality. In contrast to the ethnic and racial Other of the 'natural area', the 'marginal man' is always relatively the 'more civilized human being' (Park, 1937, p. 376). The 'marginal man' complements the environment and temperament of a modern urban civilisation because it encourages the social and intellectual freedom that traditional cultures neither support nor tolerate. Park contends that the 'half-caste people are city folk' and 'the mixed blood is the more mobile man' (Park, 1934, p. 135). Mobility and the rationalisation of social relations by the market represent the new urban environment, and the 'marginal man' finds his home in this milieu. Park's more enlightened hybrid subjects are not only 'more civilized' than other strangers, but they also encapsulate the very essence of a modern urban civilisation.

Likewise, Park provides a different evaluation of the life of the mulatto and the Negro. Cultural factors, argues Park, have played a role in making the mulatto 'the cultural advanced guard and the leaders of the Negro people'. They are 'more enterprising than the Negroes, more restless, aggressive, egocentric and ambitious [and] are often sensitive. . . . The mulatto, in spite of his smaller numbers, still largely represents the intellectual class of the race' (Park, 1929a, pp. 381, 384, 392).

Park articulates the differences between the Negro and the mulatto in essentialist terms when he compares Negro folk songs with the literature emerging out of the new race-consciousness of the mulatto. Negro folk songs are 'primitive, and less articulate', and the 'rude hymns of the slave' tend to be 'crude and elemental' (Park, 1923, pp. 286–7). The old Negro poetry, moreover, is concerned with surrender and resignation. Biological reasoning and the eugenics movement tend to influence Park's early description of the Negro. Drawing on Reuter, Park argues that 'the mulatto group thus, on the assumption of the transmission of superior mental capacity, tends to become not only a culturally but a biological superior group' (1929a, p. 385). Although Park had rejected the idea of racial inferiority before 1920, he still believed that racial temperaments were at least partly 'transmitted biologically'. The Negro temperament includes a 'general sunny and social disposition' in which he is more emotional and less rational, and Park concludes, 'the Negro is, so to speak, the lady among the races' (1919, pp. 129–30).

The racialisation of the Negro is unfortunate here and speaks to the broader views of Negroes in white society in the early part of the twentieth century.

It is also difficult to avoid the gendered nature of Park's description. The hybrid subject is described in 'masculine' terms, whereas the Negro epitomises all that is 'feminine'. In contrast to the Negro, the mulatto represents the man of 'action'. The 'masculinity' of the mulatto is particularly evident in the rebelliousness and self-assertiveness of their literature. Park concludes that 'particularly in literature and the expressive arts, the mulatto has outdistanced the Negro' (Park, 1929a, p. 384). When comparing the Negro to another marginal man such as the Jew, Park argues that whereas the Jew, 'because of his intellectuality, is a natural born idealist and internationalist', the Negro is 'pre-adapted to conservatism and to local and personal loyalties' (Park, 1919, p. 130). Unlike the hybrid subject, the Negro's main concern is with the particular rather than the universal. Park confines the Negro's worldview to his primary group and to what he previously characterised as their 'universe of discourse'. Some observers have cited Park's description of the Negro as the 'lady among the races' as evidence of his racism. This criticism is unfortunate because Park does acknowledge that unlike white immigrants in America, the black American 'has had his separateness thrust upon him because of his exclusion and forcible isolation from white society' (Lal, 1990, pp. 5–6).

Park's observation on the Negro and the racial hybrid infer that not all strangers are the same. Some like the Negro are less likely to develop that 'objectivity' that has come to be associated with the Simmelian stranger. Park's description implies that Negroes, no matter how much contact they may have with whites, are destined (biologically?) to be prisoners of their 'universe of discourse'. Bound by their life-world, Negroes, from a phenomenological perspective, are not able to transcend their natural attitude. Thus contact with those who are different, at least for Negroes, has not led to empathetic understanding or to the development of greater insights.

As mentioned in the introduction approaches to the stranger have been gender blind, and Park's notion of the marginal man is a clear example of this. The term has been used in a gender-neutral way, but the concept is intrinsically male (Deegan, 2005, p. 216). The experience of a black marginal woman – an experience that Park does not acknowledge – is different from the 'marginal man'. Not only is she 'marginalised' from the white and black community, but she is also the Other to the 'marginal man'. Women's accounts of their hybrid experiences suggest that their identities are constructed through a lack of privilege and are confronted by oppressive socio-political realities (Sparrow, 2000, p. 189). In some cases, marginal women construct their multiple identities both in response and in resistance to gendered hegemonic narratives evident in their ethnic and host communities.

In addition, marginal subjects are not only 'modern', but they are *more* 'modern' than white Americans. The temperament of the mulatto/'marginal man' can be closely associated with some of the characteristics of civilisation, for example, rationality, reason and objectivity; the Negro, on the other hand, represents civilisation's Other, for example, irrationality and subjectivism. The Negro represents what civilisation tries to deny or suppress but nevertheless needs for its own constitution. Park's hybrid self is more objective, rational and not confined to the 'universe of discourse' of the dominant or subordinate group. Hybrid subjects have a wider intellectual horizon; the marginal self transcends the particular and, like modernity, comes to represent universal attributes such as reason and objectivity. This representation of the 'marginal man' is also evident in a latter work by Stonequist (1937). He refers to the 'modern Jew' and the 'advanced Negro' as examples of marginal personalities. These individuals are 'flexible and restless', and the 'lack of provincialism enables' them 'to see the world more objectively and more abstractly' (Stonequist, 1937, p. 81). Stonequist also connects the 'marginal man' to the 'intellectual Negro' who has a 'more realistic, objective view' of race relations compared to those Negroes who cling to the past (the 'accommodating Negro') or reject it completely (the 'emancipated Negro'). According to these accounts, the marginal self epitomises the culture of Western modernity.

Conclusion: a social theory of hybridity

Park's work on race and the 'marginal man' has made a substantial contribution to a social theory of hybridity. In the social sciences, especially anthropology and sociology, the orthodox approach to understanding a premodern and/or traditional society has been to concentrate on the less mobile and tradition-bound personality type of primitive and rural communities. Evolutionary anthropology understood and constructed the 'primitive' Other as 'fundamentally primitive from a progress and evolution frame of reference' (McGrane, 1989, p. 89). Anthropology has tended to study the primitive self to expose the truth not only about the past but also about us 'moderns' (McGrane, 1989, p. 95). Sociology, on the other hand, is more often conceived as a commentary on the present, the modern, and tends to study the 'traditional' or pre-urban self of rural communities, not as an end in itself but as a means to expose the differences between the traditional and the modern. At times particular types of sociology, such as the functionalist sociology of Talcott Parsons, study the primitive self to highlight the progressive nature of modernity. This sociology of modernity studies and exposes both the rationality and autonomy of the modern subject and the so-called conformism and irrationality of the premodern self. It implies that the constitution of modernity depends on that which is different. To conceptualise and comprehend the 'modern', a sociology of modernity needs a contrasting 'past' or 'tradition' to distinguish itself.

The assumption is that studying the 'primitive' Other allows scholars to develop a deeper understanding of where we have been and where we are now. Paradoxically, although the primitive Other is different to us, it is the window to our past self. McGrane (1989, p. 97) notes that 'when we study them we study, not ourselves, but our past. And when we study them we study, not them, but our past'. Colonialism viewed hybrid individuals as 'primitive' and thus backward and savage and a threat to the purity of the European race (Young, 1995). Consequently, the only value in studying them was to highlight the present superiority and possible deterioration of the civilised, white population. Studies such as those of Park and Stonequist, however, imply that the study of hybrid individuals should focus on the psychological and intellectual repercussions of living in between two races and cultures. The 'primitive' side of the hybrid self does not inhibit social and cultural development; on the contrary the 'primitive' side of the hybrid subject contributes to the special powers of insight available to the marginal personality. The hybrid subject is able to adopt a hybrid, double consciousness not available to those confined to one racial or cultural identity. Whereas the hybrid subject is biologically connected to the Negro, and thus partly 'primitive', the marginal man is also more modern than the white American. Conversely, studying the 'marginal man', for Park, illustrates the close relation between civilisation and hybridising processes.

The association between the stranger and the 'marginal man' demonstrates how greater knowledge of our increasingly complex and heterogeneous modern world does not lie in the study of the 'primitive' self nor with those who are confined to one identity and culture but in the in-between self. The stranger via the category of the 'marginal man' opens up new ways of conceptualising racial and cultural identity, but it also contributes to the sociology of knowledge by theorising the existence of an in-between consciousness that was also evident in Simmel's account. Contemporary accounts have continued this connection between hybridity and an enlightened type of consciousness (Ang, 1994; Baldassar, 1999; Bolatagici, 2004; Butcher, 2004; Eriksen, 2003; Ichimoto, 2004; Kapchan, 1999; Sharp, 1995; Thomas and Nikora, 1996) but have paid little attention to the work of Park.

Park's ideas on culture, civilisation and marginality reveal that the relationship between hybridity and modernity is not one of incommensurability because the hybrid, as epitomised by the 'marginal man', comes to represent the key features of modernity, for example, rationality, objectivity and universalism. The hybrid subject closely resembles the rationalising dimension of modernity. The 'marginal man' occupies an ambivalent position: he is both the offspring of modern civilisation but also its harshest critic. This is not a position that the 'marginal man' has freely chosen because the ability to be both involved and detached emerges from the experience of rejection from white and black communities.

References

Ahmed, S., 2000. *Strange Encounters: Embodied Others in Post-Coloniality*. London: Routledge.

Ang, I., 1994. On Not Speaking Chinese: Postmodern Ethnicity and the Politics of Diaspora. *New Formations*, 24, pp. 1–18.

Baldassar, L., 1999. Marias and Marriage: Ethnicity, Gender and Sexuality among Italo-Australian Youth in Perth. *Journal of Sociology*, 35(1), pp. 1–22.

Bolatagici, T., 2004. Claiming the (n)either/(n)or of "Third Space": (Re)presenting hybrid identity and the embodiment of mixed race. *Journal of Intercultural Studies*, 25(1), pp. 75–85.

Bulmer, M., 1997. W.I. Thomas and Robert E. Park: Conceptualizing, Theorizing, and Investigating Social Processes. *In*: C. Camic, ed. *Reclaiming the Sociological Classics: The State of Scholarship*. Oxford: Blackwell, pp. 242–261.

Burrow, J.W., 1966. *Evolution and Society: A Study in Victorian Social Theory*. Cambridge: Cambridge University Press.

Butcher, M., 2004. Universal Processes of Cultural Change: Reflections on Identity Strategies of Indian and Australian Youth. *Journal of Intercultural Studies*, 25(3), pp. 215–231.

Deegan, M.J., 2005. Transcending "The Marginal Man": Challenging the Patriarchal Legacy of Robert E. Park. *In*: R.M. Dennis, ed. *Marginality, Power and Social Structure: Issues in Race, Class, and Gender Analysis*. Amsterdam: Elsevier, pp. 207–227.

Du Bois, W.E.B., 1903. *The Souls of Black Folk*. New York: Penguin.

Eriksen, T.H., 2003. Creolization and Creativity. *Global Networks*, 3(3), pp. 223–237.

Harman, L.D., 1988. *The Modern Stranger: On Language and Membership*. Berlin: Moutonde Gruyter.

Ichimoto, T., 2004. Ambivalent "Selves" in Transition: A Case Study of Japanese Women Studying in Australian Universities. *Journal of Intercultural Studies*, 25(3), pp. 247–269.

Kapchan, D., 1999. Theorizing the Hybrid. *Journal of American Folklore*, 112(445), pp. 239–253.

Lal, B.B., 1990. *The Romance of Culture in an Urban Civilization: Robert E. Park on Race and Ethnic Relations*. London: Routledge.

Lindner, R., 1996. *The Reportage of Urban Culture: Robert Park and the Chicago School*. Cambridge: Cambridge University Press.

Lyman, S.M., 1990. *Civilization: Contents, Discontents, Malcontents and Other Essays in Social Theory*. Fayetteville: The University of Arkansas Press.

Maines, D.R., Bridger, J.C. and Ulmer, J.T., 1996. Mythic Facts and Park's Pragmatism: On Predecessor – Selection and Theorising in Human Ecology. *The Sociological Quarterly*, 37(3), pp. 521–541.

McGrane, B., 1989. *Beyond Anthropology: Society and the Other*. New York: Columbia University Press.

Papastergiadis, N., 2000. *The Turbulence of Migration: Globalization, Deterritorialization and Hybridity*. Cambridge: Polity Press.

Park, R.E., 1916. The City: Suggestions for the Investigation of Human Behaviour in the Urban Environment. *In*: E.C. Hughes, C.S. Johnson, J. Masuoka, R. Redfield and L. Wirth, eds. *The Collected Papers of Robert Ezra Park: Volume II*. Reprint 1974. New York: Arno Press, pp. 13–51.

Park, R.E., 1919. The Conflict and Fusion of Cultures with Special Reference to the Negro. *Journal of Negro History*, 4(2), pp. 111–133.

Park, R.E., 1923. Negro Race Consciousness as Reflected in Race Literature. *In*: E.C. Hughes, C.S. Johnson, J. Masuoka, R. Redfield and L. Wirth, eds. *The Collected Papers of Robert Ezra Park: Volume I*. Reprint 1974. New York: Arno Press, pp. 284–300.

Park, R.E., 1924. The Concept of Social Distance. *In*: E.C. Hughes, C.S. Johnson, J. Masuoka, R. Redfield and L. Wirth, eds. *The Collected Papers of Robert Ezra Park: Volume I*. Reprint 1974. New York: Arno Press, pp. 256–260.

Park, R.E., 1925. The Urban Community as a Spatial Pattern and Moral Order. *In*: E.C. Hughes, C.S. Johnson, J. Masuoka, R. Redfield and L. Wirth, eds. *The Collected Papers of Robert Ezra Park: Volume II*. Reprint 1974. New York: Arno Press, pp. 165–177.

Park, R.E., 1926. Behind Our Masks. *In*: E.C. Hughes, C.S. Johnson, J. Masuoka, R. Redfield and L. Wirth, eds. *The Collected Papers of Robert Ezra Park: Volume I*. Reprint 1974. New York: Arno Press, pp. 244–255.

Park, R.E., 1928. Human Migration and the Marginal Man. *In*: E.C. Hughes, C.S. Johnson, J. Masuoka, R. Redfield and L. Wirth, eds. *The Collected Papers of Robert Ezra Park: Volume I*. Reprint 1974. New York: Arno Press, pp. 345–356.

Park, R.E., 1929a. Mentality of Racial Hybrids. *In*: E.C. Hughes, C.S. Johnson, J. Masuoka, R. Redfield and L. Wirth, eds. *The Collected Papers of Robert Ezra Park: Volume I*. Reprint 1974. New York: Arno Press, pp. 377–392.
Park, R.E., 1929b. Sociology, Community and Society. *In*: E.C. Hughes, C.S. Johnson, J. Masuoka, R. Redfield and L. Wirth, eds. *Collected Papers of Robert Ezra Park: Volume II*. Reprint 1974. New York: Arno Press, pp. 178–209.
Park, R.E., 1934. Race Relations and Certain Frontiers. *In*: E.C. Hughes, C.S. Johnson, J. Masuoka, R. Redfield and L. Wirth, eds. *The Collected Papers of Robert Ezra Park: Volume I*. Reprint 1974. New York: Arno Press, pp. 117–137.
Park, R.E., 1937. Cultural Conflict and the Marginal Man. *In*: E.C. Hughes, C.S. Johnson, J. Masuoka, R. Redfield and L. Wirth, eds. *The Collected Papers of Robert Ezra Park: Volume I*. Reprint 1974. New York: Arno Press, pp. 372–376.
Park, R.E., 1938. Reflections on Communications and Culture. *In*: E.C. Hughes, C.S. Johnson, J. Masuoka, R. Redfield and L. Wirth, eds. *The Collected Papers of Robert Ezra Park: Volume I*. Reprint 1974. New York: Arno Press, pp. 36–52.
Park, R.E., 1939. The Nature of Race Relations. *In*: E.C. Hughes, C.S. Johnson, J. Masuoka, R. Redfield and L. Wirth, eds. *The Collected Papers of Robert Ezra Park: Volume I*. Reprint 1974. New York: Arno Press, pp. 81–116.
Park, R.E., 1943. Race Ideologies. *In*: E.C. Hughes, C.S. Johnson, J. Masuoka, R. Redfield and L. Wirth, eds. *The Collected Papers of Robert Ezra Park: Volume I*. Reprint 1974. New York: Arno Press, pp. 301–315.
Park, R.E. and Miller, H.A., 1921. *Old World Traits Transplanted*. Reprint 1969. New York: Arno Press.
Pettigrew, T.F. and Tropp, L.R., 2006. A Meta-Analytic Test of Intergroup Contact Theory. *Journal of Personality and Social Psychology*, 90(5), pp. 751–783.
Pettigrew, T.F., Tropp, L.R. Wagner, U. and Christ, O., 2011. Recent Advances in Intergroup Contact Theory. *International Journal of Intercultural Relations*, 35(3), pp. 271–280.
Raushenbush, W., 1979. *Robert E. Park: Biography of a Sociologist*. Durham: Duke University Press.
Sharp, A., 1995. Why Be Bicultural? *In*: M. Wilson and A. Yeatman, eds. *Justice and Identity: Antipodean Practices*. Wellington: Allen & Unwin, pp. 116–133.
Sparrow, L.M., 2000. Beyond Multicultural Man: Complexities of Identity. *International Journal of Intercultural Relations*, 24, pp. 173–201.
Stonequist, E.V., 1937. *The Marginal Man: A Study in Personality and Culture Conflict*. Reprint 1961. New York: Russell & Russell.
Thomas, D. and Nikora, L., 1996. Maori, Pakeha and New Zealander: Ethnic and National Identity among New Zealand Students. *Journal of Intercultural Studies*, 17(1/2), pp. 29–40.
Young, R.J.C., 1995. *Colonial Desire: Hybridity in Theory, Culture and Race*. London: Routledge.

6 The hybrid of modernity

Zygmunt Bauman is a leading social theorist of modernity and postmodernity. His work is increasingly used to enhance our understanding of social, cultural and political changes in Western societies. Bauman's reputation, at least in Europe, has grown by an emergent publication industry around his work (Beilharz, 2000; Best, 2013; Poder and Jacobsen, 2008; Smith, 2000; Tester, 2004) and the establishment of the Bauman Institute at Leeds University. While Park's politics and theoretical ideas are informed by a liberal reformist agenda and US pragmatism, Bauman, a sociologist and critical theorist, emerges from the tradition of Marxism. Bauman's Jewish origins and his experience of war contrast sharply with Park's life as a native-born son of the commercial classes, raised with an understanding of US identity that was immersed in the contrasting figures of Lincoln and Jesse James (Matthews, 1977, pp. 2–3). Whereas these distinctions throw into sharper relief the cultural and intellectual differences between Park and Bauman, there are aspects of their work that bring them closer: both focus on the relationship between modern society or civilisation and hybridity, and both are influenced by Simmel and his concept of the stranger.

Simmel and Park were sociologists living through the *fin de siècle*, in which rural or traditional society was slowly being overrun by industrialisation, modernisation and urbanisation. The new social modality, for Simmel and Park, was epitomised in the life of the metropolis. The new social, political and economic arrangements within the metropolis fostered new types of subjects: the metropolitan stranger and the marginal man. Bauman's writing occurs in another *fin de siècle*, but this time we have entered a new millennium. Both the old and new *fin de siècle* generate hopes and fears (Beilharz, 1994), and these, for Bauman, are expressed through his idea of 'liquid modernity'.

Bauman's work raises pertinent questions on the nature of social and cultural boundaries under modernity. The binaries of inside and outside and the idea of the boundary are significant in Bauman's critique of solid modernity's 'will to order' and in his examination of the stranger. This ordering process manifests itself at the individual and societal levels (modernity). The idea of the stranger and the ordering process, however, are not mutually exclusive because whereas the ordering process is concerned with the maintenance of borders, the figure of the stranger transcends or threatens these very same borders. Bauman's contention is that modernity's search for a meta-order leads to the construction of boundaries and to exclusionary practices. It is the presence of the in-between stranger or what Bauman calls the 'hybrid of modernity' that threatens the certainty of order. Similar to Simmel, there are different permutations of the stranger in Bauman's work, and I critically explore these different conceptions and Bauman's contribution to the 'universalisation of strangeness' thesis. Moreover, his work on the ethical responsibility towards the Other brings a moral dimension to theories of the stranger that were previously absent in Simmel and Park. Such a dimension allows us to re-theorise the political and social conditions necessary to promote ethical cross-cultural encounters and reassess the nature of knowledge in multicultural societies.

Bauman once argued that he is 'incurably eclectic' (Kilminister and Varcoe, 1992, p. 211). This has been supported by interpretations of his work which assert that the 'aim of Bauman is to reflect life's inconsistencies in his texts – and this cannot but make heavy demand on the composition of his writing' (Nijhoff, 1998, p. 95). For Nijhoff, the inconsistency in Bauman's work is a positive trait, whereas for others it exposes the confusing and problematical nature of some of Bauman's ideas (Kellner, 1998, p. 78). This perceived inconsistency – whether one interprets it as positive or negative – might exist because Bauman draws on a variety of theoretical frameworks and writes on a broad range of subjects that are sometimes not explicitly interrelated. At times Bauman's work draws on the critical Marxist tradition and the structural linguistics of Saussure, especially as it is adopted by Lévi-Strauss. At other times his work is informed by the first- (Adorno and Horkheimer) and second-generation (Habermas) critical theorists, the ideas of Derrida and Foucault and finally the theory of ethics as expressed in the work of Levinas and Logstrup. Juxtaposed with these diverse theoretical frameworks is Bauman's interest in a wide range of subjects such as class, culture, freedom, communism, Marxism, Polish politics, modernity, the Holocaust, the stranger, hermeneutics, postmodernity, death, consumerism, sex, the 'new poor', sociology, art, religion, globalisation, education and ethics. Yet, underlying Bauman's 'inconsistency' and 'eclecticism' are recurrent themes that only emerge when the whole of Bauman's project is considered.

Whereas it would be difficult to classify Bauman as a 'systematic' social theorist, there is a conceptual framework and key ideas that underline his fragmented and diverse work. This conceptual framework encompasses Bauman's intellectual interest in the ordering impulse, his use of the idea of the stranger and the various metaphors associated with it, and his support for a specific type of freedom.

Structure, structuring and human agency

Bauman's intellectual curiosity regarding the ordering process is evident in his writings from the mid-1950s. The source of this concern may be traced back to his experience of the Communist Party in Poland and the bureaucratisation of everyday life in Poland. Bauman notes that Polish political life was undemocratic and dominated by bureaucratic rationality where red tape, predictability and control were more important than encouraging an active, aware and committed public (Satterwhite, 1992, p. 21). By the 1960s Bauman begins to build his critique of bureaucratic rationality, and the ordering process on which it is based, within a specific theoretical language. In Bauman's examination of the 'process of structurisation', he begins to differentiate between the ideas of 'structuring' and 'structure'. The structurisation process 'is comprised of two aspects: the passive, reproductive, orientational one; and the active ordering one, which involves the elimination of some alternatives and making others more probable' (Bauman, 1968, p. 30). The active ordering dimension entails a process where oppression and exclusion are necessary so that only one order reigns. At one point, Bauman has suggested, 'we feel the need of "condensing" the verb [ordering/structuring], which refers to an activity, into a noun [order/structure], because we wish to report the steadiness, regularity, resilience of the activity in question' (Bauman, 1989a, p. 44).

The distinction between structuring and structure, for Bauman, reflects micro and macro processes. In the realm of everyday life, Bauman believes that human activity is defined by its natural propensity to order. Social actors, for Bauman, are boundary-constructing beings because it is through ordering that individuals make sense of their world. He asserts that 'what is universal here is this propensity, this inner push, to structure – and not any emergent structure' (Kilminister and Varcoe, 1992, p. 211). Bauman does not believe that such a thing as a social structure exists and that there is 'some final, ultimate underlying structure of everything' (Kilminister and Varcoe, 1992, p. 211). At the macro level, Bauman argues that premodern and modern societies can be understood in terms of their need to establish an order or structure and thus alleviate the 'slimy' or the stranger that threatens the stability and coherence of this social order. Although at both the individual and societal level, structuring leads to the imposition of social, cultural and symbolic boundaries, it is at the societal level that the ordering process leads to the establishment of a meta-order, thereby suppressing and excluding any individual or group that comes to epitomise disorder or ambivalence.

In the early to mid-1970s Bauman did not view culture as a form of communication but as an ordering or 'structuralising' process (Bauman, 1973a, p. 70). Similar to de Saussure's insistence on understanding language as a system, Bauman comprehends 'the logic of culture as the logic of the self-regulating system' (Bauman, 1973a, p. 80). This was clearly evident in the anthropological notion of 'culture' particular to the British and US, which views culture as an autonomous entity standing above individuals affecting their beliefs and life-world (Bauman, 1973b, p. 115). In this version, culture refers to a meta-structure that imposes itself on the individual. Rather than accepting this oppressive view of 'culture', Bauman maintains that we should adopt a more emancipatory notion of culture in which we acknowledge the agency of the social actor. Culture, concludes Bauman, is an activity, a process, and this activity or process is linked to human praxis. Human praxis is the 'idea of creativity, of active assimilation of the universe, of imposing on the chaotic world the ordering structure of human intelligent action' (Bauman, 1973b, p. 118). Culture no longer refers to a structure that imposes boundaries but is seen as a critical process in which individuals transcend boundaries. The 'cultural stance', for Bauman, is a questioning position in which the existence of multiple realities is recognised. In *Culture as Praxis* (1973b), however, Bauman acknowledges that there is a dark side to the human praxis of structuring because, left unchecked, it can lead to imposition of a meta-structure. Cultural praxis is the propensity to structure and impose order on a chaotic world that leads to exclusionary practices, hence the centrality of strangers in Bauman's thought.

Solid and liquid modernity

The drive for a meta-structure becomes particularly violent and destructive under modernity and nationalism. Bauman's descriptive and critical interpretation of modernity entails an account of its solid and liquid dimension. His account of solid modernity refers to a historical period that began in Western Europe in the seventeenth century. It achieved its 'maturity' with the emergence of the Enlightenment and capitalist and socialist industrial societies (Bauman, 1991a, p. 3). Bauman writes that modernity 'may be best described as the age marked by constant change – but aware of being so marked. In other words, modernity is an era conscious of its historicity' (1993a, p. 592). Modernity, claims Bauman, is the self-reflective moment, the time when one becomes conscious of being conscious of the need for order for the world, for oneself and for society (1991a, p. 5). Modernity 'is about the production of order' (1991a, p. 15).

Enthused by the rationalist stream of the Enlightenment project, modernity imposes order onto a world that is chaotic, ambivalent and immersed in tradition. Modernity equals modernisation. Nevertheless, the Enlightenment's view of modernity is delusionary because it did not reflect existing social reality. In contrast, Bauman's conception of the modern, a conception stripped of its delusions, encompasses the contingent and ambivalent nature of modern life. Bauman views the modern through the lens of modernism rather than modernisation. Whereas the latter is about imposing order and predictability, the former speaks to the fragmented, the multiple, the non-linear and ambivalent view of reality. We live in a world where uncertainty and contingency constitute the very essence of the modern, and it has only been certain groups – like *les philosophes* – and processes, such as nationalism and rationalism, that have denied the fragmentary and fluid nature of the modern condition. In his later writings, Bauman has distinguished the delusionary and 'authentic' versions of the modern in terms of 'solid' and 'fluid' modernity (Bauman, 2000, 2005). The Enlightenment's solid modernity undermines premodern solids (tradition, religion and collectivism) and then replaces them with new and improved solids (science, humanism and reason). Modernity's urge to do away with past solids 'was the wish to discover or invent solids – for a change – lasting solidity, a solidity which one could trust and rely upon and which would make the world predictable and therefore manageable' (Bauman, 2000, p. 3). Bauman's critique of 'solid' modernity is really a critique of totalitarian thought that existed in both Eastern and Western Europe.

Earlier in his work Bauman contrasts solid modernity with postmodernity. If 'solid' modernity can be characterised by a boundary-constructing process which fears ambivalence and attempts to alleviate it, then postmodernity, for Bauman, is about embracing ambivalence, contingency and uncertainty and thus transcending boundaries. Similar to his description of modernity, Bauman also believes that postmodernity can be associated with a state of mind; however, this state of mind is more self-reflective and critical. At times, Bauman believes that this frame of mind is particularly evident in philosophers, scholars, intellectuals and artists (1991a, p. vii). The postmodern mind undermines the metanarratives (the belief in progress and science) and the ordering tendencies of modernity. It does not seek to replace one truth with another or one political or social ideology for another, rather 'it splits the truth, the standard and ideal into already deconstructed and about to be deconstructed.... It braces itself for a life without truths, standards and ideals' (Bauman, 1991a, p. ix). Postmodernity 'can be seen as restoring to the world what modernity, presumptuously, had taken away; as a re-enchantment of the world that modernity tried hard to dis-enchant' (Bauman, 1991a, p. ix). The postmodern frame of mind is trying to re-spiritualise, re-personalise the world; it is trying to recapture the contingent nature of the social world that the rationalisation of society has suppressed. A postmodern sensibility, argues Bauman, is a modern mind realising that it cannot satisfy its original project of universalisation and ordering and that instead of destroying ambivalence and pluralism, modernity is producing them (1991a, p. 98). Rather than viewing modernity and postmodernity as distinct social, cultural, political epochs, Bauman argues that they are inextricably linked. He argues that postmodernity can be interpreted 'as modernity conscious of its true nature . . . [or] as modernity emancipated from false consciousness' (1991b, p. 33). Bauman's theoretical discussion of postmodernity suggests that it has transcended the 'false consciousness' of the previous social modality and consequently has less need for the exclusionary practices that characterised 'solid' modernity. Nonetheless, his social analysis of the postmodern condition tends to suggest that the modern state's obsession with ordering and thus coercion and violence is now decentralised, diffused and localised within neo-tribalism. These neo-tribes are 'the contrived, made up community masquerading as a Tönnies-style' community. These 'Kantian aesthetic communities . . . have no other grounds but the individual decisions to identify with' (Bauman, 1992, p. 697, 1993b, p. 16). Neo-tribes have a tendency to intolerance and aggression because they have no solid ground to rest on apart from individual decisions. New communities are kept together under the territory classified as 'culture'.

In his later work any reference to describing contemporary society as postmodern all but disappeared. Since 2000 Bauman has distanced himself from a postmodernist reading of the contemporary world (Best, 2013, p. 101), nevertheless there are similarities in his account of postmodern and liquid life. For example, 'liquid' modernity does not set itself the task of constructing a new and better order to replace the old, defective one. Bauman states that the 'melting of solids' is the permanent condition of 'liquid modernity' and 'the liquidising powers have moved from the "system" to "society", from "politics" to "life-politics" – or have descended from the "macro" to the "micro" level of social cohabitation' (Bauman, 2000, p. 7). Liquid modernity refers to a society in which the action of actors continuously change so that they cannot ossify into habits and routines and where contemporary subjects live a precarious life under the conditions of constant uncertainty (2005, pp. 1–2).

Underlying Bauman's examination and critique of modernity, postmodernity and liquid modernity is his conception of moral responsibility. His notion of moral responsibility draws on Levinas's work and particularly the idea that 'responsibility is the essential, primary and fundamental structure of subjectivity' (Bauman, 1989b, p. 183). It is only by being responsible that we constitute ourselves as subjects. As Bauman argues, 'Morality is before ontology, for is before with' (Bauman, 1993c, p. 71). It is only 'being-for' the Other that the uniqueness of the Other can be protected, whereas when the interaction is 'being-with' the meeting is fragmentary and precarious and is the 'meeting of incomplete and deficient selves' (Bauman, 1995a, p. 50). To act morally, for example, is characterised by ambivalence because to care for another may lead to domination or paternalism that can undermine the autonomy of the Other, whereas tolerance can lead to indifference. Bauman concludes, 'no act, no matter how noble and unselfish and beneficial for some, can be truly insured against hurting those who find themselves, inadvertently, on its receiving end' (Bauman, 1989b, p. 181). Bauman theorises a primal scene where the moral self is constituted, and it is within this moral primal condition that individuals are *for* rather than *with* the Other. The actions of the moral self are not based on instrumental rationality, rather they are based on responsibility and the urge to care (Bauman, 1993c, p. 60). Not only does modernity repress and exclude the social and cultural stranger by erecting oppressive boundaries, but it also suppresses the development of the moral self. Modernity, for Bauman, has fostered a process where the distance between self and Other has steadily widened. The Holocaust could only have occurred by suppressing and neutralising the impact of primeval moral drives (Bauman, 1989b, p. 188). Bauman claims that it is by making the Other an abstract category, by effacing the 'real' Jew, that the Nazis were able to suspend moral responsibility. By increasing the distance between self and Other, a decline in moral responsibility necessarily follows (Bauman, 1989b, p. 193). At this stage in Bauman's thinking, the immoral acts of individuals seem to be the result of a particular type of societal organisation (modernity). Bauman uses a sociological explanation to understand the denial of the moral impulse. Modern society, argues Bauman, through its intellectual, social and cultural framework suppresses the moral impulse. The underlying premise of modern morality is the belief 'in the possibility of a non-ambivalent, non-aporetic ethical code' (Bauman, 1993b, p. 9). On the other hand, a postmodern ethic does not provide for any such ethical foundation. What constitutes the postmodern moral self is contingency and ambivalence. In the next section I show how this moral impulse, for Bauman, is indispensable in dealing with strangers.

Strangers, identity and the construction of boundaries

Bauman's (1982) understanding of the stranger is multidimensional. In his early writings on capitalist modernity, the working class becomes the dangerous group of the producer society. Under consumer society the 'flawed consumer' or the 'new poor' encapsulate the condition of strangeness. Finally, Bauman uses the metaphor of waste to depict the plight of the underclass as strangers in a global and neoliberal world.

In *Memories of Class* Bauman (1982) suggests that the control over the working class occurred because the dominant, bourgeois, rational self wanted to suppress the 'animal'-like sensations of workers that could threaten the social order. For Bauman, underlying this new type of power was a moral rather than an economic objective. It is in his early publication that Bauman's political economy approach of capitalist exploitation is complemented by a socio-psychological explanation. He indicates that to understand the true significance of the exploitation of the working class, one has to look beyond materialist explanations. The control and exploitation of the masses is both a desire for power and related to the fear of the stranger.

The socio-psychological perspective also informs Bauman's (1987, 1998) assessment and description of the consumer society and the stranger on which it relies on, for example, the 'flawed consumer' or the 'new poor'. Bauman contends that successful consumers are controlled by disciplinary power and become seduced by the free-market into believing they are free. The 'flawed consumers', on the other hand, are those who want to be 'successful' but, because of their economic and social conditions, can only dream of what it is like to be a successful, consuming self. The 'flawed consumers' are the by-products of consumer society, necessary for it to be sustained and reproduced (Bauman, 1988a, p. 187). These 'flawed consumers' are sometimes categorised as the 'new poor' who are disempowered because they are bureaucratically controlled and administered (Bauman, 1988a, p. 185). The 'non' or 'flawed' consumers become the strangers of the consumer society. Bauman depicts them as the 'inner demons' of consumer life that need to be repressed and metaphorically exorcised (Bauman, 1997, p. 42). The general consensus in Western societies is that the 'poor far from meriting care and assistance, deserve hate and condemnation' (Bauman, 1997, p. 43). The strangers of the consumer era (flawed consumers) are thus needed to reinforce the boundaries between the self and the stranger (Bauman, 2004).

Bauman's Marxist humanist background has always made him sensitive to the needs and plight of those on the margin of capitalist modernity and to the psychological and material mechanisms that can explain the origins and continuation of this marginalisation. It is through the fear of the stranger that Bauman finds a partial explanation for this exploitation, oppression and marginalisation. The foci of the following section will be on three essays that encapsulate how his ideas on the stranger have developed and the conceptual framework he applies to understand the role of the stranger in solid and liquid modernity. In the process I will examine the extent to which Bauman's stranger has any affinity with the 'classical stranger' and demonstrate his critical contribution to the 'universalisation of strangerhood' thesis.

The universality and particularity of strangers

In 1988 Bauman published his first systematic analysis of the stranger called 'Strangers: The Social Construction of Universality and Particularity', in which he introduces the key themes underlying the category. Unlike premodern times, modernity's will to order, argues Bauman, found it increasingly difficult to physically and functionally separate strangers because – drawing on the Simmelian stranger – they do not leave. Modernity has a difficult time dealing with the incongruities and ambiguities of strangers and their tendency to blur boundaries. The uncertainties generated by strangers can be resolved through extermination, isolation or discrediting them through stigmatisation (Bauman, 1988b, pp. 10–12). Nonetheless, stigma is at loggerheads with the values of modernity. Whereas stigma emphasises a difference that is beyond repair or 'the outward signs may be hidden, but cannot be eradicated' (Bauman, 1988b, p. 12), modernity is a revolt against that which is fated or ascribed. This contradiction reappears in liberalism's offer that individuals can take their fate into their own hands, but if one does not take advantage of this offer then the responsibility falls on the individual – hence this generates the 'victim blaming' ideology that lies at the heart of liberalism (Bauman, 1988b, p. 14). Ethnic-religious-cultural strangers accept the liberal offer of emancipation and the benefits that come with self-improvement at face value. As soon as they come close to fulfilling the liberal offer, Bauman argues that the 'dagger of racism appears from beneath the liberal cloak' (Bauman, 1988b, p. 15). Cultural or religious strangers continuously have to prove themselves to the native that they have lost their origins and are fully acculturated, but full acculturation never occurs because the 'individuality of the stranger is dissolved into the category' (1988b, p. 16). This is evident when Muslims in the West are continually asked to denounce global terrorism while advocating their allegiance to secularist and democratic values. Hence they can never escape their strangeness because any attempt to assimilate is perceived by the native as denying their culture or seen as an example inauthentic conversion; if they do attempt to stay connected and work for their cultural group, it is proof of their difference and strangeness. This situation, for Bauman, leads to the 'restlessness of the stranger', which from the native's point of view is evidence of their erratic nature.

Bauman also draws on the phenomenological approach to reinforce Schutz's argument that the presence of the stranger raises epistemological issues. Echoing the latter's position, Bauman argues that the stranger's stance to the world differs from the native's, and even when the native's world is absorbed and assimilated, this world proves useless in getting on in the world. It is this existential condition of the stranger 'which makes the native's knowledge unassimilable' (Bauman, 1988b, p. 19). One cannot assimilate what one questions, and the stranger's self-conscious attempt to absorb what the native unconsciously accepts brings the constructed nature of reality into stark relief. The fact that strangers have not been assigned an insider status means that their attempts to assimilate heighten their strangeness (Bauman, 1988b, p. 20). The very act of entering the native's world makes this world a disputed, uncertain and challenging place. Bauman, following Simmel, highlights the objectivity of strangers because of their freedom and lack of commitment to the native's way of life. This objectivity, from the native's perspective, is seen as lacking loyalty and commitment to the native's worldview. The native thus views the essence of strangeness as homelessness, but from the stranger's perspective, this is experienced as loneliness (Bauman, 1988b, pp. 20–21). It is the stranger's objectivity that makes it possible to find the universal truth that the native seeks. It is the nomadic and homeless life that allows one to identify the truth that those fixed are seeking. Drawing on the Russian-Jewish philosophy of Lev Shestov, Bauman concludes, 'Truth found inside a tightly sealed home is hardly useful outside' (Bauman, 1988b, p. 23). Ironically, the universality that the native seeks is found through the homelessness and the particularity of the stranger (Bauman, 1988b, p. 26), and this rootlessness relativises everything that is solid in the native's world.

Bauman's (1988a) essay, however, locates two distinct changes to the stranger in contemporary society. The stranger, for Bauman, can traditionally be associated with the 'modern intellectual' or Mannheim's 'free intellectual' who is a 'perpetual wanderer and universal stranger' (Bauman, 1988b, p. 25). In *Legislators and Interpreters* Bauman does envisage a role for the modern intellectual as the stranger who has the mindset to identify truth and moral right (Bauman, 1987, p. 192). Those 'free intellectuals' however, have become university professors, government consultants and bureaucratic experts who have settled and are more concerned with cultivating their own position. They can now only grasp the world through the particular. It is the knowledge class, argues Bauman, that has replaced the modern intellectual, and they have no urge for certainty (universalism) or relativism (particularity) or the contradictory relationship between them.

The second change – which is crucial for our examination of theories of the stranger – is that strangeness has become privatised and ironically universalised. The 'mode of "being a stranger" is experienced, to a varying degree, by every member of contemporary society with its extreme division of labour and compartmentalisation of functionally separated spheres' (Bauman, 1988b, p. 36). Bauman maintains that due to the poor coordination among the social, cultural, political and economic subsystems, people have developed diverse and multiple selves that are not at home anywhere. In a world on the move, there are no natives and no uncontested standards or values, and strangeness is no longer a temporary condition. This means that 'once rootlessness itself turns into a universal condition, particularity (strangeness) has been effaced' and if 'everyone is a stranger, no one is' (Bauman, 1988b, p. 39). While discussing the personal consequences of universal rootlessness, Bauman draws on Berger et al.'s (1973) *The Homeless Mind* to clarify that we do not find ourselves in an existential crisis. Instead,

Bauman moves to an existential reading of the stranger that implies the death of the stranger as Other.

His second essay, published as a chapter in *Thinking Sociologically* (Bauman, 1990), and in conjunction with an earlier chapter on 'us and them', demonstrates how Bauman's approach to the stranger is premised by binary thinking. Humans have a tendency to view the world in binary terms. In other words, the self's identity is constituted through its opposition to the Other, that is, where identity is subject to a differential logic of opposition to establish difference. Identity, like language, can only gain meaning through a system of signs. Each word or identity gains meaning through its opposition to another. This structuralist linguistic approach and its relationship to identity construction are first evident in Bauman's early English language publications (see Bauman, 1973a), and it is in the chapter on 'us and them' where Bauman highlights how binary thinking underpins our attempt to bring order into our lives. Binary thinking underlies the construction of collective identities in which groups – large and small – adopt this mode of thinking to establish an identity through difference. For example, the discourse on nationalism is particularly prone to this type of thinking. Nationalism seeks unification and homogeneity and achieves this through the act of drawing boundaries between natives and aliens (Bauman, 1992, p. 683). Nationalism and thus the '"we-ness" of friends owes its materiality to the "they-ness" of the enemies' (Bauman, 1992, p. 678).

Although some strangers play an important role in reinforcing this binary process, other strangers undermine it. In *Modernity and the Holocaust* (Bauman, 1989b) and especially in *Modernity and Ambivalence* (Bauman, 1991a), the Jewish experience captures the stranger's paradoxical position. Jews become the insiders/outsiders who have access to a different type of knowledge not available to either the insider or outsider. Like Simmel and Park before him, Bauman argues that the Jew is the exemplary stranger. The Jews epitomise the ambivalent Simmelian stranger because they are 'always on the outside even when inside, examining the familiar as if it was a foreign object of study, asking questions no one else asked, questioning the unquestionable and challenging the unchallengeable' (Bauman, 1989b, p. 53). Bauman has suggested the space that the Jews occupy is 'nowhere' and provides 'an intellectually fertile situation' where 'you are somewhat less constrained by the rules and see beyond' (Kilminister and Varcoe, 1992, p. 227–8). The Jews are therefore difficult to classify. They are neither friend nor enemy. They undermine and destabilise the comfortable antagonism between friend and enemy because the Jew can be a friend, a foe or both. From the point of view of the Gentile, Bauman suggests that the Jew as stranger 'threaten[s] sociation itself – the very possibility of sociation' (Bauman, 1991a, p. 55). In Bauman's earlier publication *Culture as Praxis,* he depicts the Jewish experience as the 'hybrid of modernity' who undermines 'the harmonious build-up of the human universe' (Bauman, 1973b, p. 135). Later he describes Jews as ambivalent people, as the 'third element' or 'the true hybrids' who cannot be classified and are unclassifiable and 'unmask[s] the brittle artificiality of division' (Bauman, 1991a, p. 58).

More recently, reflecting on Simmel's ideas of the dyad and triad, he claims, 'the appearance of the third is an evolutionary moment' (Bauman, 2013, p. 35). Unlike the enemy, this in-between stranger defies division and 'what they oppose is the opposition itself: divisions of any kind, boundaries which guard them, and thus the clarity of the social world results from all that' (Bauman, 1990, p. 54).

In *Thinking Sociologically* (Bauman 1990) these 'ambivalent strangers' are not necessarily related to the cultural or religious Other; for example, 'ambivalent people' can be natives or insiders who have turned against the group such as the deserters, religious converts, the nouveau rich and the upstart who was in a low position and now has a powerful position. In this account, the 'ambivalent person'/stranger becomes conceptually confusing and is in danger of what Ahmed (2000) argues elides the 'regime of difference' that informs this category because the ambivalent stranger is no longer confined to those who are racially and cultural different from the host but to anyone who upsets the clarity and order of the insider's world. The idea of 'ambivalent strangers' is in danger of denying difference because it collapses the in-betweenness of the religious and ethnic Other with the native's experience of in-betweenness.

This slippage is also evident when the chapter revisits the 'universalisation of strangerhood'. Bauman reiterates that we 'live among strangers, among who we are strangers ourselves. In such a world, strangers cannot be confined or kept at bay. Strangers must be lived with' (1990, p. 63). Once again being a stranger extends beyond those who are culturally, religiously and racially different and reiterates the classic argument put forward by urban sociologists that strangeness is a general condition. Compared to his 1988 paper, however, Bauman is more critical of the consequence rather than accuracy of the universalisation thesis. Through civil inattention we treat strangers as 'faceless backcloth against which the things which truly matter happen' (1990, p. 66). What we lose in an urban environment characterised by 'universal strangerhood' is the ethical character of human relationship because under 'the conditions of "universal strangerhood".... [P]hysical proximity has been cleansed of its moral aspect' (1990, p. 69). Whereas in a 'world of strangers' strangers are not treated as enemies and may not be targets of hostility or aggression, they are nonetheless 'deprived of that protection which only moral proximity may offer' (1990, p. 70). Bauman's multiple account of the stranger illustrates both how they reinforce and undermine binary thinking, but also reflect a general condition that we all share in a global urban environment. Bauman does not explicitly investigate the relationship among these three conditions of strangeness. How does a general condition of strangeness undermine binary thought? How can we identify 'ambivalent people' when we are all strangers? Does not ambivalence disappear in the general condition of ambivalence? Under what conditions can the stranger reinforce, but also undermine, binary thinking?

Bauman's (1995b) *Thesis Eleven* article on the 'Making and Unmaking of Strangers' makes no mention of 'ambivalent strangers' or of the universalisation thesis. Nonetheless, in this article Bauman makes the first and only mention of 'postmodern strangers' and focuses on the central role that fear plays in our response to strangers which later becomes a significant argument in his analysis of liquid modernity. The shift from modern and postmodern strangers, according to Bauman, reflects the change from modern to postmodern society, reminiscent of the tradition in social and cultural thought that associates personality types with different societal conditions (see Chapter 3). In this article he reiterates a familiar line of argument about how 'modern strangers were the waste of the state's ordering zeal' (Bauman, 1995b, p. 2) and how they were excluded or assimilated because they corrupted neat divisions. This continued as long at the search for order was collectivised in the hands of the state and the prospects of living with strangers were slim. These conditions, for Bauman, no longer hold in a 'postmodern' society where we live in a continuous state of uncertainty with little hope of finding solidity or continuity. In a postmodern society – in which the boundaries between the normal/abnormal, the expected/unexpected, the ordinary/bizarre, the familiar/strange and us/them have become increasingly uncertain – the role of the stranger has been transformed.

Consequently, 'strangers are no more authoritatively pre-selected, defined and set apart, as they used to be in times of the state managed, consistent and durable programmes of order-building' (Bauman, 1995b, p. 8). They are unpredictable and unsteady, erratic and volatile, as one's identity. The difference that set the self apart from the non-self and 'us' from 'them' 'is no more given by the preordained shape of the world nor by command from on high' (Bauman, 1995b, p. 8). Previously, the hybrid had upset modernity's natural order of things, but with the appearance of a postmodern society, one's position in the hierarchy of advantages has altered, and this places the stranger in an ambivalent position. Constructing the stranger is now a never-ending process, and like the slimy is hateful and feared (Bauman, 1995b, p. 10). The resentment shown to the stranger depends on the relative freedom one has and the amount of control people have over their lives. Bauman stresses that the less freedom and control that one has over one's life, the more resentment one directs towards the stranger. In return, those who have less control and freedom are in turn constructed as strangers, the new poor or the waste of modernity.

According to Bauman's assessment, under postmodern conditions the category of the stranger no longer signifies cultural or racial difference. The stranger is both the cultural stranger who is resented by those host members who have less freedom and control, but they themselves become excluded from the benefits of a global, neoliberal world. They are the new poor. Hence it is unclear whether 'postmodern' strangers are those who are part of the host society, but are excluded from the benefits of global capitalism or whether they are the culturally and religiously Other who the marginalised host members blame for their poor economic and social predicament.

This conflation continues when Bauman argues that under postmodern times, host members use postmodern strangers differently: the powerful and affluent exoticise the cultural and racial stranger for their consuming pleasure while, at the same time, setting the rules of the encounter. The powerless host, on the other hand, view the cultural and racial stranger as a threat because they experience the world as a trap with no means of escape. For the marginalised host the 'sliminess of strangers . . . is the reflection of their own powerlessness', and in this situation the 'weak meets and confronts the weak' (Bauman, 1995b, p. 11). Bauman's position here has implications for the universalisation thesis. We may live in a 'world of strangers', but the affluent host may have the means to opt out of this world and exploit the fear of the cultural and racial stranger to maintain their privileged position. Bauman argues that the privileged deflect the real causes of social and economic problems, for example, an unrestrained, neoliberal, global market onto these strangers. The powerful exploit the insecurities of the weak by identifying and excluding those who are 'security problems', consequently excluding them also from our universe of moral obligation (Bauman, 2011, pp. 57–9). Bauman concludes that the inequalities between the powerful and powerless are based on unequal freedoms, on unequal resources for identity building and unequal access to citizenship and the right of individuality. These all contribute to inequalities and the polarisation between groups. As long as this remains, there is no possibility of de-sliming strangers (Bauman, 1995b, p. 16). Yet, in light of the conflation of various strangers in Bauman's work, the question arises: which strangers have no opportunities to be de-slimed? Is it the weak, marginalised, new poor, or the cultural and racial Other? Or is it both? Unfortunately, Bauman does not explicitly provide the answers to these questions.

Overall, the three essays on the stranger demonstrate Bauman's contribution to theories of the stranger; of particular import is Bauman's account of how power relations among groups affect the construction of the stranger, something that was missing in the work of Simmel and Park. In places, however, this contribution needs conceptual refinement. This is particularly the case when he claims that strangers are 'ambivalent people', and includes those who are not culturally or racially different under this category. The experience of ambivalence for an ambivalent insider will be quantitatively and qualitatively different from the ambivalence experienced by the racial and cultural stranger/outsider, especially if the host imposes that ambivalence. Bauman's insightful analysis of how the powerful and affluent elite manipulate the fears of the new poor or the waste of modernity to deflect the real causes of global inequalities is mitigated by undifferentiated categories such as the 'slimy stranger' and 'ambivalent people'. The danger is that the idea of 'ambivalent people' hides inequalities among those who experience ambivalence. The stranger as Other needs to be retained when we speak of ambivalent, in-between actors, otherwise we lose the opportunity to say anything critical about how marginalisation and oppression are experienced differently by different strangers.

Finally, Bauman's claim that the stranger upsets the binary logic adopted by the native sits uncomfortably with the binary logic he uses to interpret the social world. Throughout his work he demonstrates how ideas have no inner essence because their meaning can be attained only through difference. For example, freedom, for Bauman, does not refer to an inherent free will, rather it refers to a relation: one cannot have freedom without dependency because to be free is to aspire to escape from a form of dependency (Bauman, 1988a, pp. 9, 15–16). Moreover, he argues that there is no design without waste and no order without chaos (2004, pp. 30–31). The first term is always privileged (freedom, solidity or order), and it is the second term (dependency, fluidity or chaos) that gives relevance and meaning to the first. Paradoxically Bauman seems to rely on this very binary system to interpret the modernist project while at the same time questioning its explanatory force through his idea of the 'ambivalent stranger'.

Community, freedom and cross-cultural dialogue

If strangers are here to stay, what conditions should exist for us to live with them as subjects rather than objects? In other words, how in a world of strangers can we stop treating others as slime, waste or collateral damage? Bauman attempts to answer this question through a notion of 'community', based on substantive 'freedom', cross-cultural dialogue and moral responsibility. Bauman's view of 'community' moves beyond the oppressive community constructed by modernity and the postmodern neo-tribes. In contrast to the consumer freedom that exists in contemporary society, Bauman's community apparently provides scope for a more substantive type of freedom to flourish where boundaries are paradoxically sustained and transcended.

He notes that part of the human condition is the desire for both security, which we gain from living in a 'community', and the need for autonomy. These two desires cannot be reconciled nor satisfied simultaneously (Bauman, 2001, p. 5). This mutual tension between freedom and community exists because 'freedom without community means madness, while community without freedom means serfdom' (Bauman, 1995a, p. 127). Nonetheless, Bauman does support a particular type of freedom that can be traced back to his contribution to the Polish revisionism of the 1950s and 1960s. Bauman was one of several Polish thinkers for whom communism and freedom occupied a central place in the conceptual framework within Polish revisionism (Satterwhite, 1992, p. 40). His passion for freedom, however, is for a more substantive type.

Bauman's main critique is directed at consumer freedom that exists in late capitalist modernity. Although consumer capitalism produces a society that provides greater choices along with an individual who is more self-assertive, this comes at a cost because the contest over power is channelled towards the consumer market. Consumer freedom does not destabilise existing power structures. In Bauman's words, 'reproduction of the capitalist system is therefore achieved through individual freedom and not through its repression' (Bauman, 1988a, p. 61). In contrast to consumer freedom, Bauman advocates a political or public freedom that can only be attained in a certain type of political association where moral responsibility and difference thrive.

In the early 1990s Bauman notes that there is not much hope for the political freedom which existed in the Greek polis to be realised in contemporary society (Cantell and Pedersen, 1992, p. 141). He is also rather pessimistic about how we can move from tolerance to solidarity in a postmodern world where there is either indifference or heterophobia directed at strangers (Cantell and Pedersen, 1992,

p. 138). Although Bauman does not explicitly put forward a systematic proposal of how solidarity can be attained, there are moments in his work where the ideas of community, solidarity and freedom become intertwined.

Bauman's political philosophy is informed by the classical republican tradition as understood by Hannah Arendt and later by the work of Castoriadis. Unlike Habermas, Arendt and Bauman believe that participation in 'politics' is important for the self-realisation of individuals (Vetlesen, 1995). Drawing on Arendt's work, Bauman (1988a) argues that the consumer freedom that prevails under late capitalism is an illusion because it is not authentic. Therefore, freedom, for both Arendt and Bauman, means freedom to take part in public affairs, which Bauman calls 'public freedom', and it is in this sense that Bauman argues 'free consumers are poor'. The importance of public freedom and its link to the classical republican view of politics is particularly evident in *Memories of Class* (Bauman, 1982, p. 197), *Freedom* (Bauman, 1988a), *In Search of Politics* (Bauman, 1999a) and *Liquid Modernity* (Bauman, 2000). Bauman attempts to rescue the notion of 'the political' from the economisation of politics that began in the 1970s under the idea of 'corporatism' (Bauman, 1982). He wants to de-economise the political and replace the metaphor of the market with the idea of dialogue that is central to the republican tradition (Vetlesen, 1995, p. 4). It is in the consumer market where the responsibility for the Other is replaced by the responsibility for oneself and where self-indulgence is justified in moral terms: what is good for me must be good for others (Bauman, 2011, p. 78).

Bauman's early work drew on Habermas's notion of communicative rationality to conceptualise the public realm or the body politic. In his formulation a political community consists of open debate and negotiation between equal groups without a structure of dominance distorting the communication (1978, pp. 243–5). Later he utilises John Rawls's theory of an 'overlapping consensus' to argue that agreement is possible when individuals, like those who used to meet in the public spaces of the polis, take responsibility for their actions and accept differences. Bauman maintains that whatever ' "overlapping consensus" there was', for the citizens of the Greek polis, 'it was their common achievement, not the gift they received – they made and made again that consensus as they met and talked and argued' (1995a, pp. 284–5). In his recent work Bauman has been explicitly concerned with the disappearance of politics or the public realm within postmodern consumer society. The realm of politics, for Bauman, is where 'private problems are translated into the language of public issues and public solutions are sought, negotiated and agreed for private troubles' (2000, p. 39) and where genuine autonomy and capacity for self-assertion is fostered (2000, p. 41).

Unlike the Greek polis, however, the political 'community' that Bauman advocates is self-reflective, less homogeneous and more ambivalent and supposedly provides the conditions where individuals can be intimately connected as autonomous, morally self-sustained citizens (Bauman, 1995a, p. 287). Unlike the postulated communities of the neo-tribes in which 'the air inside would soon get stuffy and in the end oppressive' (Bauman, 2001, p. 4), Bauman's political community attempts to foster moral responsibility towards strangers rather than suppress it.

The dialectical relationship between diversity and unity leads Bauman to conclude that an 'overlapping consensus' will allow differences to be transcended and foster an 'intimate connection' based on a 'common' moral impulse that accepts difference. Unlike the traditional sociological notion of community where there is 'no cognitive ambiguity, and so no behavioural ambivalence' (Bauman, 2001, p. 12), Bauman's conception of community is based on the dynamic and vigorous coexistence of ambivalence, boundaries and differences. In this conception of community, it may be possible for one to both transcend and maintain differences. Bauman's political community works against both the classical sociological literature on community that was first expressed by Tönnies and then later by Barth (1969) and Redfield (1971) and the community or nationalism under modernity's will to order. The constitution of community under these accounts is understood in terms of maintaining cultural and symbolic boundaries so that those within the community recognise and exclude strangers.

In response, Bauman's work suggests that a third type of 'community' can be constructed where boundaries are porous rather than fixed and where difference and universality are dialectically interwoven and autonomy and self-critique are the basis of an autonomous political society (Bauman, 1999a). It is only under these conditions that the social and cultural stranger will be accepted and effectively contribute to the life of the community. With the help of Castoriadis, Bauman theorises the existence of an autonomous society where universality is not the enemy of difference (1999a, p. 202). In an ambiguous political community, dialogue between strangers or different cultures does not result in distorted communication but in different communications. Within Bauman's community a 'cultural frontierland' exists in which cultural borders are fluid and cultures are unfinished projects, where ambivalence, confusion and uncertainty are mixed with tolerance and moral responsibility towards the Other (Bauman, 1999b: I–Ii). To rebuild this public space, we need a specific type of political education that encourages people to think about the relationship between the common and the individual as well as private and communal interests. In this old/new public space, we can encourage the development of skills, such as interacting with others, conducting dialogue, gaining mutual understanding and resolving and managing conflicts, which are a part of living with strangers (Bauman, 2005, p. 125).

Yet, this moral public space, it seems, cannot be sustained by its own moral impulse because Bauman still envisages a role for the state. But this state is 'social': the 'social' state endorses the protection of individual misfortune and its consequences and provides its citizens with social rights because they are necessary for political rights to be meaningful (Bauman, 2010, pp. 40–41). A society, for Bauman, grows as its weakest grows (2010, p. 42). This 'social' state has also a global dimension that depends on the resurgence of the socialist 'active utopia', invoking collective responsibility and collective insurance against human misfortune and misery at a global scale (Bauman, 2011, p. 26). This type of utopian thinking, characterised by its critical edge, its hope, and its ability to engage with the possible, has been evident since the mid-1970s (see Bauman, 1976, pp. 9–17). It is within this 'political autonomous community' that the cultural and religious stranger with all its ambivalent connotations finds a home and where the universalisation of strangeness loses its amoral foundation.

Conclusion

The condition of strangeness and its relationship to ambivalence allow Bauman to expose the universal and totalitarian tendencies of 'solid' modernity; to illuminate the ambivalence and contingency of postmodernity or 'liquid' modernity; to conceptualise the human condition as moral and ambivalent; and to expose the dark side of modernity. It is only in Bauman's attempt to formulate a community based on difference and 'public freedom' that the ambivalence of strangers becomes a source for moral responsibility. Overall, Bauman implies that ambivalence provides the possibility or the means with which we seek freedom – especially for the excluded – and extend responsibility to the weak and marginalised. It is only in his reformulation of community that Bauman treats ambivalence not as an ethic but as a condition in which we live.

Nevertheless, the relationship between the category of the stranger and ambivalence is not without its problems. Although ambivalence allows Bauman to effectively analyse the paradoxical effects of imposing a universal structure, the idea – when used to describe the stranger's experience – is perplexing. Whereas the Jew as insider/outsider encapsulates the experience of hybridity and ambivalence that modernity attempts to repress, this ambivalent experience is not always confined to the stranger as Other. For example, Bauman speaks about 'ambivalent people' who are not necessarily culturally and racially different to the host.

References

Ahmed, S., 2000. *Strange Encounters: Embodied Others in Post-Coloniality*. London: Routledge.
Barth, F., 1969. Introduction. In: F. Barth, ed. *Ethnic Groups and Boundaries: The Social Organization of Cultural Difference*. Boston: Little, Brown and Company, pp. 9–38.
Bauman, Z., 1968. Marx and the Contemporary Theory of Culture. *Social Science Information*, 3(3), pp. 19–33.
Bauman, Z., 1973a. The Structuralist Promise. *The British Journal of Sociology*, 24(1), pp. 67–83.
Bauman, Z., 1973b. *Culture and Praxis*. London: Routledge and Kegan Paul.
Bauman, Z., 1976. *Socialism: The Active Utopia*. New York: Holmes & Meier.
Bauman, Z., 1978. *Hermeneutics and Social Science*. New York: Columbia University Press.
Bauman, Z., 1982. *Memories of Class*. London: Routledge & Kegan Paul.
Bauman, Z., 1987. *Legislators and Interpreters: On Modernity, Postmodernity and Intellectuals*. Oxford: Polity Press.
Bauman, Z., 1988a. *Freedom*. Stony Stratford: Open University Press.
Bauman, Z., 1988b. Strangers: The Social Construction of Universality and Particularity. *Telos*, 78, pp. 7–42.
Bauman, Z., 1989a. Hermeneutics and Modern Social Theory. In: D. Held and J.B. Thompson, eds. *Social Theory and Modern Society: Anthony Giddens and His Critics*. Cambridge: Cambridge University Press, pp. 43–55.

Bauman, Z., 1989b. *Modernity and the Holocaust*. Cambridge: Polity Press.
Bauman, Z., 1990. *Thinking Sociologically*. Cambridge: Basil Blackwell.
Bauman, Z., 1991a. *Modernity and Ambivalence*. Cambridge: Polity Press.
Bauman, Z., 1991b. A Sociological Theory of Postmodernity. *Thesis Eleven*, 29, pp. 33–46.
Bauman, Z., 1992. Soil, Blood and Identity. *Sociological Review*, 40(4), pp. 675–701.
Bauman, Z., 1993a. Modernity. *In*: J. Krieger, ed. *The Oxford Companion to Politics of the World*. New York: Oxford University Press, pp. 592–596.
Bauman, Z., 1993b. Racism, Anti-Racism and Moral Progress. *Arena Journal*, 1, pp. 9–22.
Bauman, Z., 1993c. *Postmodern Ethics*. Oxford: Blackwell.
Bauman, Z., 1995a. *Life in Fragments: Essays in Postmodern Morality*. Oxford: Blackwell.
Bauman, Z., 1995b. Making and Unmaking of Strangers. *Thesis Eleven*, 43, pp. 1–16.
Bauman, Z., 1997. *Postmodernity and Its Discontents*. Oxford: Polity Press.
Bauman, Z., 1998. *Work, Consumerism and the New Poor*. Buckingham: Open University Press.
Bauman, Z., 1999a. *In Search of Politics*. Cambridge: Polity Press.
Bauman, Z., 1999b. Introduction. *In*: *Culture as Praxis*. 2nd edition. London: Sage, pp. vii–Iii.
Bauman, Z., 2000. *Liquid Modernity*. Cambridge: Polity Press.
Bauman, Z., 2001. *Community: Seeking Safety in an Insecure World*. Cambridge: Polity.
Bauman, Z., 2004. *Wasted Lives: Modernity and its Outcasts*. Oxford: Polity.
Bauman, Z., 2005. *Liquid Life*. Cambridge: Polity.
Bauman, Z., 2010. *Living on Borrowed Time: Conversations with Citlali Rovirosa-Madrazo*. Cambridge: Polity.
Bauman, Z., 2011. *Collateral Damage: Social Inequalities in a Global Age*. Cambridge: Polity.
Bauman, Z., 2013. A Conversation with Zygmunt Bauman: From Ethics to Justice: The Role of the Triad in Modern Social Imagination. *In*: I. Cooper and B. Malkmus, eds. *Dialectic and Paradox: Configurations of the Third in Modernity*. Oxford: Peter Lang, pp. 25–36.
Beilharz, P., 1994. *Postmodern Socialism: Romanticism, City and State*. Melbourne: Melbourne University Press.
Beilharz, P., 2000. *Zygmunt Bauman: Dialectic of Modernity*. London: Sage.
Berger, P.L. Berger, B. and Kellner, H., 1973. *The Homeless Mind: Modernization and Consciousness*. New York: Random House.
Best, S., 2013. *Zygmunt Bauman: Why Good People Do Bad Things*. Surrey: Ashgate.
Cantell, T. and Pedersen, P., 1992. Modernity, Postmodernity and Ethics: An Interview with Zygmunt Bauman. *Telos*, 93, pp. 133–144.
Kellner, D., 1998. Zygmunt Bauman's Postmodern Turn. *Theory, Culture & Society*, 15(1), pp. 73–86.
Kilminister, R. and Varcoe, I., 1992. Appendix: Sociology, Postmodernity and Exile: An Interview with Zygmunt Bauman. *Intimations of Postmodernity*. London: Routledge, pp. 205–228.
Matthews, F.H., 1977. *Quest for an American Sociology: Robert E. Park and the Chicago School*. Montreal: McGill-Queen's University Press.
Nijhoff, P., 1998. The Right to Inconsistency. *Theory, Culture & Society*, 15(1), pp. 87–112.
Poder, P. and Jacobsen, M.H., 2008. *The Sociology of Zygmunt Bauman: Challenges and Critique*. Aldershot: Ashgate.
Redfield, R., 1971. *The Little Community, and Peasant Society and Culture*. Chicago: University of Chicago Press.

Satterwhite, J.H., 1992. *Varieties of Marxist Humanism: Philosophical Revision in Postwar Eastern Europe*. Pittsburgh: University of Pittsburgh Press.

Smith, D., 2000. *Zygmunt Bauman: Prophet of Postmodernity*. Cambridge: Polity Press.

Tester, K., 2004. *The Social Thought of Zygmunt Bauman*. Houndmills: Palgrave Macmillan.

Vetlesen, A.J., 1995. Hannah Arendt, Habermas and the Republican Tradition. *Philosophy and Social Criticism*, 21(1), pp. 1–16.

7 The cosmopolitan stranger
Mark II

Introduction

The following discussion further develops my analysis of the relationship between the cosmopolitan and the stranger (Marotta, 2010) and contributes to a critical discussion of cosmopolitanism by examining the affinities between the cosmopolitan subject and some of the features of the stranger addressed in previous chapters. Drawing on the major characteristics of the stranger, and through an investigation of various cosmopolitan thinkers, I delineate a cosmopolitan worldview that has close affinities with specific versions of the stranger. This comparison leads to my central thesis that a new social type has emerged that can be categorised as the 'cosmopolitan in-between stranger'. A recent publication by Rumford (2013) has drawn on the cosmopolitan stranger and challenged some of my earlier assertions. This is not a place to quibble over which is the more authentic, 'real' or convincing version of the cosmopolitan stranger, but Rumford's criticism – as all constructive criticism should – allows me an opportunity to clarify and further develop my arguments. I demonstrate how within discussions of cosmopolitanism, as with certain approaches to the stranger, one can trace a cosmopolitan who develops a more perceptive, broader and keener insight than those confined to either a particular/universal or insider/outsider perspective. As a consequence of this enlightened view, these new social actors are able to undermine binary logic and the essentialism underpinning 'standpoint epistemology'. The chapter begins with an investigation of the so-called differences between the 'classical' and the cosmopolitan stranger and then provides a brief examination of the major attributes of the cosmopolitan outlook. Following this, I identify the underlying commonalities between the stranger and the cosmopolitan as a mode of being in the world. The concluding section makes several critical points: it highlights the unrealism of the realist position within contemporary cosmopolitan thought and critically evaluates the idea of openness and the passive Other embedded in the discourse of the cosmopolitan stranger.

Cosmopolitanism

Before addressing the similarities between the cosmopolitan subject and the stranger, a brief examination of cosmopolitanism is necessary. Providing a definitive definition of cosmopolitanism has its problems and thus 'no single conceptualization is adequate' (Vertovec and Cohen, 2002, p. 3). In fact, to characterise cosmopolitanism according to a set of values and principles is an uncosmopolitan act (Pollock et al., 2002, p. 1). Nonetheless, cosmopolitanism has been conceptualised in six ways (Vertovec and Cohen, 2002): as a sociocultural condition; as a philosophy or worldview; as a perspective that advocates transnational institutions; as an approach that highlights the multiple constructions of the political subject; as an attitude or disposition that is open and engaged with otherness; and finally as a propensity to be flexible, reflective and move between cultures without residing within them. Although these characteristics offer a good starting point, they do not explicitly examine the extent to which these dimensions are interrelated. Are these characteristics mutually exclusive? Is one dimension of cosmopolitanism more likely to encourage another? For example, can the cosmopolitan disposition develop or emerge in a sociocultural condition that is not cosmopolitan? These questions cannot be adequately addressed here, but they do demonstrate the need for greater clarity and conceptualisation when it comes to understanding the multiple and complex nature of cosmopolitanism. The focus of this chapter, however, is on cosmopolitanism as an intellectual disposition or outlook because it is here that the literature on cosmopolitanism and the stranger merge.

There are certain versions of cosmopolitanism, however, that view the cosmopolitan and the stranger as mutually distinct actors. This literature, for example, tends to confine itself to an investigation on how a cosmopolitan outlook encourages openness and an ethical stance towards strangers. At other times it argues that cosmopolitanism fosters a society or urban spaces where strangeness becomes universal. In these accounts, the cosmopolitan and the stranger are separate social actors with little in common. The cosmopolitan speaks about the stranger yet is not the stranger (Appiah, 2007; Iveson, 2005; Ossewaarde, 2007). It was in the mid-eighteenth century that the French philosopher Diderot connected the cosmopolitan with the stranger when he stated that cosmopolitans are 'strangers nowhere in the world' (in Jacob, 2006, p. 1). On the other hand, the classical sociological literature on the stranger makes a cursory reference to cosmopolitanism when it addresses the characteristics of the stranger. For example, Park associates the hybrid self with the stranger and in turn with cosmopolitan sentiments. Stonequist (1937) makes a passing reference to the 'cosmopolitan individual' in his assessment of the marginal man concept and its association with Simmel's stranger. The cultural anthropologist Hannerz (1990, p. 248) also implies an underlying strangeness to cosmopolitans because they are one of us (proximity) yet they are different (distance).

More recently, Chan Kwok Bun (2003, p. 154) notes that cosmopolitan encounters are encounters with strangers and makes references to Simmel's stranger and Park's 'marginal man' as a means by which these cross-cultural encounters can be understood. Ossewaarde (2007, p. 371) argues that the activities of cosmopolitanism results in the inclusion of strangers, but he also maintains that cosmopolitans enter local communities as strangers who have special knowledge, qualifications and social status acquired outside the local group. He outlines that, similar to Simmel's stranger, cosmopolitans are objective because they are able to distant themselves from local loyalties (2007, p. 374). These writers make important, tentative steps towards the formulation, conceptualisation and understanding of the cosmopolitan stranger. These positive steps, however, are undermined by Ossewaarde's and Chan's misinterpretation of Simmel's stranger and the type of 'objectivity' that it promotes.

Ossewaarde (2007, p. 372) and Bun (2003, p. 148) argue that Simmel's stranger is one who arrives today and leaves tomorrow, contradicting Simmel's own formulation. It is the fact that strangers *remain* that places them in an ambivalent position. In addition, Simmel's version of objectivity – as shown in Chapter 4 – is as much about detachment as involvement. Both Ossewaarde and Bun understate Simmel's ambivalent description of objectivity and provide an incomplete account of Simmel's stranger. These oversights make their comparison between the cosmopolitan subject and the stranger unconvincing. The next section addresses these omissions by providing a more detailed and fuller assessment of the affinities between the cosmopolitan self and what I call the in-between stranger.

The in-between stranger

I have argued that Simmel, Park and Bauman formulate an in-between stranger that destabilises binary oppositions and that this in-betweenness fosters special qualities and insights unavailable to those inside and outside the group. This in-between subject could also be associated with the experience of liminality, hybridity and *mestiza* consciousness (Marotta, 2011). Rumford (2013) claims that the 'in-between stranger' is conceptually redundant because 'the stranger is already an undecidable, an inbetweener, as constructed in the writings of Bauman and Simmel (p. 117). My discussion of Bauman and Simmel has shown that the figure of the stranger is multifaceted and thus not necessarily confined to an in-between subject. The very fact that the in-between stranger is not unique in Simmel and Bauman makes it conceptually significant. At one level, Bauman and Simmel construct the stranger as in-between, but as I have shown, this is in tension with other versions of the stranger in their work. For example, Bauman uses the stranger to highlight how it reinforces and feeds into the host's understanding of the world in binary terms. From the perspective of the host, strangers are useful in constructing the host's identity through establishing difference between oneself and others. In these terms strangers are conceptualised as non-members and thus not in between. Their exclusion and marginalisation from the 'in-group' or 'native group' depends on their status as cultural outsiders. In this conception, the function of the stranger, for Bauman, is to reinforce cultural and social boundaries and the binary opposition 'us/them'. The host adopts a binary logic to demarcate a world according to who belongs and who does not. Simmel's work also speaks to other versions of the stranger that are not explicitly related to a state of in-betweenness such as an existential condition or cultural otherness (the Greeks vs the barbarians). For Simmel, there are strangers who are associated with a 'third party' and thus undermine the search for absolute contrast; consequently, he alternates from a conception of the stranger (the barbarian) whose role is to reinforce binary thinking to one that challenges it.

Similarly, what we find in Bauman's work are multiple strangers that at times lack conceptual clarity. They both threaten (ambivalent people) and reinforce (flawed consumers or the waste of modernity) boundaries. In Bauman's work there is no guarantee that those strangers who are initially positioned as the Other will become a source of ambivalence and thus difficult to categorise. In contrast to Rumford's claim then, strangers are not already 'inbetweeners' in the work of Bauman and Simmel. We find multilayered and multifaceted approaches to the stranger that are not always reconciled and lead to various levels of ambiguity in their works.

When constructed as an in-between subject, the stranger tends to encourage a specific knowledge of the world that is not accessible to either the insider or outsider (those strangers who conform to a binary logic). The position of in-between strangers encourages a critical and 'objective' stance towards the host and one's own culture. The ability of in-between strangers to transcend the subjective perspective of the host's practices, customs and values allows them to critically reflect upon them. Because of this experience, in-between strangers like Park's marginal man are able to re-evaluate and reflect upon their own group's traditions and worldview. This is why they are in-between because they stand outside of the host and their own group; their exposure to the Otherness of the host self allows them to reassess their 'home' culture as less stable and fixed. Home as a given and natural state now becomes contingent. This alternative in-between knowledge allows strangers the ability to transcend conventional and 'situated' knowledge and, by implication, the in-between, third position permits strangers to see things more clearly and/or differently than those who occupy opposing cultural perspectives.

For example, Simmel's in-between strangers are 'objective', but this objectivity is not associated with the neutrality or value-free process that characterises positivism. As shown in Chapter 4, Simmel's in-between strangers dialectically adopt a frame of mind that could be classified as a 'subjective objectivity', which entails being both remote and near, detached and involved, and indifferent and concerned. In-between strangers have a 'bird's-eye view' and are not immersed in the particularities of the opposing parties or cultural groups. This 'bird's-eye view' allows those situated in the third position to adopt and therefore understand the particular views of both parties but be adequately detached from them to identify underlying common or universal interests.

The previous chapters have shown that theories of the stranger have postulated that there are epistemological advantages of being a social and cultural in-between subject. Park was at the forefront in theorising and linking cultural and racial hybridity to special cognitive abilities. He spoke of the in-between subject – which he linked to the stranger – as having a wider horizon, a keener intelligence and a more detached and rational viewpoint. Hybrid subjects adopt a cosmopolitan disposition because they are less nationalistic and thus 'look across national boundaries' (Park, 1934, p. 137). This alternative epistemology and perspective is not available to those immersed in the worldview of either the established or the marginal, either the native or foreigner.

The cosmopolitan stranger

Understood along these lines, the in-between stranger has some affinities with a cosmopolitan disposition as expressed in the work of Beck (2001, 2004), Hannerz (1990), Turner (2001, 2002), Rumford (2013) and Waldron (1992). These authors have attempted to think beyond the confines of their disciplines by articulating and adopting a cosmopolitan outlook. Hannerz expresses the classic statement on the cosmopolitan mind when he examines the relationship between cosmopolitans and locals. Hannerz (1990, p. 230) observes that cosmopolitanism as a state of mind refers to a mode of managing meaning that includes being involved with and open to Otherness. Such a mode of being in the world fosters the development of a cosmopolitan subject who is autonomous, masterful and expansive. The cosmopolitan subject 'surrenders' to other cultures, but this capitulation is not associated with a commitment to others (1990, p. 240). Engagement with others becomes an 'aesthetic stance of openness toward divergent cultural experiences', and consequently it comprehends other cultures as works of art (1990, p. 237). Reminiscent of the 'free floating, unattached intellectual' (Gouldner, 1979; Mannheim, 1993; Pels, 1999), the cosmopolitan adopts a 'culture of critical discourse' which is reflective, questioning and devoted to the mastery of explicit and less ambiguous knowledge (Hannerz, 1990, pp. 246–7). Cosmopolitans are those at home in a homeless world. This rootlessness is the precondition for developing a 'wider vision' because cosmopolitans reside in 'no man's land'. Cosmopolitan subjects adopt detached inquiry, they straddle the universal and particular, and they 'eschews binaries in favor of subject positions that strive towards the flexible' (Heydt-Stevenson and Cox, 2005, pp. 131, 134–5). Waldron (1992) continues the theme of the rootlessness of the cosmopolitan self in his critique of identity politics in the US.

Waldron examines the communitarian's critique of cosmopolitan subjectivity, especially their claims that the cosmopolitan self is nomadic and that it undermines the fixed and stable identities that constitute the modern subject. The outcome, according to the communitarians, is a lack of commitment and responsibility towards others. Waldron rejects these assertions because they misrepresent the 'cosmopolitan self' and they seem to hark back to, and are nostalgic for, *gemeinschaft* relations. These relations no longer reflect the 'real communities' to which most of us belong. As examples of these 'real communities', Waldron designates the international community of scholars, the scientific community, the human rights community, the artistic community and the feminist movement (1992, p. 777). Waldron concludes that the advantage of these global communities is that they incorporate diverse opinions and ideas and thus generate common solutions to common problems (1992, p. 776). It is only those who are 'citizens of the world', or what he occasionally categorises as the 'cosmopolitan self' who can resolve global problems. Similar to in-between strangers – who are not confined by particular identities – the cosmopolitan self has greater allegiance to international communities and organisations than to local cultures and communities.

The 'communitarian position', suggests Waldron, assumes that 'the social world divides up neatly into particular distinct cultures . . . and secondly, the assumption that what everyone needs is just *one* of these identities – a single coherent culture – to give shape and meaning to life' (1992, p. 782). In contrast to the communitarian subject, Waldron asserts that the cosmopolitan self is more 'authentic'. Waldron's use of the adjective 'authentic' here does not imply a return to essentialism: rather he believes that the cosmopolitan self accurately reflects contemporary multiple, playful and hybrid identities. The cosmopolitan self, concludes Waldron, is a 'richer, more honest, and more authentic response to the world in which we live than a retreat into the confined sphere of a particular community' (1992, p. 788). The cosmopolitan self, according to this formulation, is a manager who juggles several commitments and attachments. Waldron acknowledges, however, that whereas this may lead to conflict and fragmentation for the cosmopolitan self, it may also involve a sense of continuity. Cosmopolitan selves do not neglect local identities, even though they can move beyond group loyalties. Similar to the idea of the in-between stranger, cosmopolitan subjects can adopt a universal stance while incorporating and understanding local identities. They can move easily between the particular and the universal.

The work of Beck and Turner continues this connection between the cosmopolitan temperament and characteristics such as in-betweenness, reflexivity, distance, openness and a critical viewpoint. Beck develops a cosmopolitan sociology based on a dialogic imagination that incorporates rival ways of life into the experiences of individuals. By incorporating difference into one's life, one is better able to compare, reflect, criticise and understand the contradictions of modern life. The dialogic imagination fosters a meaningful engagement with the Otherness of the Other, and Beck believes that this imagination is implicit in Kant's version of cosmopolitanism as a 'citizen of the world'. The dialogic imagination contrasts with a national or monological perspective. In the latter, individuals are unable to critically reflect on their action, adopt binary thinking and are likely to exclude the Otherness of the Other in their ethical judgments.

The dialogic imagination explores the creative contradictions of cultures within and between imagined communities and adopts a methodology which rejects the either-or principle or binary thinking because conceiving the world in terms of binaries reinforces power relations between the dominant self and the subordinate other. Beck also addresses the idea of 'rooted cosmopolitanism' in which one is both simultaneously local and global. Unlike the cosmopolitanism associated with mobile elites, Beck argues that 'rooted cosmopolitanism' promotes an ethical engagement with Otherness.

Beck notes that we need rethink how we understand and approach our global world. What we need is an epistemological shift that will allow us to be *open* to pluralism and difference. The dialogical imagination encourages this epistemological shift by appealing to a 'higher amorality' which encompasses an ethical position that denies the superiority of one's own morality while being open to contrary beliefs. A dialogical imagination also involves a politics that is critical of the essentialising nature of nationalism. The cosmopolitan perspective, for Beck, thus fosters a subjectivity that is transcultural, hybrid, transnational and transgressive. This subjectivity develops a critique of our existing Western society and its intellectual foundations based on mono-dimensional, essentialist and binary thinking.

On the other hand, Turner's conception of the cosmopolitan subject has some affinities with a 'cosmopolitan virtue'. Social actors who embrace a cosmopolitan virtue adopt a mode or attitude to the world that involves an ironic distance. This entails being sceptical of grand narratives, distancing oneself from one's local culture, respecting and caring for other cultural values, especially indigenous cultures, accommodating cultural hybridisation and having an universal commitment to dialogue across cultures (Turner, 2001, pp. 148–50). This cosmopolitan mentality encourages 'thin social relationships' such as those based on email friendships and electronic networks (Turner, 2001, p. 148).

Beck's and Turner's cosmopolitan disposition echo the characteristics of the in-between stranger. First, both social actors adopt an epistemic distancing, but they also encompass the movement between particularism and universalism that is evident in Turner's idea of patriotic cosmopolitanism (2002, p. 59) and Beck's rooted cosmopolitanism. The cosmopolitan disposition allows one the ability to be both socially and ethically close but distant, which reverses the distant/proximity scheme of the classical stranger (socially distant but physically close). Second, the cosmopolitan outlook echoes the 'subjective objectivity' of Simmel's in-between stranger because it develops an intellectual attitude to the world that is not available to those confined to a particular/universal or insider/outsider position. Turner concludes that the cosmopolitan ironic stance is sceptical of grand narratives, whereas Beck and Waldron argue that rooted cosmopolitanism transcends universalist cosmopolitanism. The third position – which the cosmopolitan stranger occupies – encourages a critical view of binary thinking and the essentialist identities it fosters. Understanding the insider experience (host or local) is only possible through proximity and distance, through self-reflexivity and through an ironic dialogical imagination.

Rumford's idea of the cosmopolitan stranger dismisses this link between the cosmopolitan and the in-between stranger, and in the long tradition of trying to kill off the 'classical stranger', he argues that his version of the 'cosmopolitan stranger' has little to do with the 'classical stranger'. Rumford does have a point because traditional discussions of the classical stranger (excluding Bauman) do not contextualise it within a global context, and hence the latter cannot be 'found in predictable places' and 'does not conform to the "comes today, stays tomorrow"' (2013, p. 105) classical frame. Thus, for Rumford, in a condition of 'generalised societal strangeness' – in which we are strangers to others and ourselves – the cosmopolitan stranger may not be associated with migrants and foreigners. Nevertheless, I have suggested in Chapters 3 and 4 that the death of the 'classical stranger' is premature, especially when one acknowledges its multiple constructions. Rumford's conceptualisation of the cosmopolitan stranger differs from certain versions of the classical stranger, but like previous accounts of the cosmopolitan outlook, his cosmopolitan stranger remains within the discourse of the in-between third position.

Rumford's 'cosmopolitan stranger', in contradistinction to the 'classical stranger', potentially connects people with distant others, creates new forms of social solidarity and 'can manoeuvre in the restricted spaces caused by the social and political compression characteristic of the Global Age'. The cosmopolitan stranger is not here to stay and thus has a 'relatively short-term or fleeting existence' in which 'strangerhood can be a political resource' which 'opens up a range of possibilities under conditions of strangeness'. Cosmopolitan strangers are strangers to themselves and unlike 'classical strangers' are 'everywhere at home' and, because they 'enjoy heightened mobility' (Rumford, 2013, p. 121), are able to connect globally without leaving home. Moreover, in contrast to the 'classical stranger' – who wants to belong – the cosmopolitan stranger 'wants to be free of the ties and obligations which come from (attempted) belonging', and this disconnection from the 'clutches of community' allows the cosmopolitan stranger political clout. Being everywhere at home encourages 'a certain freedom from both physical and ideological commitment', and consequently they 'advocate a society of individuals' (Rumford, 2013, p. 123). Drawing on Haraway's 'standpoint epistemology' in which the social world cannot be understood from a single, privileged position, Rumford argues that cosmopolitanism 'encourages multiperspectivalism rather than producing "high point" thinking' (Rumford, 2013, p. 118). It is not clear in Rumford's description whether this multiperspectival position is associated with the cosmopolitan stranger, but one can assume that due to the mobility and disconnection from any community, the cosmopolitan stranger has access to multiple ways of interpreting the world.

A critique of the cosmopolitan stranger

I want to make three critical points on the cosmopolitan stranger and the intellectual and cognitive qualities it apparently fosters. First, I criticise the 'unrealism' of the realist position informing contemporary cosmopolitanism. Second, I interrogate the claim that the cosmopolitan stranger can initiate cross-cultural dialogue and be open to the Other. Third, I question the cosmopolitan stranger's construction of the Other as passive in intercultural encounters.

Early critics of ethical cosmopolitanism argued that the moral community of humankind posited by universalist cosmopolitan theorists did not reflect or mirror the reality of the human condition (Lu, 2000, p. 246). The charge of utopian idealism led to accusations that universal cosmopolitanism would undermine international and human security because the practices it advocated would divide more than they would unite (Lu, 2000, p. 247). Aware of these charges of unrealism and utopian idealism, contemporary discussions of the cosmopolitan subject adopt a realist position. In other words, the writers under consideration here speak of the cosmopolitan self as if it reflects or mirrors existing subjectivities. For example, when Waldron speaks of an 'authentic cosmopolitan subject', he assumes that it mirrors existing patterns of social interaction and current multiple and hybrid identities. Nonetheless, Waldron moves from description to prescription when he argues that the existence of a cosmopolitan self is essential for a vibrant and sound individual. It is 'the possibility of such conflict, and variety and open texture of character that make it possible . . . [and] indispensable', argues Waldron, for 'a healthy personality' (1992, p. 791). Not only does the cosmopolitan self reflect reality, but it also becomes the grounds for psychological and social well-being.

Turner, on the other hand, argues that contemporary societies characterised by a 'system of global cultures' and 'postmodern or cosmopolitan citizenship' have 'cool loyalties' and 'thin social relationships'. This type of societal configuration encourages the emergence of ironic cosmopolitan personalities. Although Turner's discussions of the cosmopolitan self is descriptive in places, one would have to question the existence of such a self, especially whether it is possible to combine all the qualities of cosmopolitan virtue. Turner provides little empirical evidence to support the description of the ironic cosmopolitan self. Further, if such personalities do exist, to what extent are they able to juggle the various demands placed upon them? How can these social actors combine the care and respect for others, with the scepticism of grand narratives, with the detachment of locality, with the accommodation of hybridisation and with a universal commitment to cross-cultural dialogue? If such a personality does exist, Turner has not clearly demonstrated how these individuals can effectively accommodate the possible tensions and complexities arising from these competing demands.

Second, if a cosmopolitan mentality and an ironic disposition encourage 'thin relationships', as evident in computer-mediated communication, then one must not assume that these are compatible with the key components of cosmopolitan virtue, such as promoting caring and respectful relationships. Online communication can be the impetus for developing online friendships which extend beyond the virtual world, but online communication is a much more ambivalent medium than Turner suggests. The Internet and online communications can be a forum for racism, sexism, terrorist organisations and paedophiles (Atton, 2006; Awan, 2007; Malesky, 2007). The analogy between a cosmopolitan orientation and online relations is problematic. Cosmopolitans may encourage 'thin relationships', but these thin relations may not necessarily foster the care and responsibility towards others that a cosmopolitan virtue is said to promote. The point here is that the work of contemporary cosmopolitan theorists on the cosmopolitan subject lack empirical examples. A further instance of this is Beck's claim that a dialogical and rooted cosmopolitanism will lead to ethical relations towards the Other; this assertion is about what should be rather than what is. Contemporary cosmopolitan thought has made implicit attempts – through its analysis of the cosmopolitan self – to resist the charge of utopian idealism, but this has led to unrealistic and unverifiable claims.

The second assertion made by cosmopolitan theorists is that openness, connection, respect and engagement with Otherness are inherent qualities of the cosmopolitan stranger. What is questionable here is how this 'openness' or 'connection' is manifested. Rumford argues that the mobility of cosmopolitan strangers enhances their ability to connect with distant Others. Yet this connection is only possible for those who shun social connection and who do not pursue 'conventional community contact' (Rumford, 2013, p. 123). It is never clear what type of connection Rumford is referring to here or what 'conventional community' means. The assumption is that this connection is 'open', but what do we mean by 'open'? In addition, if cosmopolitan strangers are wary of social contact, one would have to query what sort of openness and connection Rumford is alluding to. If one wants to be 'open' and connect with distant Others, then it seems that the ability to be 'social' and engaging would be an essential quality.

The question of what constitutes openness and its relationship with how the cosmopolitan stranger connects to the Other is also evident in Hannerz's work. He argues that a 'more genuine cosmopolitanism' relates to an 'aesthetic stance of openness' in which other cultures are seen 'as works of art'. What constitutes an 'aesthetic stance of openness', however, is left unanalysed. If we view the Other as a 'work of art', we may fall into the trap of objectifying and eroticising the Other, thereby placing undue focus on their apparent 'beauty' and 'difference' rather than their actual material conditions. Turner also draws on the idea of openness and care for the Other and notes that this openness and care 'can be conceptualized in terms of the psychoanalytic relationship, in which the neutral analyst has to listen carefully to what the other is saying' (Turner, 2001, p. 149). Using the analogy of the psychoanalytic relationship to express the openness inherent in cosmopolitan virtue is fraught with danger. First, the traditional psychoanalytic relationship is a paternalistic and unequal relationship in which we listen to the Other, but the cosmopolitan 'neutral analyst' interprets their ideas, emotions and values. The analyst is in a privileged position to provide the correct treatment and advice to the dependent patient. The psychoanalytic relationship is also a flawed analogy because it does not depend on a shared openness: the patient/Other opens up to the cosmopolitan/neutral analyst, but this is not necessarily reciprocated.

Finally, the unequal relationship between the cosmopolitan self and the Other is underscored by how the discourse of the cosmopolitan stranger constructs the Other as passive. Discussions on the cosmopolitan outlook/orientation focus on what the cosmopolitan self acquires in cross-cultural dialogues. What is unclear is whether the engagement with otherness has any benefits for the Other. Do they also develop a cosmopolitan virtue or a dialogic imagination when they encounter the Otherness of the cosmopolitan self? In the construction of cosmopolitan subjectivity, the Other becomes a passive observer whose only purpose is to foster the development of cosmopolitan virtue. The origin of the cosmopolitan virtue, therefore, exists within the Otherness of the Other. Moreover, it is assumed that the Other does not resist but welcomes the engagement and dialogue with the cosmopolitan self. Rather, there may be occasions when approaching difference leads to rejection and enclosure by the Other. Difference and Otherness are not open books in which we can draw information and knowledge when we need it. They are more like doors that can be opened or shut depending on the visitor and the context. The discourse on the cosmopolitan stranger constructs the Other as a passive social actor, which in turn becomes a source of empowerment and enlightenment for the cosmopolitan.

Conclusion

The cosmopolitan ideal and cosmopolitanism in general have been sources of contestation in the social sciences and humanities, and the preceding discussion has made a small contribution to this debate through its investigation of the cosmopolitan stranger. It has shown that contemporary scholarship on the construction and appraisal of the cosmopolitan subject can be informed through an analysis of a social theory of the stranger articulated in the work of Simmel, Park and Bauman. The idea of the in-between subject has been evident in sociological and anthropological thought for over a century (Marotta 2011) and has reappeared in the work of scholars advocating a dialogical imagination, a cosmopolitan virtue and a rooted or multiperspectival cosmopolitanism. Moreover, the literature on the cosmopolitan in-between subject is questionable because it relies on a view of the Other as passive, adopts a non-reciprocal notion of openness and uncritically accepts the transgressive powers of in-betweenness. This final point I will revisit in the final chapter.

References

Appiah, K.A., 2007. *Cosmopolitanism: Ethics in a World of Strangers*. London: Penguin.
Atton, C., 2006. Far-Right Media on the Internet: Culture, Discourse and Power. *New Media & Society*, 8(4), pp. 573–587.
Awan, A.N., 2007. Virtual Jihadist Media: Function, Legitimacy and Radicalizing Efficacy. *European Journal of Cultural Studies*, 10(3), pp. 389–408.
Beck, U., 2001. The Cosmopolitan Society and its Enemies. *Theory, Culture & Society* 19(1–2), pp. 17–44.
Beck, U., 2004. Cosmopolitan Realism: On the Distinction between Cosmopolitanism in Philosophy and the Social Sciences. *Global Networks*, 4(2), pp. 131–156.
Bun, C.K., 2003. Imagining/Desiring Cosmopolitanism. *Global Change, Peace and Security*, 15(2), pp. 139–155.
Gouldner, A., 1979. *The Future of Intellectuals and the Rise of the New Class*. London: Macmillian.
Hannerz, U., 1990. Cosmopolitans and Locals in World Culture. *Theory, Culture & Society*, 7(2/3), pp. 237–251.
Heydt-Stevenson, J. and Cox. N., 2005. Introduction: Are Those Who Are "Strangers Nowhere in the World" at Home Anywhere: Thinking about Romantic Cosmopolitanism. *European Romantic Review*, 16(2), pp. 129–140.
Iveson, K., 2005. Strangers in the Cosmopolis. *In*: J. Binnie, J. Holloway, S. Millington and C. Young, eds. *Cosmopolitan Urbanism*. London: Routledge, pp. 70–86.
Jacob, M.C., 2006. *Strangers Nowhere in the World: The Rise of Cosmopolitanism in Early Modern Europe*. Philadelphia: University of Pennsylvania Press.
Lu, C., 2000. The One and Many Faces of Cosmopolitanism. *The Journal of Political Philosophy*, 8(2), pp. 244–267.
Malesky, L.A., 2007. Predatory Online Behaviour: Modus Operandi of Convicted Sex Offenders in Identifying Potential Victims and Contacting Minors over the Internet. *Journal of Child Sexual Abuse*, 16(2), pp. 23–32.
Mannheim, K., 1993. The Sociology of Intellectuals. *Theory, Culture & Society*, 10(3), pp. 69–80.

Marotta, V., 2010. The Cosmopolitan Stranger. *In*: S. van Hooft and W. Vandekerckhove, eds. *Questioning Cosmopolitanism*. New York: Springer, pp. 105–120.

Marotta, V., 2011. The Idea of the In-Between Subject in Social and Cultural Thought. *In*: M. Lobo, V. Marotta and N. Oke, eds. *Intercultural Relations in a Global World*. Illinois: Common Ground Publishing, pp. 179–199.

Ossewaarde, M., 2007. Cosmopolitanism and the Society of Strangers. *Current Sociology*, 55(3), pp. 367–388.

Park, R.E., 1934. Race Relations and Certain Frontiers. *In*: E.C. Hughes, C.S. Johnson, J. Masuoka, R. Redfield and L. Wirth, eds. *The Collected Papers of Robert Ezra Park: Volume I*. Reprint 1974. New York: Arno Press, pp. 117–137.

Pels, D., 1999. Privileged Nomads: On Strangeness of Intellectuals and the Intellectuality of Strangers. *Theory, Culture & Society*, 16(1), pp. 63–86.

Pollock, S.H.K., Bhabha, H. Breckenridge, C. and Charkrabarty, D., 2002. Cosmopolitanisms. *In*: C.A. Breckenridge, S. Pollock, H.K. Bhabha and D. Chakrabarty, eds. *Cosmopolitanism*. Durham: Duke University Press, pp. 1–14.

Rumford, C., 2013. *The Globalization of Strangeness*. London: Palgrave.

Stonequist, E.V., 1937. *The Marginal Man: A Study in Personality and Culture Conflict*. Reprint 1961. New York: Russell & Russell.

Turner, B.S., 2001. Cosmopolitan Virtue: On Religion in a Global Age. *European Journal of Social Theory*, 4(2), pp. 131–152.

Turner, B.S., 2002. Cosmopolitan Virtue, Globalization and Patriotism. *Theory, Culture & Society*, 19(1–2), pp. 45–63.

Vertovec, S. and Cohen, R., 2002. Introduction: Conceiving Cosmopolitanism. *In*: S. Vertovec and R. Cohen, eds. *Conceiving Cosmopolitanism: Theory, Context, and Practice*. Oxford: Oxford University Press, pp. 1–24.

Waldron, J., 1992. Minority Cultures and the Cosmopolitan Alternative. *University of Michigan Journal of Law Reform*, 25(3/4), pp. 751–793.

8 The multicultural civil sphere and the universality of binary codes

Public and academic debates on who should be categorised as a 'citizen' have intensified in a period of heightened fear and moral panic over the so-called Islamisation of Europe and other Western countries. In response to the public fear of the stranger as foreigner, and a backlash to multiculturalism, many have argued that Muslims and new immigrants can be effectively integrated into Western societies if we rethink the idea of multiculturalism. Jeffrey Alexander's work has made a concerted effort to explore the normative conditions for the integration of strangers in civil society. Through a critical review of his work, I evaluate the relationship between the civil sphere and diversity with particular attention given to the role of the stranger in the composition of civil society. Alexander claims that underlining the constitution of civil society is a binary discourse that constructs some citizens as friends and others as enemies. In the first instance this chapter maps out the contours of Alexander's cultural sociology and its relevance to his conceptualisation of the civil sphere. This section critically addresses his understanding of the 'core group' and how the stranger is constituted. Second, I examine the role that recognition and cross-cultural contact play in articulating Alexander's multicultural civil sphere and suggest that his argument – that genuine incorporation of marginalised groups depends on the recognition of Otherness – overlooks their material condition. The latter part of the chapter critiques Alexander's binary discourse of civil society in the context of how the in-between stranger problematises the binary formulation underlying his essentialist categories of 'core group', 'we-ness' and the 'Otherness' of difference. Finally, Alexander's work needs to be contextualised within the sociological literature on the interconnection between solidarity and difference evident in the work of Zygmunt Bauman and theories of the stranger. Overall, whereas Alexander has made some significant advances on traditional conceptions of civil society, especially through his culturalist approach, his overreliance on binarism as an interpretative scheme creates an ambiguity in his work, especially around his formulation of a multicultural civil sphere.

Cultural sociology and civil society

Alexander's work adds a critical dimension to existing theories of civil society by raising important issues to do with the nature of marginalisation and difference and their contribution to the construction of political communities. Earlier conceptions of civil society, for Alexander, first ignored how subjective meanings operate below and above the explicit societal institutions and, second, tended to associate civil society with the organisation and working of cultural, social and political institutions. He has shown that, unlike previous competing models, civil society is an inherently ambiguous, contradictory and paradoxical idea. The constitution of the civil sphere depends on subjective and emotional processes that lead to the interplay of exclusionary and inclusionary practices; as a consequence of this subjective dimension, civil society like modernity has both a liberal and repressive undercurrent (Alexander, 2006, p. 4).

Alexander suggests that the 'civil sphere is bounded by what might be called "non-civil" spheres, by such worlds as state, economy, religion, family and community' (2006, p. 8). He adopts a sphere concept that embraces a spatial metaphor in which civil society is one of three sectors that is separate from the market, the state and its institutions (Jensen, 2006, p. 42). This account values civil society because it consists of free associations, modern democracy and pluralism. The sphere concept has generated intense debate about whether the boundaries between these spheres are porous or not and which associations and institutions should be considered a part of the state, the market and civil society (Edwards, 2014, p. 16). Alexander is silent on these issues, and his reference to civil and non-civil spheres implies that they are hermeneutically sealed categories.

Nevertheless, Alexander has been at the forefront of a cultural turn in American sociology that has seen a shift away from the positivist and materialist tradition in favour of a sophisticated appreciation of the analytic importance of 'culture' in contemporary social theory (Eyerman, 2004; Lynch and Sheldon, 2013, p. 253; Thompson, 2004). He views culture as an inherently contentious narrative discourse based on cultural codes. Drawing on Durkheim's and Ferdinand de Saussure's structuralist theory of culture (Alexander, 2013a, pp. 255–6), he argues that cultural formations should be viewed as symbolic and that cultural life practices can be understood in terms of binary symbolic codes, which foster and weaken solidarities. In particular, Alexander's conception of civil society is informed by Durkheim's idea that cultural systems or structures of meaning are based on binary oppositions such as the 'profane' and 'sacred'. He notes that 'meaning is not objective but relational; it can be made only through difference' (Alexander, 2013b, p. 538). A moral structure is not possible, for Alexander, without the identity and beliefs of a group being contrasted with what they believe to be their opposite (Alexander, 2013a, p. 260), concluding that 'such binarism is universal' (2013a, p. 261). Although 'sophisticated people' try to embrace ambiguity, for Alexander, 'simplifications are inevitable in these giant, vague collective consciousness' (2013a, p. 261). He claims that the universalism of binary thinking exists across all levels of society. The universality of binarism is both an observable behavioural phenomenon – at least for Alexander – and an interpretative scheme that he uses to formulate a theory of civil society. Throughout Alexander's examination of civil society, he slips from the former to the latter, and at times, his interpretative scheme threatens to become a metanarrative where there is little room to incorporate and acknowledge the ambiguity, contradiction or nuances of social life.

This meta-framework is particularly relevant to Alexander's description of 'real' civil societies in which the primordial qualities of 'core groups' are constructed through a polluting system of representation in which membership is determined by identifying a stranger/enemy (Alexander, 1998, p. 98). In this account he understands the stranger as the foreigner, and accepts the condition of the 'classical stranger' as one who comes today and stays tomorrow. Once we understand civil society in a more 'realist' manner, we can then establish a more critical normative theory from which to judge the deficiencies of actual existing civil societies (Alexander, 2006, p. 23). Alexander articulates the utopian normative ideal in the following terms:

> In this civil sphere, actors are constructed, or symbolically represented, as independent and self-motivating individuals responsible for their own actions who feel themselves, at the same time, bound by collective solidarity to every other member of this sphere. The existence of such a civil sphere suggests great respect for individual capacities and, at the same time, trust in the goodwill of others.
>
> (2006, pp. 402–3)

This normative 'civil sphere' will be sustained by 'public opinion, deep cultural codes, distinctive interactional practices as civility, criticism, and mutual respect' (2006, p. 31); it will be a just, inclusive society where collective obligations will coexist with the protection of individual autonomy (2006, p. 34). Inclusion in this normative account of civil society has a subjective dimension because it goes beyond social and political participation to encompass a 'felt solidarity' (Alexander, 1988, p. 79), and a form of 'incorporation' that entails reducing the inequality between strangers/outsiders and 'core group' members and allowing the expression of their respective identities in the public sphere. Thus solidarity denotes 'the subjective feelings of integration that individuals experience for members of their social group' (Alexander, 1988, p. 79, 2013b, p. 535). Alexander claims that solidarity and incorporation along these lines allows members of society to express the principles that regulate civil life, such as equality, solidarity and respect for others.

Real civil societies work against this utopian promise because they are susceptible to a binary logic that uses symbolic codes to frame understanding and reproduce unequal social practices. The binary discourse of real civil societies, for Alexander, allows the 'core group' to conceptualise the world into those who deserve inclusion – members – and those who do not – strangers. We know who the strangers are not because there is some essence to strangeness but because we can contrast them with their opposite – members/natives. In semiotic terms, it is through difference that we can identify who are the core members of civil society. The difference between strangers and the 'core group' signifies and carries meaning. Otherness/strangeness become constructed in terms of civil incompetence and are essentialised to protect what the 'core group' perceives to be the democratic nature of their political community (Alexander, 2001a, p. 373). For Alexander, the stranger is constructed in relational terms, consistent with one account of Bauman's stranger as formulated through an 'us and them' mentality.

Throughout Alexander's discussion of the binary discourse that underpins real civil societies, he gives insufficient attention to defining the 'core group'. In *The Civil Sphere* (Alexander, 2006) he provides a cursory definition when examining how the 'core group' protects their primordial identities through stigmatising the 'out-group'. Alexander outlines a list of characteristics that outsiders, according to the 'core group', need to possess to satisfy what the 'core group' considers to be 'civil competence'; for example, being Protestant, Anglo, white and North-west European (2006, p. 422). In a later work Alexander associates 'core group' qualities with being Western, white, modern and Christian (2013b, p. 541). Alexander accepts these categories at face value and ignores how they may be internally differentiated along class, gender, sexual or regional lines. He assumes that the 'core group' is easily identifiable and stable, but in the case of the US, from where Alexander draws most of his examples, the identity of this 'core group' is becoming increasingly problematic. For example, the claim that the 'core group' is associated with whiteness ignores the contested nature of 'whiteness' in the US. Bonilla-Silva believes that the 'white group' 'will include "traditional" whites, new "white" immigrants and, in the near future, totally assimilated white Latinos' (2004, p. 932). If the white 'core group' becomes internally differentiated, then it may have difficulties in identifying who is a stranger and who is a friend; consequently the theoretical import of binary codes for conceptualising civil society becomes increasingly fragile. It is uncertain whether Alexander is imposing these essentialist qualities onto the 'core group' or whether these are self-imposed. In other words, who is simplifying the world here? Is it Alexander or 'core group' members? If we cannot escape simplifications, as Alexander has stated, then the danger is that he may succumb to the very processes that he imparts onto the 'core group'. The metanarrative of binarism may make it difficult to locate the ambiguities and nuances underlying the category of the 'core group'.

When it comes to defining Otherness/difference, things are no less obscure. The constitution of Otherness and hence exclusion, for Alexander, has been traditionally understood by US and European social scientists such as Weber, Simmel and the Chicago School as a result of external encounters 'between a relatively well-integrated social system on the one side and an unfamiliar, physically and geographically separated group on the other' (2006, p. 411). These accounts, argues Alexander, have been confined to behavioural processes and effects (2006, p. 413). He asserts that we need to go beyond these behavioural approaches and focus on the 'internal structures of society in reaction to which outsiders are placed'. It is not the encounter itself that will determine the type of incorporation adopted towards the stranger, rather it will depend on whether the 'outsider enters rigid "state" societies . . . or more independent civil societies' (2006, p. 414). How civil societies are structured, for example, whether thin or thick (2006, p. 415), autonomous or dependent, will determine how we understand and incorporate outsiders. In other words, it is the nature of the social system and not who we encounter that determines our attitudes to difference and diversity. The more society is 'civil', the less likely it will adopt exclusionary practices. The logic of this argument sounds plausible; for instance, the more society is open and inclusive, the more hospitable and just it will be towards outsiders. There is, however, some tension or uncertainty in Alexander's position. If binary simplifications constitute subjectivity and larger collective identities, then behavioural processes – such as those that occur in our encounters with Otherness – cannot be ignored. Binary thinking has an impact on how we *behave* towards the Other, and this binary thinking is triggered – because it is universal – when we encounter difference, whether the social system is 'civil' or not. Alexander's cultural sociology, premised on the 'subjective' and emotional dimension of encounters, shifts his analysis away from a systemic examination of difference. His earlier work suggests a way around this intellectual quandary because he argues that the subjective dimension must be understood with reference to social structural constraints (Alexander, 1988, p. 84). This relationship between the subjective and structural dimension of civil society has not been sufficiently developed in his later work on the binary discourse of civil society. If we cannot escape behavioural processes – such as adopting binary thinking and simplifications in our encounters with strangers – then privileging the internal, systemic structures of civil societies suggests a conceptual tension between the systemic (thick and thin views of civil society) and the behavioural approaches to the stranger.

A multicultural civil sphere

The close relationship among civil society, solidarity and difference is evident in Alexander's examination of different modes of 'incorporation' and 'inclusion'. These inclusionary practices take on three ideal types: assimilation, hyphenation and multiculturalism (Alexander, 2001b) that in practice can blend and coexist (Alexander, 2006, p. 456). In different historical contexts one form may take precedence over others. Assimilation is evident when outsiders or foreigners are allowed to participate fully in civil life on the condition they shed their primordial identities in public (Alexander, 2006, p. 429). Incorporation based on hyphenation becomes possible when the 'core group' tolerates difference to the extent that there is some interchange between 'core group' and marginal groups that contributes to creation of a common collective identity that is neither core nor peripheral but rather hybrid. Alexander, however, still believes that there is a significant amount of stigmatisation that occurs under hyphenation because the qualities of the stranger are still valued less than the 'core group' (2001b, p. 245). The drawback to hyphenation is that whereas it provides a positive recognition of the stranger's qualities, these qualities are not equally valued because 'there remain powerful, if less clearly demarcated, hierarchies in the valuation of primordial qualities . . . [and] hyphenation incorporation does not truly promote the valuing of difference as such' (Alexander, 2006, p. 451). In his use of terms such as 'hyphenation' and 'hybridity', Alexander never explores what these new identities would entail and assumes that hybridity/hyphenation is the coming together of two distinct essentialised identities.

The shift towards a utopian, normative vision of civil society is evident, for Alexander, when societies adopt a multicultural mode of incorporation. Here he joins a growing tradition that attempts to formulate a multicultural civil sphere; however, current accounts of civil society view pluralism in terms of a variety of interests and associations. They tend to assume that 'citizens' within civil society are devoid of race, ethnicity, gender and sexuality. Existing discussions of 'multicultural civil society' just add another layer of diversity such as religion, culture and 'race' to 'associational ties'. For example, the contention is that pluralism in civil society should not only include associational but also communal ties. Lehning argues that by 'broadening our perspective in this way, we can also include in our analysis of civil society aspects of multiculturalism' (1998, p. 224). Walzer, contemplating the types of divisions that may exist in civil societies and the role of a strong state in overcoming them, asserts that the 'multicultural character of contemporary civil society' acknowledges divisions based on race, ethnicity and gender and the politics of identity embedded in these divisions (2002, p. 40). These references to the 'multicultural' dimension of civil society highlight the tokenistic nature of theories of civil society towards difference and diversity. In other words, these accounts of mostly liberal democracies do not adopt a radical 'multicultural' approach that questions and seeks to change the ethnocentric and Eurocentric basis of civil society; rather, it is an approach that seeks a superficial incorporation of difference. Although Alexander moves beyond these superficial accounts, he does not embrace, and actually rejects, the radical multicultural position advocated by Iris Young. According to Alexander, she has an unrealistic view of how civil societies actually work, is sociologically naïve and reverts back to the idea of 'civic impartiality' that she initially critiqued (2006, pp. 398–402).

Alexander does acknowledge there are different faces of multiculturalism (2013b, pp. 532–3); however, in much of his work on civil society and its relationship to multiculturalism, he draws heavily on US examples (2001a, pp. 374, 396, 2001b, pp. 245–6, 2006, pp. 450–457, 2010, p. 125). The US version has historically incorporated non-immigrant demands such as those made by gay, women and civil rights movements. This version differs to the Australian model, where it has been traditionally associated with 'ethnic' programs and policies, or the Canadian case, where multiculturalism while referring to the incorporation of immigrants has sometimes incorporated other nationalist (French) or indigenous demands. Due to these cross-national differences, our capacity to generalise about a 'multicultural civil sphere' and the 'core group' is limited.

Unlike the previous inclusionary models, Alexander argues that the multicultural mode of incorporation has the potential to enhance and revive an authentic civil sphere because it encourages genuine inclusion and hence equality, respect for and understanding of strangers. The multicultural mode of incorporation values the qualities of outsiders and, through interaction with Otherness, encourages cross-group identification based on difference and common experiences. This particular type of multicultural interaction, in Alexander's words, 'expands the range of imagined life experiences for the members of a society's core groups. In doing so, it opens up the possibility not just for acceptance but for understanding, and as a result the boundaries between core and out-group become blurred and the notions of particularity and universality become increasingly intertwined' (2001b, p. 246, see also 2006, p. 451). Incorporation into this multicultural civil sphere – in which the discourse of liberty has the ascendancy and the normative dimension is flourishing – allows 'groups to publicly assert their right to be admired for being different' (Alexander, 2001b, p. 248). Drawing on Charles Taylor's notion of recognition, Alexander occasionally confines recognition to the public display and performance of difference (Alexander, 2001b, p. 246, 2006, p. 452). This is exemplified through 'multicultural pop culture', through the 'Black is beautiful' slogan that inverts negative racial identifications, through public display and performances of religious, sexual and gender identities and through increasing intermarriage rates (Alexander, 2006, pp. 452–3). Multicultural forms of incorporation reside in between assimilation and hyphenation and allow the development of a normative civil society in which groups utilise the 'binary discourse to publicly assert the right to be admired for being different'. A multicultural civil sphere strengthens rather weakens the ties between 'collective obligation and individual autonomy' (Alexander, 2006, p. 457) and encourages – through our increasing contact with Otherness – inclusiveness, collectivism and individual autonomy. The following section will critically assess how this 'inclusiveness', for Alexander, is encouraged through greater contact and recognition of strangers.

Recognition and cross-cultural contact

There is a long-running debate over the role of recognition in social theory that Alexander overlooks and needs to be addressed if we want to develop a more sophisticated and complex understanding of a multicultural civil sphere. If membership of a multicultural civil sphere is confined to public performances of identity and 'inclusion' is reduced to the 'core group' tolerating these, then this places little obligation on the part of the 'core group' to redress the economic inequalities experienced by strangers. In other words, as Fraser (2000, 2001) has argued, the politics of recognition ignores the politics of redistribution and what is required is a multilevel approach that adequately encompasses the politics of both distribution and recognition. The identity theory of recognition, which Alexander uncritically embraces, is silent on the subject of economic inequality. A more radical conception of a 'multicultural civil sphere' – which is serious about justice and equality – would need to address the economic inequalities experienced by non-'core groups'.

Although the binary discourse is universal, Alexander implies it has both a positive and a dark side. That is, binary codes are used for constructive and destructive ends. The oppressive side is evident when 'core groups' pollute the identities of strangers, and the normative dimension is apparent when strangers use it to advance more just and inclusive goals. This multidimensional nature of binary thinking is never fully explored by Alexander. For example, what guarantees do we have that in the process of advocating for their rights to be recognised, marginalised groups will not in turn use binary thinking as a source of repression and exclusion? They may exclude the voices – such as women or the young – inside or outside their group who are competing for the same economic and political resources. One needs to acknowledge that the enabling dimension of binary thinking that marginalised groups utilise can easily be used for oppressive ends. Alexander's work provides a corrective to traditional approaches to civil society, but we need to locate under what social, political and economic conditions the use of binary codes become a source of ethnocentric and racist attitudes or conversely the conditions for justice and equality. In other words, is Alexander implying that binary thinking only becomes oppressive when adopted by 'core groups'?

Alexander also assumes that one of the conditions necessary for a multicultural civil sphere to emerge is the existence of cross-cultural contact. In Alexander's multicultural civil society cross-cultural contact allows 'core group' members to feel solidarity with strangeness and thus to adopt the perspective of the other (Alexander, 2006, p. 451). The ability and desire to empathise becomes a key quality of 'core group' members under a multicultural civil sphere. If binary thinking is universal, then the 'core groups' do not necessarily stop thinking in binary terms just because they live with difference. In fact living with difference may allow the destructive side of the binary discourse to thrive. Yet, Alexander's argument implicitly accepts the 'contact hypothesis' – as did Park (see Chapter 5) – in which hostility and prejudice is fuelled by separation and lack of knowledge about the other and that, under favourable conditions, cross-cultural contact encourages the reduction of prejudice and tension between different groups (Brewer, 1997). This may not always be the case, especially when the exposure and contact to difference occurs without consultation with 'host' members such as when governments place new immigrants in certain suburbs without community consultation or when immigration continues in difficult economic and political times.

Civil society and the hybrid stranger

As I have shown, there is a danger that Alexander's theoretical scheme on binary thinking may downplay the ambiguity, contingencies and nuances of social reality. For Alexander, the constitution of 'real' civil societies and their treatment of the stranger rely on binary oppositions. This binary code does allow us to understand why those who are different are treated the way they are, and it captures the diversity of the world within their either/or framework. It also promotes greater understanding of the emotional and subjective factors that underlie solidarities. Nevertheless, binary thinking is often a crude and reductionist way of establishing meaning (Hall, 1997, p. 235). To accept that binary thinking is universal oversimplifies the conceptual framework for understanding the constitution of civil society and the identities of 'core' and marginalised groups within it. Simplifications may be a universal human trait, but this does not mean that we should simplify what is a contingent and fluid social reality. Binary oppositions may allow us to understand how 'core groups' construct their identities and the rationale behind their treatment of those they fear, but it tells us very little about how the 'core group' deal with those who slip through binary systems.

Underlying the discourse of repression is a particular attitude towards strangers. Strangers are a threat to the order and stability of civil society. Alexander's approach to the stranger is conceptualised through a dichotomous symbolic structure. This is particularly the case when he criticises Simmel's stranger. Alexander contends, as discussed in Chapter 3, that Simmel's stranger cannot be associated with those who are excluded, such as the poor and new immigrants. To reiterate, for Alexander, Simmel's stranger is not capable of understanding the representational systems informing the 'core group's' understanding of individuals – in terms of polluted representations such as 'us and them'. According to Alexander, Simmel's account focuses too much on the underlying commonalities between the stranger and the host rather than their differences. Alexander's reading of Simmel's stranger becomes increasingly ambiguous when he later contends that Simmel's idea is closely connected to a constructed notion of Otherness that seems to allude to difference rather than commonality (Alexander, 2013c, p. 79). He concludes that Simmel's account of the stranger is 'more cultural and more complex than the negative categories' expressed by Marx's proletarian class, Weber's subordinated status group, Durkheim's egoist, the anomic and criminal, and the functionalist construction of the deviant. However much this may advance classical notions of marginal groups, it is undermined by Simmel's overreliance on structural forces such as spatial and ecological processes to construct the stranger as a social status (Alexander, 2013c, p. 81). In contrast to the spatial and behavioural relation of Simmel's stranger, Alexander wants to focus on the 'cultural interpretation of social structures' that will allow us to see how difference rather than commonality make potential marginal groups into dangerous ones that are strange (Alexander, 2013c, p. 83). Yet, Alexander's criticism – as I demonstrated in Chapter 3 – assumes a one-dimensional representation of Simmel' stranger. Alexander wants to confine the experience of strangeness to those 'marginal groups' who threaten the subjective identity of the 'core group' (Alexander, 2013c, p. 86). It is only under these conditions that strangeness can be assigned and binary thinking is activated (Alexander, 2013c, p. 87). The subjective, cultural and polluting processes are evident, for Alexander, in the Orientalist discourse, in the racialisation and polluting of the black underclass and in the ways nations construct each other as strange and different (2013c, pp. 88–92).

The second problem with Simmel's stranger, according to Alexander, is that whereas all excluded groups can at some stage be interpreted as being in (physically close), but not a part, of their host society (socially distant), this explanation does not acknowledge that 'structural marginality need not be accompanied by strangeness' or a sense of commonality (2013c, p. 84). To support this claim Alexander argues that the 'functional importance' of black slavery in the

US did not 'produce abstract feelings of commonality'. In addition, many black middle-class Americans may have been economically integrated, but 'their common humanity still remains suspect to many Americans, if not the majority' (2013c, p. 84). These criticisms are based on a narrow reading of Simmel's stranger essay that understates the rich and multiple manifestations of the 'classical stranger'.

This multiplicity is particularly evident in the role that commonality plays in Simmel's essay. To reduce Simmel's idea of 'commonality' to common human characteristics is to simplify his idea of strangeness. As discussed in Chapter 3 there is an existential dimension to the stranger that alludes to the loss of uniqueness (individuality) in the face of overwhelming universal forces (commonality). Commonality is not solely confined to what we share with others but to a moment when we become aware of the loss of our uniqueness. My reading of Simmel's stranger shows that 'commonality' and difference are not mutually exclusive. There is a sense that the stranger promotes both sameness and difference because the 'general qualities in common' are overshadowed by the differences that are evident in 'organically connected persons'. Ignoring the dialectics of commonality and difference underlying the category of the stranger leads to some inconsistencies in Alexander's position. For example, in places he argues that Simmel's stranger has some affinities with Seidman's postmodern idea of Otherness (Alexander, 2013c, p. 79). Here Otherness is about difference, not commonality, and obscures rather than illuminates Alexander's position on Simmel. If Simmel's stranger has some resonance with Seidman's idea of Otherness, as Alexander claims, then it has greater affinities with Alexander's 'cultural interpretation of social structures' in which marginal groups are seen as dangerous and thus strange.

Moreover, what can upset this normative civil order, and Alexander's conceptual framework, is when things turn up in the wrong category or when things fail to fit any category such as the 'hybrid in-between stranger'. For Alexander, the debate centres on whether the stranger can be aligned with either commonality or difference, and thus he adopts binary thinking to resolve this issue. Certain theories of the stranger argue that, although the stranger enforces social and cultural boundaries, this is not always the case, especially when the stranger becomes difficult to classify. In this situation boundaries become porous and unstable. Rather than reinforcing boundaries, the stranger who cannot be classified problematises them. The hybrid stranger epitomises an in-between or ambivalent position. It is those in-betweens, the insiders/outsiders, who threaten the binary logic of the 'core group's' identity; as stated by Bauman, they are the 'third element' or 'the true hybrids' who are unclassifiable. In Alexander's paper on rethinking the stranger (2004) and in his articulation of the binary discourse of civil society, he has no space for this 'third element'. The stranger, for Alexander, is closer to Schutz's stranger as foreigner because it constitutes difference from the host.

If the hybrid stranger not only questions the opposition between friend and enemy but also the very principle of opposition, then they can unmask the brittle artificiality of division and thus the binary discourse on civil society. Alexander's interpretative model may have difficulties in dealing with strangers that do not conform to the binary model. For example, in a 'real civil society' like the UK how would Alexander understand the reaction of the 'core group' – who are prone to simplifications and binary thinking – to those 'British Muslims' who speak and act like Britons but are not Protestants or Catholics, white or Western, and therefore may self-identify as simultaneously 'British' and 'Muslim' and thus occupy a 'third space' in terms of their self-identity (Mythen, 2012). In the US there are categories such as 'Asian Americans' who are defined as neither 'real' Americans nor 'real Asians' (Chong, 2015; Tuan, 1999) and thus 'float ambiguously in some unstable, dangerous hybrid zone of indeterminacy in-between' (Hall, 1997, p. 236). What interrupts the binary discourse of civil society are those that are out of place. Alexander's cultural sociology, with its overreliance on the binary code, may have difficulties in explaining how 'core groups' deal with the existence of hybrid strangers in a multicultural civil sphere.

Bauman and the sociology of community

In this final section I want to take issue with one of Alexander's key claims. In a recent paper Alexander argues that both classical and modern 'sociological theory has not been well prepared to discuss matters of solidarity and difference, especially when they relate to the dark side of modernity' (2013b, p. 536). This statement is significant because it attempts to distinguish his argument from previous accounts but is somewhat unfair to a particular body of scholarship on the stranger that I have identified and that has solidarity and difference as its central concern – the work of Zygmunt Bauman. The fact that he neither acknowledges this work nor engages with it in a rigorous and systematic manner does not negate the originality of Alexander's work on civil society. Rather my point is that by not giving this scholarship its due recognition, Alexander has lost the opportunity to contribute to a critical conversation with this broader literature.

Alexander in a footnote is aware of Bauman's work (Alexander, 2006, p. 425) but criticises it for adopting the behavioural approach rather than the systemic perspective to conceptualising the stranger. Bauman's work on modernity's will to power has not only shown us the dark side of modernity but also how this dark side and the solidarity on which it was built were premised on the suppression and marginalisation of strangers. To reiterate, Bauman's modernity is about the production of order, and this search for order is associated with the suppression and exclusion of strangers. The stranger, from the perspective of the 'will to order', epitomises chaos and thus is a potential threat to the stable and fixed boundaries modernity seeks to impose. If social and cultural boundaries are fluid, then clarity, certainty and predictability are threatened. At the very heart of the modern project is a paradox. Modernity seeks to eliminate chaos and ambivalence but reproduces them. Chaos and ambivalence, for Bauman, represent the true nature of the modern social world. The imposition of order, for Bauman, is based on polluting binary thinking, thus there are similarities between Bauman and Alexander's arguments. Where they differ however, is that Bauman conceives the contingency and ambiguity of modern life as working against the universality of binary thinking. In other words, whereas Alexander views simplifications and binary thinking as 'natural' universal processes, Bauman understands them as myths perpetuated by 'core groups', such as Enlightenment thinkers, to impose an order where none exists.

In addition, although Alexander's cultural sociology has made an important contribution to reconceptualising the relationship among civil society, solidarity and Otherness, he has not given sufficient weight and acknowledgment to the literature on the sociology of community that argues that political and cultural communities are constructed across difference. A body of sociological literature does exist which implicitly adopts the idea that meaning is relational and that when theorising community, one needs to examine the relationship between estrangement and solidarity. Torrance (1977, p. 128) argues that those who may have nothing in common apart from their shared difference find a basis of solidarity in their rejection from the 'core group'; at the same time the solidarity of the 'core group' is based on a sameness contrasted to the outsider. Consequently, a binary discourse develops based on an 'us and them' mentality, and this serves the purpose of maintaining and establishing the identity and boundary of the 'core group' and their political community.

The sociological literature on community also contends that to develop and maintain a sense of community, both physical and symbolic boundaries are erected so that the core community is able to differentiate itself from strangers. Cohen, in his influential sociological text on community, insists that 'community assertiveness' is not stimulated by the need to express the inherent character of a community 'but, rather, from a felt need to discriminate it from some other entity' (1985, p. 110). In this case, estrangement and solidarity are dialectically interwoven. The construction of a symbolic community also depends upon identifying and labelling strangers through a binary discourse. Other scholars have shown that in the use and construction of political enemies, 'core groups' are 'manifestly defining themselves and their place in history' and that to define those who are different as evil is to define oneself as virtuous (Edelman, 1988, p. 76). Past sociological studies – and Alexander becomes part of this long tradition – have highlighted the cultural subjective dimension of the civil order (community) and shown how the identities of 'established members' have been dependent on the construction of outsiders (strangers). In the 1960s sociologists and anthropologists such as Elias and Scotson (1965) and Barth (1969) argued that the exclusion and stigmatisation of outsiders would allow the established group to maintain their identity, assert their superiority and preserve cultural boundaries.

What is disappointing is not that Alexander ignores these previous studies on the relationship between estrangement and solidarity but that he overlooks the opportunity to investigate the possible theoretical affinities between his binary discourse on civil society and the sociology of community. There are important similarities and differences between the way that the ideas of community and civil society are constituted. For example, both Alexander and the scholarship on community argue that collective identities depend on the classification of the stranger as the cultural and/or racial Other, and they accept that meaning is relational. Alexander and scholars within the sociology of community also essentialise and fix the identities of the 'established' and 'core group' members. On the other hand, what Alexander brings to the sociology of community is a more active role for outsiders in the construction of solidarities. The sociology of community is silent on how outsiders can use binary thinking or an 'us and them' mentality to change their subordinate position. For Alexander, this agency was evident in the civil rights movement in the US (Alexander, 2010, p. 121). Unlike the sociology of community, Alexander emphasises the agency of marginalised groups because they actively use binary thinking to promote their own primordial identities and goals in the face of structural forces imposed by the host society.

Conclusion

Alexander's binary discourse has made a substantial contribution to theories of civil society. What has been missing in this theory, however, is how certain types of strangers elude easy characterisation into the binary discourse of civil society. The theories of the stranger that I have outlined in this book can highlight how estrangement and solidarity are mutually constitutive, but they can also question the very basis of this relationship and the binary discourse on which it depends. Whereas Alexander's idea of the binary discourse of civil society allows us to move beyond traditional non-culturalist interpretations of civil society, its interpretative potential – as shown – is weakened by the appearance of 'the in-between stranger'. The either/or framework underlying the binary discourse of civil society may have difficulty in categorising individuals and groups who fall in the gaps and blur the social, cultural and political boundaries of society. 'Core group' solidarity, as Alexander has shown, is dependent on both the discourse of repression and inclusion, but the in-between stranger can highlight the tenuous and brittle nature of this discourse.

Alexander's multicultural civil sphere also needs to be contextualised within the broader theories of the stranger, the sociological literature on community, Bauman's notion of modernity's 'will to order', and contact theory. Such an analysis will deepen our understanding of how classical and modern sociological theories have understood matters of solidarity and difference. It will also highlight the gaps in this scholarship and provide a more sophisticated theory of a multicultural civil society where contingency, ambiguity and contradiction coexist with and challenge the universality of binary thought.

References

Alexander, J., 1988. *Action and Its Environments: Towards a New Synthesis*. New York: Columbia University Press.

Alexander, J., 1998. Citizen and Enemy as Symbolic Classifications: On the Polarizing Discourse of Civil Society. In: J.C. Alexander, ed. *Real Civil Societies: Dilemmas of Institutionalization*. London: Sage, pp. 96–114.

Alexander, J., 2001a. The Long and Winding Road: Civil Repair of Intimate Injustice. *Sociological Theory*, 19(3), pp. 371–400.

Alexander, J., 2001b. Theorizing the "Modes of Incorporation": Assimilation, Hyphenation, and Multiculturalism as Varieties of Civil Participation. *Sociological Theory*, 19(3), pp. 237–249.

Alexander, J., 2004. Rethinking Strangeness: From Structures in Space to Discourses in Civil Society. *Thesis Eleven*, 79, pp. 87–104.

Alexander, J., 2006. *The Civil Sphere*. Oxford: Oxford University Press.

Alexander, J.C., 2010. Power, Politics and the Civil Sphere. *In*: K.T. Leicht and J.C. Jenkins, eds. *Handbook of Sociology and Social Research*. New York: Springer, pp. 111–126.

Alexander, J.C., 2013a. The Sociology of the Sacred: A Conversation with Jeffrey Alexander. *Culture and Religion*, 14(3), pp. 253–267.

Alexander, J.C., 2013b. Struggling over the Mode of Incorporation: Backlash against Multiculturalism in Europe. *Ethnic and Racial Studies*, 36(4), pp. 531–556.

Alexander, J.C., 2013c. *Dark Side of Modernity*. Oxford: Wiley.

Barth, F., 1969. Introduction. *In*: F. Barth, ed. *Ethnic Groups and Boundaries: The Social Organization of Cultural Difference*. Boston: Little, Brown and Company, pp. 9–38.

Bonilla-Silva, E., 2004. From Bi-racial to Tri-racial: Towards a New System of Racial Stratification in the USA. *Ethnic and Racial Studies*, 27(6), pp. 931–950.

Brewer, M.B., 1997. The Social Psychology of Intergroup Relations: Can Research Inform Practice? *Journal of Social Issues*, 53(1), pp. 197–211.

Chong, K.H., 2015. "Asianness" Under Construction: The Contours and Negotiation of Panethnic Identity/Culture among Interethnically Married Asian Americans. *Sociological Perspectives*, Published online before print 9 December 2015, DOI: 10.1177/0731121415611682.

Cohen, A.P., 1985. *The Symbolic Construction of Community*. London: Tavistock Publications.

Edelman, M., 1988. *Constructing the Political Spectacle*. Chicago: University of Chicago Press.

Edwards, M., 2014. *Civil Society*. Cambridge: Polity.

Elias, N. and Scotson J.L., 1965. *The Established and the Outsiders*. Reprint 1994. London: Sage.

Eyerman, R., 2004. Jeffrey Alexander and the Cultural Turn in Social Theory. *Thesis Eleven*, 79, pp. 25–30.

Fraser, N., 2000. Rethinking Recognition. *New Left Review*, 3, pp. 107–120.

Fraser. N., 2001. Recognition without Ethics? *Theory, Culture & Society*, 18(2–3), pp. 21–42.

Hall, S., 1997. The Spectacle of the "Other". *In*: Stuart Hall, ed. *Representation: Cultural Representations and Signifying Practices*. London: Sage, pp. 223–290.

Jensen, M., 2006. Concepts and Conceptions of Civil Society. *Journal of Civil Society*, 2(1), pp. 39–56.

Lehning, P.B., 1998. Towards a Multicultural Civil Society: The Role of Social Capital and Democratic Citizenship. *Government and Opposition*, 33(2), pp. 221–242.

Lynch, G. and Sheldon, R., 2013. The Sociology of the Sacred: A Conversation with Jeffrey Alexander. *Culture and Religions*, 14(3), pp. 253–267.

Mythen, G., 2012. Identities in the Third Space? Solidity, Elasticity and Resilience amongst Young British Pakistani Muslims. *The British Journal of Sociology*, 63(3), pp. 393–411.

Thompson, K., 2004. Durkheimian Cultural Sociology and Cultural Studies. *Thesis Eleven*, 79, pp. 16–24.

Torrance, J., 1977. *Estrangement, Alienation and Exploitation: A Sociological Approach to Historical Materialism*. London: The Macmillan Press.
Tuan, M., 1999. Neither Real Americans nor Real Asians? Multigeneration Asian Ethnics Navigating the Terrain of Authenticity. *Qualitative Sociology*, 22(2), pp. 105–125.
Walzer, M., 2002. Equality and Civil Society. *In*: S. Chambers and W. Kymlicka, eds. *Alternative Conceptions of Civil Society*. Princeton, NJ.: Princeton University Press, pp. 34–49.

9 The cyborg stranger and posthumanism

The phenomenological stranger has been conceptualised in terms of the meeting of co-present actors and predicated on face-to-face interaction. During Simmel and Schutz's time letter writing, telegraphs, radio and the telephone were being used as dominant forms of communication across time and space. Although Schutz mentions different types of electronic mediations, he did not apply them to situations of human contact and to the realms of human relations (Zhao, 2004, pp. 97–8). In particular, Simmel and Schutz did not contemplate how via letter writing, the telegraph, radio, television and telephony social interaction of co-present, disembodied strangers could be possible, nor did they examine how strangeness could be conceptualised differently as a consequence of different communication technologies (Virnoche, 2002). In contrast, the burgeoning literature on computerised technology and cyberspace has led to a rethinking of the nature of subjectivity and social interaction, and concomitantly the figure of the stranger has also become an object of inquiry.

A chapter that includes the idea of the cyborg and posthumanism cannot do justice to either concept. My intention is not to add anything new to the literature on the cyborg nor on posthumanism but rather to investigate how these ideas have and can inform our investigation of the 'classical stranger' and what contribution these ideas can make to theories of the stranger. More specifically, I am interested in how the stranger – as an analytical category – has been reconceptualised as a consequence of computer-mediated communication and the use of mobile technologies. This chapter examines the ideas of posthumanism, transhumanism and the cyborg first by considering the association between posthumanism and transhumanism and their relationship to the cyborg. I will then analyse how the category of the stranger has been incorporated and conceptualised by Internet scholars. I pay special attention to the impact that computer-mediated technology has had on our understanding of the embodied stranger, which forms the basis of classical accounts. The final section ponders whether computer-mediated communication has led to a rethinking of the category of the stranger, and to what extent the stranger has become disembodied. I do this by revisiting the stranger's racial and gendered body, arguing that these physical dimensions have not been erased in cyberspace. Indeed, the emergence of 'digital strangers' suggests that the material world continuous to inform how our online relations are conducted and theorised, and thus, we cannot disregard our ethical responsibility to the embodied stranger.

Posthumanism, transhumanism and subjectivity

Before we consider the contribution of the cyborg stranger to theories of the stranger and whether the cyborg can be conceptualised as posthuman or transhuman, we need to bring some clarity to our discussion. For example, the conflation of transhumanism with posthumanism has led to conceptual confusion. In an entry to the encyclopaedia of bioethics, transhumanism and posthumanism are characterised as worldviews or philosophies in which the replacement of human beings by biologically and technically superior beings is seen to benefit humanity (Hook, 2004, p. 2517). Although these terms have been used interchangeably, there are important differences, especially when we examine their relationship to what is understood as classical or rational humanism. Whereas both terms are interested in the role of technology, theorists associated with these perspectives tend to articulate the value of the relationship between technology and humans differently (Miah, 2008, p. 76). Transhumanism is usually associated with the augmentation of human intellectual, physical and emotional abilities; echoing the Renaissance Humanism and Enlightenment ideals of human perfectibility, rationality and freedom. Hence transhumanism has its origins in 'rational humanism', in which the human subject is seen as rational, in control, free and male (Wolfe, 2009, p. xiv). Those advocating the transhuman continue to believe in the perfectibility of the human and claim that the limitations of the body can be rectified through technology so that more intelligent, quicker, longer-living bodies become possible (Nayar, 2014, p. 16). In contrast, the 'cultural posthumanist' or 'critical posthumanist' (Nayar, 2014) – which has its origins in critical theory and cultural studies – focuses on disrupting the liberal humanist subject and the anthropocentric view that designates humans as the superior species in the natural order and separate from the non-human and natural environment. It rejects human exceptionalism: the position that humans are unique and have a right to control and destroy the natural world (Nayar, 2014, p. 19). Overall, to simplify what are complex sets of views, transhumanism is concerned with the value of using technology for human enhancement and perfectibility, whereas cultural or critical posthumanists are interested in technology because it is part of the societal changes that have occurred in the new millennium. Consequently, the cultural posthumanist focuses on human subjectivity and embodiment as the 'focal point for these analyses of change, rather than the prospect of human enhancement or species transgressions' (Miah, 2008, p. 79). Rosi Braidotti (2013) has recently articulated this cultural/critical posthumanist position, which amounts to a critique of the liberal, gendered and essentialist subject underlying Enlightenment humanism or what she calls 'classical Humanism'. Braidotti's posthumanism does not revert back to a humanist position where she replaces the 'man' of liberal humanism with the 'man' of socialist humanism or the 'woman' of radical feminists. Posthumanism is about understanding the human subject in terms of its multiplicity and difference, for example, acknowledging that the self is gendered, sexualised and racialised. It moves beyond the subject of modernity that positions racialised and gendered selves as Other (Braidotti, 2013, p. 38). Braidotti's 'critical posthuman subject' is relational, internally differentiated with multiple attachments, and works across difference. This subject is embodied and embedded, whereas its non-unitary dimension promotes a greater sense of interconnectedness between the self and Other, including the 'non-human or 'earth' Others; adopting a post-anthropocentric view (2013, p. 49). In light of these distinctions, a cultural posthumanist is critical of transhumanism because it reinforces the 'classical humanist' essentialist position that humans are rational beings who can become – with the help of technology – perfect.

The cyborg in transhumanism and posthumanism

Discussions on transhumanism and posthumanism refer to the idea of the cyborg, but they have different conceptions of the cyborg, which stem from the cyborg's relationship to 'classical humanism'. The roots of the transhuman cyborg can be found in the ideas of two National Aeronautics and Space Administration (NASA) researchers who originally coined the category of the cyborg in the early 1960s (Benanti, 2012, p. 191). It designated how machine-like parts control the functions of an organism so that it can better adapt to the new environment of outer space. The objective of the cyborg is to integrate robotlike behaviour and actions into the human organism so that human beings have greater potential to expand their social and intellectual abilities and thus gain greater freedoms from the constraints of their environment (Benanti, 2012, p. 191). The NASA researchers identified five different levels to the machine-human nexus (Benanti, 2012, p. 192). Cyborg I is a human with a prosthetic organ, but the addition does not change 'human nature'. Cyborg II begins to integrate human with machines and does not conceive of them as two independent systems. Their integration has an impact on the physical and emotional state of humans. Cyborg III has been genetically transformed to improve human nature so that they are less destructive and more creative. Cyborg IV represents the fusion of human with technology that will be transmitted through generations and lead to drastic changes to human beings and human nature. Finally, Cyborg V is the complete fusion of human-machine in which the mind is linked to devices and media, making the body obsolete. Human consciousness continues without the constraints of the body and evolves greater functionality, feeling and empathy. A popular Hollywood representation of Cyborg V can be seen in the film *Transcendence* (2014) starring Johnny Depp. The main character, Will, has been shot by the terrorist group 'Revolutionary Independence From Technology', and to save his 'life' his wife uploads Will's consciousness to a computer. Will's consciousness survives the death of his body, and to increase his capabilities and knowledge, he requests to be connected to the Internet. At this stage the transhuman cyborg signifies a 'triumphal disembodiment' where the transhuman cyborg can now be categorised as posthuman in the sense that it comes 'after' our embodiment has been transcended (Wolfe, 2009, p. xv).

In contrast, the posthumanist cyborg does not refer to a disembodied subject, although it draws on the idea that humans are mediated through technology. Haraway's notion of the cyborg, for example, is not 'posthuman' but rather is embedded in posthumanism, wherein classical humanism's notion of the human is interrogated and transgressed. The cyborg myth is a way of providing an alternative ontology and epistemology that works against binaries and universalistic tendencies. It is 'about transgressing boundaries, potent fusions and dangerous possibilities which progressive people might explore as one part of needed political work' (Haraway, 2007, p. 37). These transgressions are not evident in the universal and essentialist accounts of women informing critical or socialist feminist approaches because they have a totalising view of woman's experience that disregards the internal difference within the category 'woman' (Haraway, 2007, pp. 41–2). In her words, 'there is nothing about being "female" that binds women' (2007, p. 38). Rather than using gender as the unifying category in a world where computer technologies and biotechnologies are recrafting their bodies, the affinities among women could instead be based on an 'oppositional consciousness' (2007, p. 39). Cyborg feminists, drawing on the metaphor of the cyborg, should rethink the Western self and focus on the disassembling and reassembling of subjectivity. In particular, women's bodies are situated within networks of technological and scientific discourses (2007, pp. 44–5), and hence women become cyborgs because existing political, gender and organic boundaries blur. Cyborg feminists do not interpret power relations 'from a standpoint of "identification", of a unitary self' (2007, p. 49) but from a point of dispersion in which there is no totalising point. Haraway's cyborg is anti-foundationalist in that it rejects the humanist and feminist foundationalist subject which 'presumes, fixes and constrains' (Nayar, 2014, p. 28). Haraway's arguments about the cyborg are not concerned with enhancing humanity but disrupting universal ideas about what it means to be human as well as the social and political entitlements that come with this dominant masculine view of the human (Miah, 2008, p. 78). The posthuman cyborg draws on the ideas within transhumanism – such as the way in which our sense of self is informed by our use and relationship to technology – to question the privileged position of the liberal male humanist subject and the rationalistic and totalising knowledge that underpins it. For Haraway, this totalising view extends to the radical and socialist feminist accounts of women.

The stranger in a computer-mediated world

Drawing on some of these observations, this section analyses the changing nature of the stranger in cyberspace. Meyrowitz (1997) was one of the earliest social scientists to explore the link between technology and the stranger. He argues that the stranger's role and function has changed in traditional, modern and postmodern societies. Meyrowitz assumes that these societies are self-enclosed entities in which there is little or no overlap and that there has been a smooth transition and break from one type of society to another. Nonetheless, for Meyrowitz, the transition from traditional, modern and postmodern society has altered the balance and meaning of 'us' and 'them', and this has been exacerbated by the changing nature of communication (1997, p. 62). Meyrowitz acknowledges how different forms of media – whether it is writing, the telegraph or landline phones – have altered social interaction and the relationship between self and other. For Meyrowitz, computer-mediated communication has continued this trend and has resulted in a rethinking of what constitutes subjectivity, identity and strangerhood. While he agrees with urban sociologists that with the shift from *Gemeinschaft* to *Gesellschaft* relations, we are now living in a 'world of strangers' (Lofland, 1973), this experience cannot be confined to one specific society. All three societies, claims Meyrowitz, could be described as populated by a 'world of strangers'; the difference between them is in terms of the 'relative place, definition and experience of strangers' within each society (Meyrowitz, 1997, p. 62).

He proposes that in 'postmodern electronic societies' group differences become less prominent because 'electronic information and experience is shared across demographic categories' (Meyrowitz, 1997, p. 65). Place is less important in 'electronic societies' because new technologies allow one to virtually travel to distant places and see different people. Electronic media, notes Meyrowitz, foster broader but shallower sense of 'us' because we cannot experience the whole world as we would our neighbourhood. Information technology allows us to share more information and behaviour across time and space and thus become similar, while these very same processes are creating greater differences within people of the same age, sex and level of authority (Meyrowitz, 1997, p. 66). Computer networks and satellite links create 'no places' in which there is a diminished control over mobile people and capital. This global mobility, for Meyrowitz, leads to greater access to difference and ironically 'the more borders are crossed, the greater the similarity of once different social arenas' (1997, p. 66). Echoing the universalisation thesis, Meyrowitz notes that this blurring of boundaries and 'global similarities' makes the category of the foreigner increasingly less 'foreign' (1997, p. 67). Paradoxically the growing 'global familiarities', argues Meyrowitz, has led to people having less in common with once familiar people in their neighbourhoods. In 'postmodern electronic societies', those who are physically far are more familiar to me than those who are co-present and potentially culturally and socially familiar. Strangers are no longer those who come today and stay tomorrow, rather it is those who are already physically here who become social and cognitively distant to our online selves. Those who were once one of 'us' and thus spatially and socially close have now become strangers to the digital self. 'Electronic societies' generate off-line strangers who are physically close but socially distant to the digital self, and what emerges is the 'strangeness of local others' and the dissolution of local mutual interconnectedness (Meyrowitz, 1997, p. 69). In Meyrowitz's account the classical stranger can still be applied to those who were once considered part of 'us'. The 'us' is no longer – if it ever was – based on similarities and cultural and social proximity. Our online lives have made those who once were physically, socially and culturally close ('us' or natives) increasingly socially distant and hence strangers.

Meyrowitz's discussion demonstrates how online communication impacts our off-line encounters and how the category of the classical stranger can still be used to explain our changing relationship to our own native community. Our online encounters have turned what was once familiar ('us') into strangers ('them'). While Meyrowitz's work cannot be understood within the extreme versions of transhumanism, in which the online self becomes dissolved into the technology, his work does suggest that we should not conceive humans and machines as two independent systems (Cyborg II). This interdependence has had an impact on human relationships and who is categorised as a stranger. Meyrowitz's online self is also distinct to the posthuman subject that challenges the gendered, racial and rational subject of classical humanism. In other words, whereas Meyrowitz's online self blurs physical boundaries, it is still embedded in global forces that foster homogeneity and sameness. For example, 'global similarities' create homogenous cultural and social online spaces in which the online self is distinct from the local embodied stranger. Although the binary between the online self and the distant 'foreigner' collapses in 'postmodern electronic societies', new binaries emerge between the online self and the off-line local stranger. Meyrowitz continues to view the world through a binary logic that sits uncomfortably with Braidotti's posthuman subject.

Recent work by Feldman (2011, 2012) revisits the relationship between the stranger and new technologies but, unlike Meyrowitz, is more interested in how online encounters with people make them strange rather than familiar. She proposes that Simmel's classical stranger is still valuable for interpreting social interaction on social media. Mediated subjects are socially close because they participate in computer-mediated communication whether this is a blog, a Facebook entry, or being involved in a web forum; whereas they are remote in that they are physically distant. Social media thus produces the essential characteristic of the Simmelian stranger; it produces relations that engender both nearness and remoteness. It is 'the general nature of these bonds that results in estrangement' (Feldman, 2012, p. 309). Similar to Meyrowitz before her, Feldman frames her understanding of the stranger in cyberspace in terms of 'us and them'. Reinforcing the universalisation thesis, she argues that what emerges in cyberspace is a shared Otherness because 'in social media there is only Otherness . . . "Them" equals "us" and the Other becomes indistinguishable from the self' (Feldman, 2011, p. 119), and thus the insider/outsider binary has become redundant. Nonetheless, Feldman paradoxically argues that social media platforms still demonstrate that 'one is created through the other' (Feldman, 2012, p. 310). In her account of online strangeness, Feldman's work does focus on human subjectivity and embodiment, but she still relies on a binary notion of identity (us/them) to conceptualise Otherness and thus implicitly accepts a unitary dimension of self and Other that cultural posthumanist finds problematic.

Whereas Meyrowitz and Feldman occasionally suggest that the stranger/Other is becoming obsolete in describing online social interaction, the death of the classical stranger in cyberspace takes a drastic turn in which the category of the stranger dissolves into the virtual system to such an extent that we cannot distinguish the stranger from the medium. Urry believes 'hybrid strangers since cyberspace not only dissolves the distances between people (the "stationary wanderer") but, more importantly, between persons, machines and organic and technical systems' (2002, p. 267). Stationary wanderers behind the screen have become less human because, according to Bogard, they are linked to 'a relation of nerves and silicon' (1999, p. 24). The stranger is now a disembodied cyborg who is 'a bio-circuit in network of bio-circuits, each node hooked to every other node in an internal matrix of connections, each mirroring others' (Bogard, 1999, p. 24). The emphasis is now on the technological rather than merely biological and psychological dimension of strangeness. Strangers become the digital networks, screens, simulation technologies and virtual systems.

In cyberspace, according to Bogard, social distance is indeterminate, and thus there is no contradiction between inside and outside to resolve because every node connects to every other. Close and far have lost their meaning in cyberspace and the 'cyborg has no social or group "identity" in the normal sense, i.e., an inside counter posed to an outside (or a Self and Other)' (Bogard, 1999, p. 25). Identity is no longer seen as relational but is a process in which one simulates a connection to an off-line world (reality). As Bogard notes, there 'is no contradiction between inside and outside to resolve, since every node connects to every other' (1999, p. 25). The cyborg is a simulated stranger because the only connections to an outside are the ones that are replicated and hence not real. There is no outside in a mediated world because it becomes what Baudrillard calls a 'simulation reference' and 'Cyberspace communications only generate the appearance of an Other, which means they also only simulate the form of strangeness' (Bogard, 1999, p. 26). In contrast to Simmel's stranger, the cyborg stranger is not a bridge between inside and outside 'but the technical system of communication, i.e., the cyborg medium itself' (Bogard, 1999, p. 26). Thus virtual travel collapses the very difference between inside and outside, and the dialectic between mobility and immobility that is epitomised by Simmel's stranger is resolved by virtual (imaginary) space.

Bogard adds that when understood as a mediator, Simmel's stranger fosters communication between two opposing parties; it refers to a 'calculating objectivity and empty indifference of a role whose only function is to transmit messages and connect systems of communication' (1999, p. 28). Within cyberspace the stranger becomes the medium between different systems of communication. This movement, for Bogard, is an illusion of movement because the stranger does not physically move, rather 'he is the virtual form of movement (or mutation)' (1999, p. 29).

In postmodern communication strangeness is reconceptualised to refer to the function of the computer-operator interface or system of interfaces. It no longer describes the dialectical relation between embodied agents but the 'cyborgian network of machine-body interfaces we call cyberspace. The stranger is not just the individual message bearer anymore, but *entire message bearing system*' (Bogard, 1999, p. 32, emphasis in the original). Simmel's embodied stranger has disappeared in the simulated world of cyberspace, but its central features persist.

Similar to the embodied strangers in which we confide because they are strangers, cyber communication includes elements of strangeness because in cyberspace 'persons confide in the medium itself. . . . [T]he medium becomes like a stranger, a kind of surrogate friend, someone (something) to tell our secrets' (Bogard, 1999, p. 32). Technology promotes interactions that are strange, and hence the medium itself has become strange.

Drawing on Haraway and cybernetics, Bogard postulates that it has become increasingly difficulty to identify what is on the other side of our interaction: we can never be certain whether it is the operator on the other side or the machine. In our postmodern communications the line between real people and the online persona has become blurred, and now we talk to the machine as much as we talk to others at the end of the line. It collapses nearness and farness, closeness and remoteness, as the basis for categorising in-groups and out-groups. Bogard's argument that strangeness not only dissolves distance between individuals, but between person and machine, makes his approach to the stranger closer to the transhumanist position. It is this blurring of the technology with the embodied subject which makes strangeness technological rather than merely biological or human.

The disembodied stranger

The embodied stranger in cyberspace is now ironically out of place. If there is no inside and outside, if the boundaries between self and other have been dissolved in computer-mediated communication, and if the medium has now become the personification of the stranger, is Otherness passed its use-by date? As discussed in Chapter 3 there is an established and increasing body of literature advocating the death of the 'classical stranger', and the idea of the cyborg stranger has continued this tradition. This, as I have shown earlier, is premature. Accounts of the cyborg stranger suggests that the very notion of what constitutes being human is now questionable, whereas others like Meyrowitz and Feldman argue that the binaries that constitute the classical stranger no longer hold in cyberspace. For Feldman, this does not mean that social media alleviates the features of distance and proximity. What is obscure here is the extent to which Feldman's use of distance and proximity reflects Simmel's use of distance and closeness in his account of the classical stranger.

The classical stranger produces relations that encompass both nearness and remoteness, but for strangeness, according to Simmel, to exist nearness is constituted spatially, whereas remoteness is constituted socially and culturally. Whereas classical strangers are physically close and socially distant, Feldman's mediated subjects are physically distant but socially close. Both the classical stranger and Feldman's mediated subjects produce relations of distance and proximity, but what is meant by distance and proximity in each case is different. Simmel did not define the stranger as that individual who is physically distant but socially close. To conflate the classical stranger with mediated subjects as Feldman does means confusing Simmel's use of proximity and distance in his account of the stranger.

As clarified in Chapter 4, for Simmel nearness refers to spatial distance and proximity to metaphoric distance.

Feldman's analysis is also conceptually confusing: to what extent can Simmel's stranger allow us to understand online social interaction, when she claims that the distinction between self and other collapses? Who is the stranger in this situation? Moreover, if the insider/outsider dualism has now been transcended, as Feldman claims, how can the self also be created through the Other? Feldman wants to move beyond binary logic but in the end cannot escape it. Feldman's work has little affinity with the transhumanist account of the cyborg stranger because she still assumes that there is an embodied subject behind the screen whose experiences of distance and proximity have changed. On the other hand, her work cannot be understood within the cultural posthumanist position because she remains committed to binary thinking to conceptualise online Otherness.

Although Bogard's cyborg stranger assumes a process of disembodiment that goes against the cultural posthumanist position, there are times when the body slips through the back door. The cyborg stranger is described as having an identity that 'cannot be called a contradictory identity, but rather a multiplicity of partial identities that proliferate internally as copies of each other' (Bogard, 1999, p. 30). If the stranger is the medium (inanimate object), then using words such as 'identity' speaks of an animate object. This slippage is clearly evident when others draw on the disembodied stranger in investigating online and off-line stranger disclosure. For example, Virnoche agrees with Bogard that 'the technology of cyberspace is the stranger' because it creates varying degrees of closeness and remoteness (Virnoche, 2002, p. 347). Nonetheless, her observations and research concentrate on how social interactions between embodied strangers reflect some of the key characteristics of the Simmelian stranger, such as 'not belonging, mobility, objectivity, and abstract commonality' (2002, p. 346). In other words, the attempt to erase the embodied stranger while retaining its core qualities leads to some confusing observations. For example, if the medium creates strangeness, rather than the embodied stranger, then the body behind the screen would become less important to research. Yet, this is not the case in Virnoche's work. She continues to use anecdotes from co-present students and colleagues to support some of her conclusions; therefore, some of her data tends to focus on her conversations with other bodies. The danger in conflating the medium with strangeness is that it overlooks how the stranger's body continues to have material and political ramifications. In other words, how we use the medium (social media) may rely on the stranger's body behind the screen and on online representations and construction of the racial and gendered body.

Discussions of the cyborg stranger uncritically accept that the body has been transcended in cyberspace or that through the use of our mobile technologies, we become disembodied subjects. Although supporters of the cyborg stranger claim that it transcends binary logic, the idea is still premised on the binary opposition between mind and body. Conceptualising the medium as strangeness relies on the belief that we can transcend and liberate ourselves from our material and embodied experience. The assumption that it is only minds which are relating to each other in cyberspace and that we have moved beyond our material and corporeal constraints 'conceives the relation between virtual or cyberspace and real space as a relation of mind and body, and rests on the patriarchal, hierarchical privilege accorded to the mind in western thought' (Ilter, 2010, p. 640). The erasure of the body and the privileging of the mind have some conceptual and political flaws. The body behind the iPhone, iPad or the laptop still needs to eat, drink and defecate. In their analysis of the embodied online subject, Lupton (2007, p. 425) and Stone (2007, p. 452) argue that life is lived through the body. It is not easy to escape the body while interacting online, and occasionally the body obstructs individuals from performing their online selves. Using a laptop, mobile phone or a digital device at home, at work or in public does not necessarily mean disconnection from other bodies. One's body and the bodies of others place demands on you. You share the physical space with others who call your body into action: you may have to rise from your laptop to answer the door, you may have to stop messaging to respond to a friend's question, or you may have to stop tweeting on public transport because of an altercation between strangers. The embodied physical world impinges on our ability to escape from it in cyberspace. More importantly, if the stranger becomes the medium, and the boundaries between 'us and them', the native and the stranger, are erased, what happens to the voices of women and minorities who continue to be harassed online or are appropriated and 'misrepresented'? If you forget the body in cyberspace, you silence the various voices of women and minorities (Stone, 2007, p. 452) and specifically the critical feminist argument that 'the body' is essential in understanding knowledge production (Boler, 2007).

Feminist and postcolonial writers have shown that the stranger's gendered and racial body has been marginalised and suppressed by a patriarchal and white society, and this continues in computer-mediated communication. It has been shown that on role-playing sites, where the user's body (usually white and male) is disconnected from the personae that they create, online racial bodies are constructed that conform to off-line racial stereotypes. For example, an Asian male personae is constructed which aligns with the Orientalised male persona that is 'potent, antique, exotic and anachronistic' (Nakamura, 2007, p. 299). On other occasions these white male users are said to be involved in 'computer cross-dressing' where they adopt an Asian female personae in which the Asian female body is constructed as a submissive, passive, and sexual plaything (Nakamura, 2007, p. 301). In this situation, whereas the body of the white male user has been erased, the representation of the (Asian) body as the stranger as Other still informs the user's view. Old racial hierarchies connected to 'white', 'black' and 'yellow' bodies are restated and rearticulated, and thus racialisation and Othering – practices that make certain bodies strange – still occur online. For example, hate speech, racial profiling and exclusionary practices are prevalent over the Internet. As a recent publication on race in cyberspace argues, 'race matters in cyberspace precisely because all of us who spend some time online are already shaped by the ways in which race matters offline, and we can't help but bring our own knowledge, experiences, values with us when we log on' (Kolko et al., 2010, pp. 4–5). We may all be strangers when we log on because we experience both proximity and distance, or the medium may reflect the characteristics of the stranger, but paradoxically the stranger's body while absent is still present. This paradox is expressed as the 'digital Cartesianism with a twist', where the online context promises untainted, disembodied communication but still requires the body (the twist) to understand textual communications (Boler, 2007, p. 154). The disembodied white user reflects this 'digital Cartesian twist' because it requires an understanding of the stranger's (Asian and gendered) real-life body to inform and construct textual communication.

The hype regarding the death of the classical stranger and the blurring of the lines between us and them on the Internet has not meant that the stranger as Otherness has become conceptually redundant. In other words, binary thinking has not disappeared when theorising about Otherness/strangeness in computer-mediated communication. Whereas a body of work endeavours to dismiss the value of the classical stranger for understanding social interactions in cyberspace, other literature continues to draw on the stranger as the Other and the binary thinking that underpins it. For example, there has been a lively debate around Prensky's (2001) argument that there are qualitative and quantitative differences between teachers' and students' use of computer technology (Bayne and Ross, 2011; Bennet et al., 2008). He categorised students as 'digital natives', that is, '"native speakers" of the digital language of computers, video games and the Internet' (2001, p. 1), whereas teachers were represented as 'digital immigrants' who learn

> like all immigrants, some better than others – to adapt to their environment, they always retain, to some degree, their "accent", that is their foot in the past. The "digital immigrant accent" can be seen in such things as turning to the Internet for information second rather than first, or in reading the manual for a program rather than assuming that the program itself will teach us to use it.
>
> (Prensky, 2001, p. 3)

It is worthwhile noting here how Prensky's description speaks to the phenomenological stranger in which the life-world of the 'digital immigrant' is at odds with the life-world of the 'digital natives'. The common knowledge of the digital immigrants' everyday world arises from their shared perspective of the role and usage of the Internet. The life-world of digital natives is in stark contrast to digital immigrants because the latter speak a different language and are a 'population of heavily accented, unintelligible foreigners' (2001, p. 3).

There are many problems with these ideas, but specifically the 'digital native' is an Othering concept that sets up a false binary between 'natives' and 'immigrants' and reinforces the anxieties around migration, integration and cultural and religious diversities in Western societies (Brown and Czerniewicz, 2010). This binary – like all binaries – assumes that these are essentialist, incommensurable categories, and thus it reinforces the phenomenological approach that the stranger's and native's life-world and 'natural attitude' are fundamentally different.

For my purposes, what is important in this debate is that the use of the classical stranger reappears in terms of its materialist and Othering proprieties. For example, not satisfied with Prensky's arguments, Brown and Czerniewicz (2010), in their study of how South African students use the Internet for educational purposes, introduce the idea of the 'digital stranger'. They contend that some South African students have less access to computer technology due to their race, gender and class. What we have in South Africa is a 'Digital Apartheid', where students are not 'digital immigrants' but are outsiders to the digital world and hence 'digital strangers' (Brown and Czerniewicz, 2010, p. 363). The notion of the 'digital stranger' continues to be used as one who is physically close – in the sense that they reside in South Africa – but, due to race, gender or class, are socially distant from the digital world of the elite.

The digital stranger as opposed to the cyborg stranger is still premised on the binaries between inside and outside: but the inside is the world of the Internet and all the educational advantages that it brings, whereas the outside is the material world with its inequalities based on the body (gender and race) and economic conditions (class). The digital stranger is an embodied individual, hence not transhuman, but neither does it echo the characteristics of the posthuman subject because the digital stranger is conceptualised in terms of either class, gender or race, contrasting with the posthumanist idea of the digital stranger as linked to multiple attachments and multiple marginalisations. The distinction between 'digital stranger' and the 'cyborg stranger' suggests that theories of the stranger cannot ignore the embodied subject. The hype over the death of the classical stranger that continues in online studies reinforces the binary between mind and body, in which the mind is privileged over the body. This position has political consequences because it erases how hierarchies of difference based on the embodied racial and gendered Other inform online relations.

Conclusion: the virtual stranger and ethical responsibility

The literature on cyberspace and the stranger has shown that the classical stranger needs to be re-theorised because 'strange encounters' are moving beyond face-to-face communication. We are no longer encountering strangers as embodied actors, and the transhumanist cyborg stranger has been pivotal to this reformulation. Moreover, the discussions of online strangers have suggested that the boundaries between 'us' and 'them' – which were essential in the construction of stranger as foreigner – have now collapsed in cyberspace. As was discussed previously, Internet scholars have indicated that the transhumanist cyborg stranger has blurred the line between machine and human and that computer-mediated communication has obscured the line between self and Other. The latter argument has some affinities with the universalisation thesis, but as Bauman has argued, if we accept this position, then our moral responsibility may be overlooked.

The paradoxical nature of strangers that are both insiders and outsiders raises ethical questions in virtual communities. Introna and Brigham (2007) critically analyse the morality-based conception of community characterised by calculative reciprocity and an ego-centric self. This community is based on coercion and incorporation; in contrast the authors want to advocate a community that entails critical and ethical involvement (2007, p. 167). They advocate a move away from a community of sameness to one that involves ethical involvements and the inclusion of the Other. Drawing on the work of Levinas, they invoke Levinas's position that community should be concerned with maintaining the primacy of the Other's singularity. The debate about virtual communities centres on the extent to which they lead to ethical and committed relations.

The virtual encounter with the stranger continues to raise perennial questions of who we are or want to be as individuals, communities and societies (Introna and Brigham, 2007). Scholars agree that the Other in the virtual world is not one that you face as an embodied entity; the virtual anonymous encounter is placeless and faceless. This means the ethical question of hospitality towards, and responsibility for, the Other becomes even more urgent. We cannot delete messages or deny Others access to our Facebook page based on their Otherness and strangeness, as Introna and Brigham note, '[W]e cannot delegate justice to technology' (2007, p. 176). The persistence of racial and gendered bodies in online encounters suggest there is a danger that the idea of the cyborg stranger erases the role of moral proximity. If the medium becomes strange, where does moral responsibility lie? Can the machine call forth our moral responsibility? Or can a machine be moral? If strangeness is disembodied, then our responsibility to the Other has no material grounding. We cannot be responsible to that which has no embodied Otherness. Yet as I have shown, this loss of an embodied Otherness is a myth, and racial and gendered bodies and what they signify are still crucial in understanding online interaction. Our moral responsibility as outlined by Bauman becomes increasingly important under these circumstances.

References

Bayne, S. and Ross, J., 2011. "Digital Native" and "Digital Immigrant" Discourses: A Critique. *In*: R. Land and S. Bayne, eds. *Digital Difference: Perspectives on Online Learning*. Rotterdam: Sense Publishers, pp. 159–169.

Benanti, P., 2012. The Cyborg and Cyborgization. *In*: J. Giordano ed. *Neurotechnology: Premises, Potential, and Problems*. London: CRC Press, pp. 191–198.

Bennet, S. Maton, K. and Mervin, L., 2008. The "Digital Natives" Debate: A Critical Review of the Evidence. *British Journal of Educational Technology*, 39(5), pp. 775–786.

Bogard, W., 1999. Simmel in Cyberspace: Strangeness and Distance in Postmodern Communications. *Space and Culture*, 4/5, pp. 23–46.

Boler, M., 2007. Hypes, Hopes and Actualities: New Digital Cartesianism and Bodies in Cyberspace. *New Media and Society*, 9(1), pp. 139–168.

Braidotti, R., 2013. *The Posthuman*. Cambridge: Polity.

Brown, C. and Czerniewicz, L., 2010. Debunking the "Digital Native": Beyond Digital Apartheid, Towards Digital Democracy. *Journal of Computer Assisted Learning*, 26, pp. 357–369.

Feldman, Z., 2011. Reading the Stranger in the Age of Social Media. *Cultural Policy, Criticism and Management Research*, 5, pp. 112–126.

Feldman, Z., 2012. Simmel in Cyberspace. *Information, Communication & Society*, 15(2), pp. 297–319.

Haraway, D., 2007. A Cyborg Manifesto: Science, Technology and Socialist-Feminism in the Late Twentieth Century. *In*: D. Bell and B.M. Kennedy, eds. *The Cybercultures Reader*. 2nd edition. Oxon: Routledge, pp. 34–65.

Hook, C.C., 2004. Transhumanism and Posthumanism. *In*: S.G. Post ed. 3rd edition. *Encyclopaedia of Bioethics*. New York: Macmillan, pp. 2517–2520.

Ilter, T., 2010. The Otherness of Cyberspace, Virtual Reality, and Hypertext. *In*: Jae-Jin Kim, ed. *Virtual Reality*. Available from: http://www.intechopen.com/books/virtual-reality/the-otherness-of-cyberspace-virtual-reality-and-hypertext.

Introna, L.D. and Brigham, M., 2007. Reconsidering Community and the Stranger in the Age of Virtuality. *Society and Business Review*, 2(2), pp. 166–178.

Kolko, B., Nakamura, L. and Rodman, G. eds., 2010. *Race in Cyberspace*. London: Routledge.

Lofland, L.H., 1973. *A World of Strangers: Order and Action in Urban Public Space*. New York: Basic Books.

Lupton, D., 2007. The Embodied Computer User. *In*: D. Bell and B.M. Kennedy, eds. *The Cybercultures Reader*. 2nd edition. Oxon: Routledge, pp. 422–432.

Meyrowitz, J., 1997. Shifting Worlds of Strangers: Medium Theory and Changes in "Them" versus "Us". *Sociological Inquiry*, 67(1), pp. 59–71.

Miah, A., 2008. A Critical History of Posthumanism. *In*: B. Gordijn and R. Chadwick, eds. *Medical Enhancement and Posthumanity*. Dordrecht: Springer, pp. 71–94.

Nakamura, L., 2007. Race in/for Cyberspace: Identity Tourism and Racial Passing on the Internet. *In*: D. Bell and B.M. Kennedy, eds. *The Cybercultures Reader*. 2nd edition. Oxon: Routledge, pp. 297–304.

Nayar, P.K., 2014. *Posthumanism*. London: Polity.

Prensky, M., 2001. Digital Natives, Digital Immigrants Part 1. *On the Horizon*, 9(5), pp. 1, 3–6.

Stone, A.R., 2007. Will the Real Body Please Stand Up? Boundary Stories about Virtual Cultures. *In*: D. Bell and B.M. Kennedy, eds. *The Cybercultures Reader*, 2nd edition. Oxon: Routledge, pp. 433–455.

Urry, J., 2002. Mobility and Proximity. *Sociology*, 36(2), pp. 255–274.

Virnoche, M., 2002. The Stranger Transformed: Conceptualizing On and Offline Stranger Disclosure. *Social Thought & Research*, 24(1–2), pp. 343–367.

Wolfe, C., 2009. *What Is Posthumanism?* Minneapolis: University of Minnesota Press.

Zhao, S., 2004. Consociated Contemporaries as an Emergent Realm of the Lifeworld: Extending Schutz's Phenomenological Analysis to Cyberspace. *Human Studies*, 27, pp. 91–105.

10 Conclusion
Intercultural knowledge and the 'professional stranger'

The examination of different theories of the stranger has underscored that certain types of strangers develop special powers of observation due to their spatial and social position. Their physical proximity and their social and cultural distance generate specific cognitive qualities. The phenomenological approach suggests that the process of strangeness and familiarity is in fact general categories of our interpretation of the world (Schutz, 1976c, p. 105). The following discussion explores the implications of these special insights into the social world on the production of intercultural knowledge, specifically an intercultural knowledge that incorporates the view and voice of both the self and Other. Theories of the stranger have alluded to in-between strangers such as 'ambivalent people' (Bauman), the genius (Simmel), the marginal man (Park) and the cosmopolitan, who develop a type of hybrid knowledge or hybrid consciousness that challenges conventional knowledge based on binary and essentialist thinking. These in-between strangers, however, are not always associated with the stranger as Other or foreigner. For example, I have examined how Simmel's work alludes to the historian and genius, and Park mentions 'urban dwellers', whereas Bauman's 'ambivalent people' do not necessarily denote immigrants or foreigners. As opposed to the 'classical stranger', which has come to be associated with the immigrant and foreigner, these in-between strangers can be categorised as 'professional strangers' (Ahmed, 2000). They are professional strangers because Otherness does not define their difference. In intercultural encounters the relationship between professional strangers and the stranger as Other is an unequal one because the construction of meaning, and understanding is skewed towards the former. By contrast, in what follows I ponder how critical intercultural hermeneutics rethinks the construction of intercultural knowledge where the role of the stranger as Other, if not at the forefront, is at least an equal partner in the construction of meaning.

'Professional strangers' and epistemic privilege

Whereas we have located 'professional strangers' in various theories of the stranger, it is in the discipline of ethnology where the 'professional stranger' makes its first appearance. The 'ethnologist stranger' is capable of detached involvement, is not prone to perceptual distortions, can look from the inside out, and can tolerate

Conclusion 121

ambiguity, inconsistency and unpredictability (Nash, 1963, p. 161). These qualities are reminiscent of Simmel's 'subjective objectivity' adopted by the historian/ genius to interpret the past. Echoes of the professional stranger also appear in Pels's third interpretative position, associated with the 'social epistemology of the stranger' (Pels, 1999, p. 73). He stresses that strangerhood or 'existential distance' provides a 'fruitful entrance to an anti-methodist and non-universalist view of critical distanciation and intellectual autonomy' (Pels, 2000, p. 205). This epistemology of critical distanciation, for Pels, recovers a critical intuition and performs a rupture with 'common sense', allowing for alternative insights into the social world. He is critical of the perceptual distortion that occurs from the perspective of the stranger as Other or 'standpoint epistemologies'. Standpoint theories based on class, gender and race argue that the dominated or marginal not only 'see differently', but they also 'see better and more' (Pels, 1996, p. 68). Pels asserts that such a position ignores the essentialist nature of standpoint epistemologies and, further, that intellectuals' 'marginal standpoint' differs from those they supposedly represent. In particular, Marxists' and feminists' standpoint theories, according to Pels, conflate their own contradictory and marginal position with those they 'represent' (1996, p. 77).

To overcome the epistemological problem of the 'marginal position' that is connected to the stranger as Other, Pels claims that 'intellectual strangers' can transcend the dualistic thinking of the first and second position, for example, bourgeois/proletariat, male/female, white/black, dominant/dominated and insider/ outsider. In other words, by privileging dualistic frameworks and the contest between the first and second position, standpoint theories tend to silence a third voice (Pels, 1996, p. 78). Pels notes that 'marginal standpoints by themselves do not suffice; they must be intellectualized, pass through theory, which evidently requires the guiding presence of the professionals of theory themselves' (1996, p. 78). Standpoint epistemology therefore depends on the work of the intellectual spokesperson's third position. It is 'their representational work', writes Pels, 'that ultimately "defines the situation" for "situated knowledge"' (1996, p. 87). The intellectual spokesperson or 'the outsider within' mediates between the margin and centre; they are neither a 'nowhere (wo)man', a universal or particularised subject, nor are they firmly rooted. Pels's intellectual stranger has close affinities with the in-between stranger because both move between inside and outside and are able to transcend the confines of their cultural position. This insider/outsider intellectual position is not possible for those strangers positioned as the Other or foreigner because they are imprisoned by their marginal essentialist position. Consequently, in defining the situated for the 'situated knowledge', professional strangers treat the stranger as Other, that is, as an object rather than a subject of knowledge. The ethnologist, professional, intellectual stranger turns strangeness into a technique for the accumulation of knowledge of the Other (Ahmed, 2000, pp. 59–60). In other words, they exploit the proximity and distance of their position as a means not only to construct knowledge of the stranger as Other but also to construct knowledge for the Other. The distinction is between strangers as the Other, who are objects of knowledge, and the professional stranger, who is the subject of knowledge. The latter is the knowing stranger, whereas the former is the unknowing Other. The stranger is redefined from an ontological lack (the Other) to an epistemic privilege (intellectual stranger) (Ahmed, 2000, p. 60). How can we re-envisage the relationship between the professional stranger and the stranger as Other in which the latter is not erased through interpretative process but becomes essential to cross-cultural knowledge construction? Critical intercultural hermeneutics allows us to rethink the interpretative process so that epistemic privilege is not found either within the self or the Other but in their interrelationship.

Gadamer and intercultural understanding

Gadamer's analysis of the interpreter's approach towards the text is a useful point of departure for conceptualising an intercultural mode of interpretation. He notes that when approaching a text, the premise of hermeneutics is the 'polarity of familiarity and strangeness' (1960, p. 262). It is simultaneously the text's strangeness and familiarity to us or the play 'between being a historically intended, separate object and being part of a tradition' which suggests to Gadamer 'the true home of hermeneutics is in this intermediate area' (1960, p. 263). This intermediate position, for Gadamer, clarifies the conditions of 'true' understanding. Nonetheless, the hermeneutical in-between situation does not lead to a definitive understanding of the other's standpoint and horizon because, for Gadamer, interpreters are never confined by one standpoint, and hence horizons are not closed or fixed. They are 'something into which we move and that moves with us' (1960, p. 271). In other words, the Gadamerian hermeneutical practice adopts a particular epistemological stance that dialectically intertwines proximity/familiarity and distance/strangeness and arrives at a 'better' and more genuine understanding of social reality.

Gadamer's hermeneutics potentially sheds light on the nature of an intercultural mode of interpretation and the role of the stranger as Other in this process. The issue with Gadamer's philosophical hermeneutics is that it tends to confine itself to the intra-cultural rather than intercultural construction of meaning, and it downplays the role of power in meaning making. For example, in an increasingly globalised world in which unequal intercultural encounters occur, is a Western hermeneutical theory still relevant (Xie, 2014, p. 4)? It has been in the field of critical intercultural hermeneutics that the issue of difference and power has played a significant role in understanding the conditions for cross-cultural knowledge.

Drawing on Gadamer, intercultural hermeneutics emphasises the non-universal and non-essentialist forms of interpretation. Recent attempts to formulate an intercultural hermeneutics, however, tend to marginalise the stranger as Other in conceptualising the conditions for cross-cultural knowledge. Ariarajah (2005) explores the nature of this intercultural hermeneutics and notes that it entails a theory and method of understanding that occurs cross-culturally. Yet the idea that intercultural hermeneutics refers to a method or a set of rules and procedures goes against the spirit of Gadamerian hermeneutics because the 'intermediate position in which it operates' does not develop a method or a set of procedures, but seeks 'to clarify the conditions in which understanding takes place' (Gadamer, 1997, p. 263). Leaving aside this tension for the moment, Ariarajah (2005) concludes that intercultural hermeneutics includes a willingness, and one would assume an ability, to cross cultural boundaries, which could lead to a 'double belonging'. Others have also drawn on this type of intercultural hermeneutics to construct professional strangers as cross-cultural subjects with a plethora of characteristics. Cross-cultural subjects can effectively communicate across cultures and are capable of moving from the particular to the universal. They have a special affinity with the unfamiliar, appreciate difference, are open to alternatives, can transcend the narrow concerns of the group, move beyond the tribal to the universal needs of humanity and are sensitive to the unity and diversity of the human condition (Roy and Starosta, 2001, p. 16). These characteristics refer to what the professional stranger can bring to the cross-cultural table, thus the interpretative process is heavily weighted towards the self (professional stranger). In contrast to these versions of intercultural hermeneutics, a school of thought known as critical intercultural hermeneutics devotes a greater role for the stranger as Other in the construction of meaning.

Critical intercultural hermeneutics

Like intercultural hermeneutics, critical intercultural hermeneutics is not infallible; it is a process that can also lead to tensions, contradictions and miscommunication, which means that it cannot always provide positive results for both self and Other. Nonetheless, critical intercultural hermeneutics uncovers what is hidden and unconscious in the contact between cultures, allowing access to these unarticulated presuppositions for understanding, examination and transformation (Xie, 2014, p. 5). Through testing, contesting and interrogating assumptions of both the professional stranger and the stranger as Other, both can develop a self-reflexivity of their own historicity. Unlike the position adopted by the professional stranger, critical intercultural hermeneutics does not assume that the stranger as Other can be intelligible only through the world of the professional stranger. The professional stranger adopts a psychologistic understanding of empathy that attempts a psychological reproduction of the Other's authentic intentional meaning within us. This, however, would not allow us to fully experience the Other's views, practices and events in the same way as the Other experiences them (Kögler, 2014, pp. 279–80). The phenomenological approach to the stranger reverses this empathetic understanding because it acknowledges that the stranger as foreigner also adopts an empathetic stance when forced to see themselves from the host's perspective. Whether an empathetic mode of understanding is adopted by the stranger as Other or the professional stranger, it assumes that an unmediated reproduction of an Other's worldview is possible.

In the process of translating the Other, in terms that we can understand, we need to preserve the difference and not simply reduce them to our own criteria. Simmel and Park fall into this trap. While acknowledging, as Gadamer does, the role of the historian/interpreter's 'personality' or subjectivity in understanding another person, the 'other person's life-world is assumed to be translatable in terms of the interpreter's subjectivity. Park's depiction of racial hybrids aligns well with the professional stranger or ethnographic stranger because of their ability to place themselves in various cultural positions and thus more effectively interpret white and black culture. In these accounts, the voice of the stranger as Other is silenced. For Simmel, the historian's interpretation of the stranger as Other is located in the past where they cannot speak back, whereas for Park, the Negro's voice is not only silenced but is constituted as irrational and 'uncivilised' and thus cannot speak the language of the 'marginal man'. In contrast, a mode of understanding informed by a critical intercultural hermeneutics should demand a space and voice for the stranger as Other. Such a voice would force the non-Other to ask important questions about their own culture. As Xie contends, '[I]nternal evaluations need to be supplemented and complicated by evaluations that other traditions offer' (2014, p. 7). In contrast to the interpretative process adopted by the professional stranger, self-distancing and self-displacement should acknowledge the power relations that exist between unequal interlocutors and how this inequality is based on historical relations (Ahmed, 2000). The problem with the position of the professional stranger is that it adopts an 'objectifying theoretical framework' in which the 'epistemic relation is between the interpreter (subject) and interpretee (object)' (Kögler, 2014, p. 214).

Moreover, the discourse on professional strangers suggests that they encourage anti-essentialist practices. In-between strangers question the essentialist idea of 'absolute contrasts' (Simmel) and binary thinking (Bauman), which promotes clear and fixed distinctions between self and Other. The tendency here is to assume that essentialism is destructive and that the dichotomous mentality is corrosive and oppressive. This view, although plausible if we accept that political and social hierarchies maintain essentialism and binary thinking, still needs qualification. Essentialist practices have led to hierarchies in which one side of the distinction – man, white, and native – is described in positive terms whereas the other side – woman, black, and stranger – is conceived as both negative and subservient to the first term. Professional strangers reject repressive and exclusionary distinctions, but this does not lead to the eradication of all distinctions and the essentialist practices on which they depend. The experience of 'dwelling among' requires the awareness of other cultures, hence the need to make distinctions; further, once professional strangers make distinctions, they by necessity adopt a dichotomous mentality. Being conscious that one is moving between cultures presupposes an awareness of separate and distinctive cultures. Without distinctions the 'inter' in the 'intercultural' would be incomprehensible. The idea of the intercultural here does not eliminate the need for essentialist practices and hence distinctions. A critical intercultural hermeneutics acknowledges some commonalities between self and the stranger as Other but leaves room for ways in which they are significantly different. This difference does not involve a negative construction of the stranger as Other but rather challenges the professional stranger's way of life (Wong, 2014, p. 177). Thus a form of essentialism occurs – through finding commonalities – but they should not be used to exclude and repress the Other but as a means to respect and value them on their own terms. As Spinosa and Dreyfus stress, 'Dwelling within an essentialist telos need not produce the ethically deplorable exclusions of essentialism' (1996, p. 763). In contrast to previous accounts, we need to rethink the idea of professional strangers and their relationship to essentialist practices. As understood here, professional strangers draw on essentialist categories, but these should provide the conditions in which we can recognise, value and give voice to the stranger as Other, even when the stranger's Otherness challenges our assumptions and way of life.

The ideology of the third position

The idea of the 'the third' has gained increasing relevance in the social sciences to such an extent that entire societies have been described in terms of thinking in twos or threes. Some have claimed that eighteenth-century societies thought in twos or in binary oppositions such as heaven/hell, mind/body and the like, whereas modernity thinks in threes wherein the figure of the third agent upsets the binaries of the old world (Malkmus and Cooper, 2013, pp. 1–2). There have also been suggestions that there has been a Third Turn in social theory initiated by – as I have shown – Simmel and, for Fischer, Freud (Fischer, 2013, p. 88). Bauman's version of modernity as the 'will to order' that reinforces binaries rather than upsetting them, suggests that classifying societies in terms of a mode of understanding is questionable, especially when what constitutes the modern has been problematised in social theory. Nonetheless, there is ample evidence that the idea of the third – in its various manifestations – has become an important idea in social theory.

Yet, is such a third position – a dwelling between the insider and outsider perspective, between the local and global, between the particular and universal – possible? The discourse on the professional stranger implies that this is possible; however, I want to raise some reservations about this discourse through a critique of the cosmopolitan stranger that I examined in Chapter 6. Similar to the professional stranger the cosmopolitan stranger straddles a third position that is not possible for locals, native/nationalist and the Other because they are confined within their epistemological framework or prison. Cosmopolitan strangers can synthesise and have access to a 'total perspective' not available to those immersed in their essentialist particular/local or global/universal frameworks. Cosmopolitan strangers are able to transcend 'standpoint epistemologies'. Due to their flexibility, reflexivity and mobility, they develop a 'double perspective' or what Rumford categorises as 'multiperspectivalism' that encourages an alternative mode of thinking unavailable to those who are fixed within their particularistic or universalistic framework. Cosmopolitan strangers have the intellectual mindset to float between the local and the global, between the particular and the universal, and thus transcend the politics of location.

Rumford contends that this 'high point', conflated with the cosmopolitan stranger, is 'the antithesis of cosmopolitanism' (2013, p. 118) and that in fact cosmopolitanism encourages multiperspectivalism. I do not find this a convincing argument because it is this very perspective that places the cosmopolitan stranger in a position *above* those confined by a single or mono-perspective. Adopting a multiperspectival view of the world may be more difficult from a position that does not allow you to see above the crowd. Rumford's description implies that the cosmopolitan stranger has a special or privileged perspective compared to those deceived by the dominant ideologies of their community. Here we see the critique of the situated reappear. The assumption is that mobility in itself encourages a multiperspectivism not available to those who are sedentary. Although advocates of the cosmopolitan stranger claim that it can transcend standpoint epistemologies, the in-between multiple perspective collapses into another standpoint. In other words, whereas the role of the cosmopolitan stranger, as I have shown in Chapter 7, can be closely associated with the ability to be both distant and close and to be subjective and objective – cosmopolitan strangers are not devoid of what Gadamer calls 'prejudice' or fore-meanings. In their interpretation of the social world and through their connection with distant Others, they bring preconceived ideas and values. Interpreters are not completely in control of the interpretative process because they may be unaware of the prejudices and fore-meanings that constitute the interpreters' consciousness. In Gadamer's words, the interpreter 'cannot separate in advance the productive prejudices that enable understanding from the prejudices that hinder it and lead to misunderstanding' (1960, p. 295).

Cosmopolitan strangers may find it difficult to be free-floating and multiperspectival because they are embedded in the prejudices – in the hermeneutical sense – of their empirical social world. The discourse on the cosmopolitan/professional stranger downplays the role of preexisting meanings and ignores how these strangers are embedded; they are historical beings who are immersed in the attitudes, values and prejudices of their time and place. They do not occupy a boundless social and cultural vacuum. They may be 'homeless', but one is never socially or culturally homeless because your 'home' – in terms of your values, prejudices, ideas, traditions and customs – are always with you, even if they change. Something of the past sticks to you however hard one tries to peel it off. 'Home' may be a moveable feast, but the ingredients for the feast are there before you. Cosmopolitan strangers are not ahistorical social actors who float above those who are socially and historically located. Customs, traditions and prejudices form social actors' understanding of the world. The idea of the cosmopolitan stranger assumes that one's historical, social and cultural position can be placed on hold or is left behind when analysing and engaging a social world that is immersed in essentialist and binary thinking.

It is the ability not only to bracket off one's values and norms but to think in non-essentialist and non-binary terms that allows cosmopolitan strangers – at least for those thinkers discussed in Chapter 6 – an alternative view of social reality not available to insiders and outsiders. Their privileged third position allows them to transcend the ideology of essentialism and binary thought evident in the world of non-cosmopolitans. On the contrary, one's cultural horizons, prejudices, 'standpoints' and the ideologies that inform them contribute and hinder the process of understanding. To be an in-between stranger is to place oneself within the intercultural encounter and not to dwell above it.

Thus the 'fallacy of the possible middle' or the 'Turn to the Third' in social theory alludes to the transcendence of insider/outsider and assumes that incommensurability between the insider's and outsider's cultures can be overcome by the third. It is those who occupy the middle or third position who can reason, converse and understand others because they are more in tune with a diverse and global world. Yet, occasionally cultural practices are grounded in particular reasons, and these reasons may not always be shared or made commensurable (Mehta, 2000, p. 620). For example, shared understanding in the case of female excision is highly unlikely, even after we have a deep understanding of those cultures that practice it. We may understand its cultural, symbolic and social context but for some – and I would include cosmopolitan/professional strangers – it will not appear 'rational' or 'morally good' (Kögler, 2014, p. 282). At some level, ethnocentrism is epistemologically unavoidable because when the third compares the practices of the cultures of the insiders and outsiders, it requires the third's experience of those practices as a reference point (Simpson, 2014). Discussions of the cosmopolitan/professional stranger tend to underplay the incommensurability of cultures and treat cultures as open books waiting to be understood by those who are capable and have the requisite intellectual skills. I do not want to suggest that we cannot communicate across cultures, but one can never completely overcome differences in cross-cultural dialogue because differences or 'moments of sameness' (Marotta, 2008) are important in understanding the constitution of the self and Other. Ironically, these moments of sameness allow us to feel different from others. There are times in which the need for predictability, order, sameness and homogeneity become paramount, and these may be expressed through collective identities or by engaging in group practices; they can also be articulated through a narrative of the self in which we recount or reconstruct our past in terms of a continuous, linear story. The concern would be when these 'moments of sameness' become the only means by which we define ourselves and Others and become the sole bases of an intercultural hermeneutics. In their eagerness to transcend an essentialist and binary mode of thought or a mono-perspective, accounts of the cosmopolitan/professional stranger downplay these 'moments of sameness' in which group and individual differences allow social actors to establish both a sense of continuity and difference.

In developing a critical intercultural hermeneutics, the role of the stranger as Other becomes pivotal in moving beyond the ideology of the third. This ideology marginalises the power relationship underlying the construction of intercultural knowledge. By advocating a more positive role of the stranger as Other in this process, it allows one to re-conceptualise intercultural knowledge within a materialist framework, something that has been missing in certain accounts of the stranger.

The central thesis of this book is that the idea of the stranger should be at the forefront of our rethinking knowledge construction and in social theorising about our diverse and global world. It is an idea that has a history, but this history is not a coherent one. It is a contested category that has served particular theoretical and political functions. It has been adopted to reveal our psychic condition, it has been utilised to shed light on the increasing alienated and isolated modern subject and it has been reconceptualised to depict a universal condition. Whereas the 'classical stranger' may no longer refer to those who are here to stay, the category of stranger has not become superfluous.

Whether we define it as the foreigner, the Other or the in-between subject, or whether we conceptualise it in terms of an intra or inter mode of interaction, the idea continues to resonate with how both scholars and the public try to make sense of their world. A genealogy of the stranger is both an attempt to trace the development of the idea through various theoretical traditions, but this genealogy is not the search for origins, for example, the 'classical stranger'. In addition, I have shown that the construction of the stranger is not a linear development but has a plural and sometimes contradictory past that reveals traces of various power relations. If the idea of the stranger has no beginning and no end, then this book represents an intellectual moment. It is a moment that reflects on the discourses of the stranger and contributes both to the coherence and fragmentation of these discourses.

References

Ahmed, S., 2000. *Strange Encounters: Embodied Others in Post-Coloniality*. London: Routledge.

Ariarajah, S.W., 2005. Intercultural Hermeneutics – A Promise for the Future. *Exchange*, 34 (2), pp. 89–101.

Fischer, J., 2013. Turn to the Third: A Systematic Consideration of an Innovation in Social Theory. *In*: I. Cooper and B.F. Malkmus, eds. *Dialectics and Paradox: Configurations of the Third in Modernity*. Oxford: Peter Lang, pp. 81–102.

Gadamer, H.G., 1960. *Truth and Method*. Reprint 1997. New York: Continuum.

Kögler, H., 2014. Empathy, Dialogue, Critique: How Should we Understand (Inter)Cultural Violence? *In*: M. Xie, ed. *The Agon of Interpretations: Towards a Critical Intercultural Hermeneutics*. Toronto: University of Toronto Press, pp. 275–301.

Malkmus, B.F. and Cooper, I., 2013. Triadic Concepts in the Humanities and Social Sciences – An introduction. *In*: I. Cooper and B.F. Malkmus, eds. *Dialectics and Paradox: Configurations of the Third in Modernity*. Oxford: Peter Lang, pp. 1–22.

Marotta, V., 2008. The Hybrid Self and the Ambivalence of Boundaries. *Social Identities*, 4(3), pp. 295–312.

Mehta, P.B., 2000. Cosmopolitanism and the Circle of Reason. *Political Theory*, 28(5), pp. 619–639.

Nash, D., 1963. The Ethnologist as Stranger: An Essay in the Sociology of Knowledge. *Southwestern Journal of Anthropology*, 19(2), pp. 149–167.

Pels, D., 1996. Strange Standpoints: Or, How to Define the Situation for Situated Knowledge. *Telos*, 108, pp. 65–92.

Pels, D., 1999. Privileged Nomads: On Strangeness of Intellectuals and the Intellectuality of Strangers. *Theory, Culture & Society*, 16(1), pp. 63–86.

Pels, D., 2000. *The Intellectual as Stranger: Studies in Spokespersonship*. London: Routledge.

Roy, A. and Starosta, W.J., 2001. Hans-Georg Gadamer, Language, and Intercultural Communication. *Language and Intercultural Communication*, 1(1), pp. 6–20.

Rumford, C., 2013. *The Globalization of Strangeness*. London: Palgrave.

Schutz, A., 1976. The Stranger: An Essay in Social Psychology. *In*: A. Brodersen, ed. *Alfred Schutz Collected Papers II: Studies in Social Theory*. The Hague: Martinus Nijhoff, pp. 91–105.

Simpson, L., 2014. Critical Interventions: Towards a Hermeneutical Rejoinder. *In*: M. Xie, ed. *The Agon of Interpretations: Towards a Critical Intercultural Hermeneutics*. Toronto: University of Toronto Press, pp. 252–274.

Spinosa, C. and Dreyfus, H.L., 1996. Two Kinds of Antiessentialism and their Consequences. *Critical Inquiry*, 22(4), pp. 735–763.

Wong, D.D., 2014. Reconciling the Tension between Similarity and Difference in Critical Hermeneutics. *In*: M. Xie, ed. *The Agon of Interpretations: Towards a Critical Intercultural Hermeneutics*. Toronto: University of Toronto Press, pp. 165–186.

Xie, M., 2014. Introduction: Towards a Critical Intercultural Hermeneutics. *In*: M. Xie, ed. *The Agon of Interpretations: Towards a Critical Intercultural Hermeneutics*. Toronto: University of Toronto Press, pp. 3–22.

Index

absolute contrasts 41, 82, 124
acculturation 67
Adorno, Theodor 13, 61
aestheticism 39–40
Agnew, J. 6
Ahmed, Sara 20–1, 70, 120
Alexander, Jeffrey 33, 91; vs. Bauman 101–3; binary discourse of 91–5, 97–103; on civil society 91–5
Alphen, E. 12
ambivalence 7, 12, 52–3, 57, 62–5, 70, 72, 81, 100–1; and strangeness 75–6
ambivalent people 7, 69, 70–4, 82, 87, 120
anthropology, evolutionary 56
Arabs, as Other 10; *see also* Muslims
Archaeology of Knowledge (Foucault) 4
Arendt, Hannah 74
Ariarajah, S.W. 122–3
assimilation 16, 48, 62, 67–8, 71, 94, 95, 97
The Authoritarian Personality (Adorno et al.) 13
authoritarianism 13
autonomy 23, 56, 62, 65, 73, 74, 75, 83, 93, 121

Barth, F. 75, 102
Bauman, Zygmunt 6, 7, 81, 91, 100, 120; and the ambivalent stranger 82; on boundaries 66–7; on community and freedom 73–6; on modernity 60–1, 63–5; and the sociology of community 101–3; on structuring and culture 61–3; theory of the stranger 91; on the universality and particularity of strangers 67–73
Beck, U. 25, 83, 84, 85, 87
Berger, P.L. 19, 21, 23, 68
Bevir, M. 5
binary discourse 91–5, 97–103, 124

binary thinking 2, 32, 33, 69–70, 82, 84–85, 92, 114, 116, 124
Bogard, W. 112, 113, 114
Bonilla-Silva, E. 94
boundaries 73, 100, 102; blurring of 110; and community 75; social 24
boundary construction 66–7
Braidotti, Rosi 107–8, 111
Brigham, M. 117
Building Dwelling Thinking (Heidegger) 18

Camus, Albert 18
Castoriadis, Cornelius 74, 75
Chan Kwok Bun 80–1
Chicago School 94
citizenship 91
civil rights movement 103
civil society: binarism in 92–5, 97–8, 100–101; and the hybrid stranger 98–101; theories of 91–5
civil sphere, multicultural 95–7, 103
The Civil Sphere (Alexander) 94
civilisation: catastrophic theory of 51; vs. culture 46
colonialism 56
commonalities 12, 33, 35, 38, 40–3, 49, 79, 99–100, 114, 124, 125
communication 49; computer-mediated 106; cross-cultural 127; in cyberspace 110–13; and modern technology 110–13; online 87; postmodern 112–13
communism 61, 73
community and communities 73, 83–4, 117–18; double 53; political 74–5, 92; sociology of 101–3; virtual 118
consciousness: double 53, 125; hybrid 52–4, 120; racial 47; third type of 33–4, 37–8, 101, 121, 125–7
consumer society 66

consumers, flawed 66
contact hypothesis 98
contextualist method 4
core groups 93–4, 97–8, 101, 103
cosmopolitanism 37, 52–3, 79–81, 125–6; ethical 86; and the stranger 83–9; *see also* strangers, cosmopolitan
cross-cultural contact 13, 32, 49, 61, 80, 91, 97–8
cross-cultural dialogue 73–6, 127
cross-cultural knowledge 7, 122
cross-cultural subjects 123
cross-group identification 96
cultural sociology 91–5, 101–2
cultural studies 1, 36, 46
culture: and binary codes 92–5, 97–8, 100–101; vs. civilisation 46; and the ordering process 62; structuralist theory of 92; of whites 7
Culture as Praxis (Bauman) 63, 69
cybernetics 113
cyberspace 106, 109, 111–17
cyborg: levels of the machine-human nexus 108; and post-/transhumanism 108–9; as stranger 7, 113–17

decolonialisation 1
deconstruction 13
democracy, modern 92
Derrida, Jacques 10, 13, 61
Dessewffy, T. 23
de-territorialisation 28
Diderot, Denis 80
digital immigrants 116
digital natives 116
distance 4, 9, 25, 30, 38, 40, 46–7, 84–5, 112–13, 116; existential 121; geometric vs. metaphoric 34–5, 114; between self and Other 65; social/cultural 15, 26, 29, 47–9, 53, 112, 120; spatial 24, 114; *see also* proximity
diversity 6, 27, 91, 95, 96, 98; super 1, 32; vs. unity 75, 123
Dostoevsky, Fyodor 18
double consciousness/perspective 53, 125
double perspective 125
Du Bois, W. E. B. 53
Durkheim, Émile 92, 99

Elias, N. 102
empathy 48, 49, 108, 123
Enlightenment 63
epistemologies, standpoint 40–4, 86, 121
essentialism 124–5

estrangement 2, 12, 13, 17–20, 26–7, 29, 36, 102–3, 111; self- 12, 18, 27, 36
ethical responsibility 117–18
ethnic studies 46
ethnocentrism 98, 127
ethnology 120–1
exclusion 11, 13, 55, 61–4, 81, 92, 94, 95, 98, 101, 102, 115, 124–5
existentialism 6, 17–20, 23, 28, 36
exploitation 33, 66, 72, 121

Feldman, Z. 111, 113–14
feminism 115, 121; cyborg 109
Fischer, J. 125
foreigners 20; as strangers 91, 100, 120; vs. strangers 10
Foucault, Michel 4, 61
Frankfurt School 27
Fraser, N. 97
free associations 92
free will 72
freedom 27, 51, 54, 61, 68, 71–4, 76, 86, 107, 108
Freedom (Bauman) 74
Freud, Sigmund 11–12, 125
Fromm, Erich 27
frontier cities 50, 52–3

Gadamer, H. G. 123, 126; and intercultural understanding 122–3
genius 39–40, 120, 121
global mobile workforce 28
globalisation 7, 26–7, 29, 61
The Great Chain of Being (Lovejoy), 3

Habermas, Jürgen 61
Hannerz, U. 80, 83, 88
Haraway, D. 42, 86, 109, 113
Harding, S. 42
Harman L. D. 17, 21, 23–5, 27, 46
Hausheer, R. 3
Heidegger, Martin 13, 18–19, 21
hermeneutics 13, 61; critical intercultural 123–5, 127; intercultural 122–3
historians 3–5, 34, 38–9, 40–3, 51, 53, 120, 121, 124
historical realism 38
history, and the marginal man 51–2; *see also* historians
History of Ideas 2–7
Holocaust 7, 61, 65
The Homeless Mind (Berger) 68–9
homelessness 18–20, 28–9, 53, 68
Horkheimer, Max 61

hosts 1, 13, 15–18, 23, 25, 26–9, 35, 38, 46–8, 50, 52–5, 70, 76, 123; affluent 71–2
Human Migration and the Marginal Man (Park) 51
human rights 1, 83
humanism 66; classical 107, 108, 109, 111; liberal 107; rational 107; *see also* posthumanism; transhumanism
Husserl, Edmund 10, 13, 14
hybridity 46, 69, 81–3; cultural 49–52; gendering of 55; racial 52, 54–6; social theory of 56–7
hyphenation 95, 97

identification, cross-group 96
identity/identities 19, 20, 46, 66–7; binary notions of 111; cultural 57; of the cyborg 112; gender 97; group 23; and hybridity/hyphenation 95; and language 69; local 84; and place 28; racial 57; religious 97; sexual 97
identity construction 1, 69
identity politics 83–4
immigrants 20, 94, 116, 120
In Search of Politics (Bauman) 74
inclusiveness 93, 95, 97
incorporation 41, 91, 93–7, 118
individualism (new) 36
individuality 36–7
individualization 25, 51
inequalities 72, 97
intellectuals, free 68
international students 1, 28
interpretation, intercultural mode of 122
intersubjectivity 46; *see also* subjectivity
Introna, L.D; 117
Islamisation 91
Islamophobia 28

Jenks, C. 2
Jews 55, 56, 65, 69, 76

Kafka, Franz 18
Kant, Immanuel 84
Kearney, R. 10
Kierkegaard, Søren 14
knowledge: construction of 41, 42–3, 121, 123, 127; cross-cultural 122; Enlightenment view of 41; historical 39, 43; hybrid 120; sociology of 40–1, 46, 48, 57
Kristeva, J. 11–13, 21

language: of membership 24; reflective theory of 4; of strangeness 24
Legislators and Interpreters (Bauman) 68
Letter on Humanism (Heidegger) 18
Levinas, Emmanuel 10, 13, 61, 65, 118
Levine, D. 33
Lévi-Strauss, Claude 61
liberalism 67, 92
life-world 14–15, 48, 116
liminality 81
Lipman, M. 36
Liquid Modernity (Bauman) 74
Logstrup, Knud Ejler 61
The Lonely Crowd (Riesman) 27
Lovejoy, Arthur O. 2–4, 5

machine-human nexus 108; *see also* cyborg
Mannheim, Karl 41, 48, 68
marginal man 6–7, 33, 46, 51–2, 57, 120, 124; and hybrid consciousness 52–4
marginalisation 7, 66, 81, 91–2, 101, 117
marginality 40, 57; *see also* marginal man
marginality theory 32–3
Marx, Karl 99
Marxism 60, 61, 66, 121
Massey, D. 29
McLemore, S.D. 32–3
Memories of Class (Bauman) 66, 74
Merleau-Ponty, Maurice 13
mestiza consciousness 81
Meyrowitz, J. 109–11, 113
migrants, temporary 28–9
mobile technologies 106, 115
modernity 7, 25, 57, 67, 92, 101; capitalist 18–19, 166, 73; social and cultural boundaries under 60–1; sociology of 56; solid and liquid 63–5, 66, 76
Modernity and Ambivalence (Bauman) 69
Modernity and the Holocaust (Bauman) 69
modernization 49
morality 65; and virtual strangers 117–18
multiculturalism 7, 91–103; and the civil sphere 95–7
multiperspectivalism 125–6
Muslims 67; as Other 10

nationalism 1, 63, 69, 75, 85; exclusionary 13; fanatical 53
Negroes 54–6, 124
neoliberalism 66, 72
neo-tribalism 64
neo-tribes 73–4
Nisbet, Robert A. 2–3
non-governmental organisations (NGOs) 1

objectivity 39, 40–1, 42, 57, 81, 82, 121
ordering process 61–2
Orientalist discourse 99
Ossewaarde, M. 80–1
Other: defining 10–11; exotic 23; representation of 42; stranger as 69, 72, 121–2, 123, 124; vs. stranger 10, 20; uncanny 12; in the virtual world 118
Othering: psychology of 13; of the stranger 35–6
Otherness: constructions of 99; engagement with 87–8; interaction with 96–7

Papastergiadis, N. 25, 26
Park, Robert E. 6–7, 32–3, 60, 80, 123, 124; on hybrid consciousness and ambivalence 52–4; on hybridity 56–7, 82–3; on the hybrid self 49–50; and the marginal man 51–2, 120; on the Negro and the racial hybrid 54–6; and the sociology of space 46–8; spatial concepts 48–9
Parsons, Talcott 56
Pels, D. 40, 121
phenomenology 6, 10, 13–17, 47, 67, 120
Philosophy of Money (Simmel) 37
pluralism 92, 96
polarisation 72
political participation 74
politics 74–6
post-anthropocentrism 108
postcolonial studies 36
postcolonialism 6, 20–1
Poster, M. 4
posthumanism 106–7, 111; cultural 114; and the cyborg 108–9; and transhumanism 107–8; *see also* humanism
postmodernism 7, 29, 64–5, 70–1, 73, 100, 109
postmodernity 61, 64
power relations 72
pragmatism 60
prejudice 47–8, 98, 126
Prensky, M. 116–17
privilege, epistemic 120–1
proletarian class 99
proximity 30, 38, 40, 41, 46, 80; cultural 110; distance and 9, 15, 25, 34, 46–9, 53, 85, 113–14, 116, 121–2; moral 70, 118; physical/spatial 24, 26, 29, 70, 120; social 24, 48, 110
psychoanalysis 6, 11–13, 29, 88

racism 13, 52, 67, 98, 115
rationalisation 50, 54
rationalism 63
rationality, bureaucratic 61–2
Rawls, John 74
recognition 91, 95, 97–8
Redfield, R. 75
refugees 1, 19, 28
Reich, Wilhelm 27
relationships, psychoanalytic 88
repression 12, 73, 98–9, 103
Reuter, Edward B. 46
Ricoeur, Paul 13
Riesman, David 23, 27
rootlessness 68; *see also* homelessness
Rumford, C. 25, 26, 79, 81, 83, 85–8, 125

Sartre, Jean-Paul 18
Saussure, Ferdinand de 61, 92
Schutz, Alfred 13–18, 21, 23, 28, 48, 100, 106
Scotson, J.L. 102
security issues 72
Seidman, S. 10–11, 13, 21, 100
self-consciousness 48, 53
self-estrangement 12, 18, 27, 36
self-reflexivity 85
self-representation 42–3
Semonovitch, K. 10
Shestov, Lev 68
Shields, R. 29–30
Simmel, Georg 6, 23, 26, 30, 37, 49, 54, 60, 68, 94, 100, 106, 120, 121, 123, 124, 125; and differentiated individuals 37–40; marginality theory 32–3; misinterpretations of 81; on the sociology of knowledge 40–1; standpoint epistemologies 40–4; and the stranger 34–7, 99–100; and the 'third way' 33–4, 37–8, 41, 42, 70, 81–2
simplification 92, 94, 95, 98, 100–2, 107
Skinner, Q. 3–4
slavery 99–100
social change 51–2
social distance 34–5
social interaction, and modern technology 106
social media 111, 113, 114
social organization 23–4
social relationships, thin, 85, 87
social state 75–6
social theory 1, 23
society: modern 23–4; other-directed 24; tradition directed 24; Western 27

sociology 1, 6; of community 101–3; cosmopolitan 84; cultural 91–5, 101–2; functionalist 56; of knowledge 7, 40–1, 46, 57; of modernity 56; scientific 50; of space 46–8; unit-ideas in 2–4
solidarity 24, 73–4, 86, 91, 93, 95, 98, 101–3
spatiality 46–7
standpoint epistemologies 40–4, 86, 121, 125; feminist 41
stereotypes 115
Stichweh, R. 25
stigmatisation 67, 95, 102
Stonequist, E.V. 56–7, 80
strangeness 49; classical idea of 9; globalisation of 26; universalisation of 25, 27–30, 35, 76
stranger(s): ambivalent 70, 72–3, 76, 82, 100, 120; and boundary construction 66–7; in cities 50; classical (sociological) 5–7, 17, 23–30, 34, 37, 29–30, 67, 85, 93, 110, 113–14, 116, 128; in a computer-mediated world 109–13; construction of 71; cosmopolitan 83–9, 120, 125–6; cultural 67, 71–2; as cultural Other 21; cyborg 106–18; defining, 9–10; digital 117; disembodied 113–17; existential 17–20, 23, 29, 52; fetishisation of 21; as foreigner 16, 91, 100; gendered nature of 7–8; and History of Ideas, 2–7; hybrid 98–101; in-between 7, 81–3, 100, 120, 124, 127; inclusion of 95; incorporation of 95–6; integration of 91; intellectual 121–2; marginalisation of 115; modern 25, 30; as Other 69, 72, 121–2, 123, 123; vs. Other 20; Otherness of 49; perspectives of 9; phenomenological 13–17, 29, 106, 120; postcolonial 20–1, 29; postmodern 70–1; professional 120–1, 123–4; psychoanalytic 11–13, 29; racial 71–2; religious 67; Simmelian 34–7, 51, 111, 114; and technology 109–13; understandings of 1–2; universality and particularity of 67–73; virtual 117–18
strangerhood, universalisation of 23, 67, 70
structuralist linguistic approach 69
structurisation 62–3
subjectivism 38–41, 55

subjectivity/ies 20, 65, 82, 85–7, 111, 121, 124; hybrid 53; and modern technology 106; and post-/transhumanism 107–8
super diversity 1, 32

Taylor, Charles 97
technology: and communication 110–13; and the stranger 109–13
Teggart, Frederick 46, 51
theories of the stranger 6, 9, 100, 120; Ahmed 20–1; Bauman 60–76, 81–2, 91; Berger 19, 21, 23; Harman 17; Heidegger 18–19; Kearny and Semonovitch, 10; Kristeva, 11–13, 21; Park 46–57; Schutz 13–18, 21; Seidman 10–11, 13, 21; Simmel 32–44, 54, 81–2, 99
Thesis Eleven (Bauman) 70
Thinking Sociologically (Bauman) 69, 70
third position 33–4, 37–8, 101, 121, 125–6, 127
Transcendence (film) 108
transhumanism 106, 107–8, 111, 117; and the cyborg 108–9; *see also* humanism
transnationalism 1, 6, 26, 28, 29, 80, 85
Turner, B.S. 83, 84, 85, 87

universalisation thesis 6, 17–20, 21, 23, 25, 27–9, 70, 72, 117
universalism 35, 57, 68, 85, 92
unrealism 86
utopian idealism 86, 93, 96

victim blaming 67
Virnoche, M. 114

Waldron, J. 83, 85, 87
Watier, P. 35
Weber, Max 94
Weinstein, D. 33
Weinstein, M. 33
women: and cyborg feminism 109; and the cyborg stranger 115; hybrid experience of 55; as Other 10
workforce, global mobile 28

xenophobia 13
Xie, M. 124

Young, Iris 96

zones of transition 50